A
HOLY
PURPOSE

STRATEGIES FOR

MAKING CHRISTLIKE

DISCIPLES

EDITED BY
BILL WIESMAN

BEACON HILL PRESS
OF KANSAS CITY

Library of Congress Cataloging-in-Publication Data

A holy purpose : five strategies for making Christlike disciples / edited by Bill Wiesman.
　　p. cm.
　Includes bibliographical references.
　ISBN 978-0-8341-2614-5 (pbk.)
　1. Discipling (Christianity) 2. Church growth. 3. Church renewal. I. Wiesman, Bill. II. Title.
　BV4520.H655 2011
　254'.5—dc22

2010051630

10 9 8 7 6 5 4 3 2 1

DEDICATION

First, this book is dedicated to the pastors and lay leaders of the USA/Canada Church of the Nazarene who faithfully serve our Lord Jesus in the mission "to make Christlike disciples in the nations" with the hope that this will be a valuable support resource in your ministry.

Second, to my beautiful wife, Sharon. As her mother says, "Beautiful inside and out."

Last and most importantly, to my Lord and Savior Jesus who changed my life completely on June 18, 1973, at the altar of the Bellflower Church of the Nazarene under the ministry of Wallace Renegar.

CONTENTS

FOREWORD

The late George Bernard Shaw said, "Some men see things and ask why. I dream things that never were and ask why not."

You are holding in your hands the insights and imaginations of such dreamers! This is not so much a "how to" kind of book as it is a "why not" kind of book. Transformed by a Holy God, captured by His holy purpose, and empowered by His Holy Spirit, these visionary dreamers and thinkers set before us both their stories and God's truth with the confidence that He will inspire all of us to embrace a "why not" missional lifestyle.

For over one hundred years God has given the Church of the Nazarene leaders and laypersons who were willing to dream of things that never were. His holy purpose has so laid hold of these men and women that they have been willing to cooperate with Him in holiness movements of New Testament proportions. When we remember the great eighteenth-century Holiness revival in the United States and Canada, the subsequent movements of God in Korea, the Horn of Africa, South Asia, Bangladesh, Sri Lanka, Peru, Brazil, and so many other places, we are reminded that God is still on His throne in heaven and indwelling His church on earth!

This is not the time to circle the wagons and hope for the best. Now is the time to raise the banner of holiness and charge headlong into the fray! The battle is ours; victory is assured! Our God is the God of "immeasurably more" (Ephesians 3:20).

Every now and then as you read, stop and ask yourself, "Why not?" Why not here? Why not now? Why not my church? Why not me? Dream a new dream. Let God's holy purpose lay hold of your heart and mind. Let Him set you aflame with holy passion.

May God open the eyes of our hearts to see "what is the hope of His calling, . . . the riches of [His] glory . . . , and what is the surpassing greatness of His power toward us who believe" (Ephesians 1:18-19, NASB).

—Dr. J. K. Warrick
Chairman, Board of General Superintendents
Church of the Nazarene

Acknowledgments

The concept for this book began nearly three years ago with the 2008 Evangelism Summit when a group of missional pastors from USA/Canada gathered in Kansas City under the leadership of Jim Dorsey. Six of the chapters in this book represent papers presented at that Summit. Thank you to all who participated and to Jim for his leadership.

More recently, under the leadership of Dr. Bob Broadbooks, USA/Canada Regional director, our District Superintendents Advisory Committee (DSAC) met with the ministry leaders from the Global Ministry Center to talk about what the church in the United States and Canada needed in order to move forward. Hundreds of leaders across USA/Canada offered insight and feedback during the Pastors and Leaders Conferences held on our nine regional universities during the summer of 2010. Five key strategies are developing and we share them with you. There is great potential for the Church of the Nazarene in USA and Canada and these strategies will help us achieve it. Thank you to Bob; the DSAC; the other district superintendents of the USA/Canada Church of the Nazarene; and the countless pastors and other leaders who contributed to these important conversations.

An expression of appreciation needs to be given to several groups who partnered in this project. First, special thanks go to the leaders who shared their experiences and enthusiasm for Making Christlike Disciples in these chapters. Thank you to Shelma Warner, Evangelism Ministries assistant at the Global Ministry Center, for her work behind the scenes to make this new resource a reality. Dale Jones, Rich Houseal, and Laura Lance form a great team in our Research Department at the Global Ministry Center. Thank you for your excellent contributions. Thank you to Bonnie Perry, Richard Buckner, and the Beacon Hill Press editors and staff for their patience and guidance and their willingness to "go the extra mile."

Thank you to public school English teacher, Christian education minister, pastor's wife and my daughter, Dori Ingram, for her invaluable contributions about split infinitives, dangling participles, parallelism, voice, and so on! Thank you, Dori.

Each chapter's author bio contains an e-mail address. Our hope is that this resource will be the starting point of many conversations as we partner and collaborate and learn from each other to fulfill our mission of making Christlike disciples in USA/Canada.

—Bill Wiesman
January 2011

Bob Broadbooks is director of the USA/Canada Region Church of the Nazarene. Bob served as pastor of four Nazarene churches in Kansas, Colorado, and Florida before being elected as district superintendent of the Alabama North District, where he served for six years. In 2003 he was appointed district superintendent of the Tennessee District, where he served for six years before being elected to his present position. Bob is a graduate of MidAmerica Nazarene University (BA) and Nazarene Theological Seminary (MDiv). MidAmerica honored him with a doctor of divinity degree in 2000. Bob has two grown children and two grandsons. He and his wife, Carol, live in Shawnee, Kansas. rbroadbooks@nazarene.org

INTRODUCTION
THE INVINCIBLE POWER OF A HOLY PURPOSE
BOB BROADBOOKS

It is an unnerving experience. In Birmingham, Alabama, across the street from the 16th Street Baptist Church is a beautiful park. In that park is a metal sculpture of three life-sized dogs raised up on their back legs. The leashes around their necks are restraining the animals from attacking. Their teeth are bared as they appear to be lunging toward their prey. It's possible for the viewer to walk through the dogs as if he or she were the one being attacked. It's a disconcerting experience to imagine being attacked by the dogs. Of course, the statue pulls the viewer back to the 1960s and the civil rights work accomplished in that city.

Many miles away in Memphis, Tennessee, it's possible for you to visit the Lorraine Motel and stand on the balcony where Martin Luther King Jr. was assassinated. On April 3, 1968, on the eve of his assassination, Dr. King preached his final sermon at a church in Memphis. He talked about the events in Birmingham and about Bull Connor, the man who was responsible for public safety in Birmingham. In that powerful sermon Dr. King said this:

I remember in Birmingham, Alabama, when we were in that majestic struggle, there we would move out of the 16th Street Baptist Church day after day; . . . And Bull Connor would tell them to send the dogs forth, and they did come; but we just went before the dogs singing, "Ain't gonna let nobody turn me around." Bull Connor next would say, "Turn the fire hoses on." But Bull Connor didn't know history. . . . that there was a certain kind of fire that no water could put out. And we went before the fire hoses; we had known water. . . .

That couldn't stop us, . . . and we'd just go on singing, "Over my head I see freedom in the air." And then we would be thrown in the paddy wagons. . . . and old Bull would say, "Take them off," and they did; and we would just go in the paddy wagon singing, "We Shall Overcome." And

. . . we'd get in the jail, and we'd see the jailers looking through the windows being moved by our prayers and being moved by our words and our songs. And there was a power there which Bull Connor couldn't adjust to; and so we ended up transforming Bull into a steer, and we won our struggle in Birmingham.[1]

Dr. King called it "the majestic struggle." These are two words that I wouldn't think to put together, odd but so descriptive. What would enable men and women to go through such a fight? How could they muster such courage to withstand attacking dogs, high-pressure water hoses, and public humiliation? What was the power that kept them going even against the threat of imprisonment and beatings? The answer is simple but profound. They were captivated by the invincible power of a holy purpose. They decided that they didn't want to live in slavery. They wanted a better life for their children and their children's children. They wanted *freedom*.

Consider the invincible power of a holy purpose. Perhaps you haven't had to face attacking dogs, high-pressure hoses, and public humiliation, but you have had your share of high pressure and humbling problems. You see, as a leader in the Church of the Nazarene, you are in a "majestic struggle." You are called to similar work, so shouldn't you be gripped with similar intensity? Isaiah describes your calling with these words:

The Spirit of the Sovereign LORD is on me, because the LORD has anointed me to preach good news to the poor. He has sent me to bind up the brokenhearted, to proclaim freedom for the captives and release from darkness for the prisoners, to proclaim the year of the LORD's favor and the day of vengeance of our God, to comfort all who mourn, and provide for those who grieve in Zion—to bestow on them a crown of beauty instead of ashes, the oil of gladness instead of mourning, and a garment of praise instead of a spirit of despair. (Isaiah 61:1-3)

When you are captivated by a holy purpose, absolutely nothing can stop you.

We celebrate what God has accomplished and is accomplishing among our churches and districts on the USA/Canada Region in the last hundred years. He has blessed our efforts. We rejoice in what He has done, and we look forward to what He will do among us.

A Holy Purpose Will Challenge Great Leaders

Look around the Church of the Nazarene. We have some of the finest leaders in the Church of Jesus Christ. We have great lay leaders, teachers, pastors, missionaries, and professors. Thousands of people have been won to the Kingdom through your efforts and the grace of Christ. You didn't answer God's call for the money. When you joined the cause of Christ, you knew that you wouldn't be famous. What was it that captured your imagination? It was a holy purpose.

When you accepted the call from Christ to work in His Church, you didn't know it would be this tough. Why do you keep on? You do so because the holy purpose has chained you to the task. You know that these "high-pressure hoses" are just the circumstances of the work that He has called you to. They are just distractions to the mission. We have a world to win. Satan would love to keep you always consumed with the details and the disturbances. But great leaders are consumed with the holy purpose. They are somehow always able to keep their concentration on reaching people and loving God. They never lose their prophetic voice. They refuse to allow trivial matters to captivate their hearts. They will always find a way to keep their focus on the real reason for the Church's existence.

Did you ever think you might like to have served in the earlier days of our church? It was easier back then, or so it seems. But you are not there. You are here. And either God put you where you are right now on purpose, or it was a fluke. Either He is adequate to help you or He is not. I choose to believe that He put you where you are right now and is adequate to help you. You have certain gifts and abilities that are needed right now. May God help each of us to focus on the holy purpose. A holy purpose is the only thing that can truly challenge a great leader.

A Holy Purpose Will Produce Results

God is blessing the Church of the Nazarene today. We are seeing Acts 2 movements in places like Bangladesh and the Horn of Africa. But God is also working here in the United States and Canada. In 2009, 60,000 people found Christ in our churches. Every three and a half days we started a church. Perhaps our growth isn't as dramatic as some other places in the world, but we are moving forward here. Tom Ranier says that if a church has a ratio of twenty to one, that is twenty congregants to win one person to Christ, it is a fairly strong evangelistic church. He says that of the 400,000 Christian churches in the United States and Canada, only 3.5 percent reach this threshold. Our research says that when you consider the attendees in our Nazarene churches, the ratio is nine to one. We are producing new Christians and discipling them. We rejoice in every victory God gives us.

But we know that in the United States and Canada in our church, as in most other denominations, our growth rate has slowed. We can keep soothing ourselves with the above statistics and never admit that the "emperor has no clothes." The fact is that last year our membership just slightly increased. The last few years we have not kept pace with population growth. We could sit back and quickly give reasons for this, like "Our church is a hundred years old, and many of our other congregations are aging," "There is an increasing distrust for organized religion in the US and Canada," and "Postmoderns are not attracted to church." You've heard the litany. We could keep rehearsing it, or we could be captivated once again by our holy purpose and driven to our knees pleading for God's help. We could decide again that we have a message the world needs. We could once again be brokenhearted by the sin and hurt around us. We could determine to establish strategies and plans that would signal that there will be no more business as usual. And we could decide that we are going to do everything we can to see this trend change.

You say, "Well, perhaps we could see it change, but how will we do that?" I am glad you asked. Recently our District Superintendents Advisory Committee met with the ministry leaders from the Global Ministry Center and we talked about what the church in the United States and Canada needed in order to move forward. Hundreds of leaders across the United States and Canada offered insight and feedback during the Pastors and Leaders Conferences held on our nine regional universities during the summer of 2010. Five key strategies are developing, and we share them with you. There is great potential for the Church of the Nazarene in the United States and Canada, and these strategies will help us achieve it.

1. **INTENTIONAL LEADERSHIP DEVELOPMENT**. We must develop, train, and release passionate leaders with a Wesleyan-Arminian focus.
2. **VIBRANT CHURCH RENEWAL**. We must help each local church discover new life.
3. **CLEAR AND COHERENT THEOLOGICAL IDENTITY**. We must facilitate communication and collaboration among the Global Ministry Center, educational institutions, ministers, and laity through print, electronic media, civil conversation, and clear preaching.
4. **PASSIONATE MISSIONAL OUTREACH**. We must release and encourage our people to embrace with open arms and hearts both the needy and the new people groups among us.
5. **MULTIFACETED NEW CHURCH DEVELOPMENT**. We need to continually foster an environment and enthusiasm for starting new churches through our districts and local churches.

These five strategies are represented in the five sections of this book. Leaders have written chapters that offer insight, illustration, and importance to the strategies.

We are moving forward in this direction, believing that God will help us. Do you remember the Old Testament story in 2 Kings 7 about the four lepers? They were sitting at the gates of the city starving. They had a choice to enter the city, where the people were also starving, or go to the enemy camp of the Arameans, where they could get killed. They made their decision. They said, "Why sit here until we die?" They thought, "We might get killed over there, too, but at least we will try." You know the story. They went to the enemies' camp and discovered the enemy had left. Thinking they were being attacked, the Arameans had all run away, leaving their food and valuables. The four lepers now had everything they needed. What had happened? The Lord saw that the lepers were moving, so He went before them and helped them. This is an incontrovertible mission principle. You will find the workers and the resources in the harvest field. We just need to make our move. It is still an important question—"Why sit here until we die?"

These are our five key strategies, and together we are developing initiatives for each one. Your involvement will be important to the success of this adventure. We plead for your prayers. We plead for your engagement. A holy purpose will produce results.

A Holy Purpose Is Absolutely Unstoppable!

In my library I have a copy of the 1836 Discipline of the Methodist Episcopal Church. This book was published less than fifty years after the death of John Wesley. They made it small and inexpensive so that it could easily fit in a person's pocket and be available to every Methodist home in the United States. It begins with an interesting few lines: "Dearly beloved brethren, we think it expedient to give you a brief account of the rise of Methodism both in Europe and America." (This is a quote of John and Charles Wesley themselves.) "In 1729, two young men in England reading the Bible saw they could not be saved without holiness: followed after it, and incited others so to do. In 1737, they saw, likewise, that men are justified before they are sanctified: but still holiness was their object. God then thrust them out to raise a holy people."

Notice it says, "God thrust them out to raise a holy people." They were thrust out, or compelled, by Christ to take the message to hurting and helpless people. They knew the dangers and the difficulties of this majestic struggle, but they were totally captivated by God to do this work. John and Charles Wesley believed the Bible taught that men and women needed to be holy before they could enter heaven. They believed that we could be sanctified after we were justified, and this holy purpose thrust them into their world. A holy purpose is absolutely unstoppable.

The five thousand churches and eighty districts of the Church of the Nazarene in the United States and Canada continue this holy march. Perhaps you are saying, "But I am just one—one person, one church, one district. We don't have much influence. We can't imagine ourselves as a mighty army." Nothing could be farther from the truth, my friend. Many of our individual churches may be small, but together we are a mighty army. Together we gave over $65 million to missions in 2009. Together we won over 60,000 to Christ. Together we started new churches. Together we educated future ministers and laity. Together we saw young people find Christ and their calls to ministry. Together we took the message of heart holiness to people of all colors.

Together we sent out mission teams all over the world. Together we are a mighty force for God.

What makes us unstoppable is that we are consumed by a holy purpose. If our purpose for being a church is not a holy purpose, we will not make progress. One influential leader in Evangelical circles today said, "Don't worry about the growth of your church, focus on fulfilling the purpose of your church." He is right. Our purpose is not to grow the church. Our purpose is to introduce people to Jesus and His abundant life. Our purpose is not to build big buildings. Our purpose is not to have great worship experiences. Our purpose is not to provide religious activities and great programs. All of these are good things, but they cannot be our purpose. Our purpose is to lift up Jesus and His message of holiness. Our purpose is to make Christlike disciples. People will come to our churches to see Jesus. They may come once to see a new building, but the only thing that will bring them back consistently is if they see Jesus while there. Dear friend, if your purpose is anything less than holy, you will not find progress. God knows the motives of our hearts, and we must be certain that we are working for a holy purpose. If your purpose is to win some award, it is not invincible. If your purpose is to further your own career or just make it long enough to retire, it is not invincible. But if your purpose is to meet the deep needs of people by lifting up Christ, you will be invincible.

Eventually we must come to the point where we stop thinking of our own welfare and think about those who desperately need God. Do you remember the story of the Good Samaritan? The Levite looked at the man in need lying on that "dangerous road" and asked, "If I stop to help this man, what will happen to me?"[2] "But then the Good Samaritan came by [and reversed] the question: 'If I do not stop to help this man, what will happen to him?'"[3] That's the question we must ask ourselves in the United States and Canada; not what about me but what about him? What about her? What are their needs? We must be captivated by the thought that if they are to make it to heaven, they will need to be holy. As Nazarene leaders, we have the answer to their deepest needs.

What I want to say to you is, we must march again. We must not let anyone stop us. Oh, there will be naysayers. Some will say, "My church is too small. We can't do anything for God. We have no money. We are not big enough to offer programs for the whole family. Our building is not adequate. We have a shortage of parking. We don't have enough qualified workers." The naysayers will be with us always. But if we could just be consumed by our holy purpose, we could march on. No church is too small to reach people. Every district can grow. No economic crisis can stop us. No disappointing demographic can keep us from reaching people. There may be a Nazarene church in every city in your state, but they haven't reached all the lost people yet. We will need churches of all kinds and sizes to reach them. On our region, every other person we pass on the street isn't on any church roll. Probably 50 percent of the people in your area are not known by any church. There are people out there that need God.

Dogs and fire hoses couldn't stop the march of the holy purpose called freedom. In the same way, economic crises, aging congregations, ebbing budgets, disappointments and discouragement cannot stop the march of the holy purpose of Jesus Christ. They laid Him in a cold, damp tomb. With tears, they rolled the stone, locking Him away. But a holy purpose is absolutely unstoppable. He burst forth from that tomb and the march of resurrection power continues to this day. We must not be sidetracked, held back, or prevented in any way from following through with His holy purpose. With the power of the resurrected Christ flowing through our lives, nothing shall be able to stop us from reaching men and women with the gospel of Christ and the message of heart holiness. May the same Spirit that thrust John and Charles Wesley upon their world, thrust us forward to take our message to the hurting people of the United States and Canada.

STRATEGY NO. 1
INTENTIONAL LEADERSHIP DEVELOPMENT

*We must recognize, develop, train, and release
passionate leaders with a Wesleyan-Arminian focus.*

Every great endeavor begins with God searching for a willing leader. He has chosen to work through called men and women. The apostle Paul recognized the absolute necessity of passionate, capable leaders, so he prayed for the leaders in the church at Colosse: "Since the day we heard about you, we have not stopped praying for you and asking God to fill you with the knowledge of his will through all spiritual wisdom and understanding" (Colossians 1:9). The Church of the Nazarene in the United States and Canada is intentionally praying for leaders of all nationalities to be called, developed, and trained. We are praying that these leaders will be infused with soul passion as they experience the cleansing, empowering work of entire sanctification. We are also praying that God will give wisdom to the church to release these new leaders into the waiting, bountiful harvest field.

The present reality is that a growing number of our leaders are being trained at various district training centers. Many years ago, the vast majority of our leaders were trained in one of our educational institutions. This served us very well, but with increasing economic challenges, additional educational providers, and the need for on-the-job training, many of the educational and training opportunities have become more localized. Part of the exciting challenge we face today is helping leaders train leaders in the local church and on our districts. Leadership development aims to cultivate a clergy or lay leader's capacity to "be," to "know," and to "do" what is involved in influencing others to make Christlike disciples.

Chapter 2: "Making Christlike Disciples," by Stan Toler

Stan Toler uses the acronym D-I-S-C-I-P-L-E to describe a simple, eight-step plan that will enable pastors and teachers not only to make converts but also to lead those converts into becoming living examples of Christ.

Chapter 3: "Developing New Ministry Leaders," by Manoj Ingle

Manoj Ingle encourages existing leaders to challenge people to act on the call of God in their life for full-time Christian ministry.

Chapter 4: "Creating a Climate for Women in Ministry," by Rondy Smith

Rondy Smith shows the importance of adopting a clear and comprehensive strategy for the intentional development of women clergy.

Chapter 5: "Preparing for Ordination," by Dan Copp

Dan Copp affirms the biblical understanding of the priesthood and ministry of all believers and the ordination of some called to a more official and public work of ministerial leadership. His focus is specifically on the process of equipping those called to prepare for ordination.

Stan Toler, a general superintendent in the Church of the Nazarene, was chosen for the highest elected office in the church at the 27th General Assembly in Orlando, Florida, in July 2009 after serving for forty years as a pastor in Ohio, Florida, Tennessee, and Oklahoma. He has written over seventy books, including his best-sellers, *God Has Never Failed Me, but He's Sure Scared Me to Death a Few Times; The Buzzards Are Circling, but God's Not Finished with Me Yet; God's Never Late, He's Seldom Early, He's Always Right on Time; The Secret Blend; Richest Person in the World; Practical Guide to Pastoral Ministry; The Inspirational Speaker's Resource; ReThink Your Life*; his popular *Minute Motivator* series; and his newest book, *If Only I Could Relate to the People I'm Related To.*

Toler for many years served as vice-president and taught seminars for John C. Maxwell's INJOY Leadership Institute, training church and corporate leaders to make a difference in the world. Recently he was honored with a doctor of divinity degree by Southern Nazarene University. He and his wife, Linda, an educator, have two married sons and one grandson. stoler@nazarene.org

■■ 2 ■■
MAKING CHRISTLIKE DISCIPLES
STAN TOLER

Jesus Christ gave a commission to the church that has not changed over the course of history: "Go and make disciples" (Matthew 28:19). Making Christlike disciples is the critical objective of the Church. Yet by most accounts we are not doing well at our primary task. It has been estimated that in North America it takes the combined efforts of eighty-five Christians working over an entire year to produce one convert. Nearly half of the churches in the country do not add a single person to their number as a result of evangelism in any given year. If we struggle on the front end of this commission—leading people to the point of conversion—we have an even more serious problem in delivering on the back half of the commission: developing those converts into fully formed, Christlike followers of Jesus Christ.

This is our primary task, and we cannot afford to fail. But where do we start? Here's a simple eight-step plan that will enable you not merely to make converts but also to lead those converts into becoming living examples of our Lord and Savior. Just remember the word D-I-S-C-I-P-L-E.

D: Develop Intentional Relationships

In order to influence people, you must get to know them. The old adage is true: nobody cares how much you know until they know how much you care. When you have gained trust, your leadership will be accepted. For making disciples, relationships must be intentional, focused associations that ultimately lead to a greater common knowledge of the Lord Jesus Christ.

Look for the Intentional Moment

Relationships don't just happen. You must be intentional about creating them. Jesus' own ministry shows this intentionality: "The Son of Man came to seek and to save what was lost" (Luke 19:10). His eyes were peeled for those who needed a way out of the condition they were in. He also advised His disciples to stay alert: "Open your eyes and look at the fields" (John 4:35). Be alert for opportunities when people are open to relationships, such as when they have expressed a need, a serious problem, or a life-changing opportunity.

Identify the Prospect

You cannot develop a relationship with everyone. You can develop a relationship with someone. Who is the person (or people) whom you will get to know in order to lead them in discipleship? The prospects for intentional relationships in discipleship may include—

- Pre-believers who express an interest in church affiliation
- New believers who are just starting their faith journey
- Believers who are struggling with personal or family faith issues
- New church attendees who are in need of friendship
- Small-group attendees who express spiritual needs

Friendships are intentional relationships. And they are strengthened one step at a time.

Take Intentional Risks

You have heard it said of people who show great interest in others— "They're always there when you need them." "Always" is a risky word. It means that for the sake of the relationship one may rearrange his or her schedule. An intentional relationship includes willingness to spend the time necessary to let that person know you are sincerely interested in him or her.

You may also find yourself risking rejection in order to form relationships. Not all of the people whom you will wish to disciple will want to be led by you. All relationships carry a degree of risk, and that is just as true in the Church as in the family, workplace, or community.

Minister like Jesus

Discipleship is a very personal ministry. You will be ministering to very human people who have very human characteristics. Meet people at their point of need. Help them to become better than they currently are. Point the way out of hopeless situations. Give to them with no thought of return. Make compassion for others the cornerstone of your ministry, and never, never, never give up on people. Discipleship is a *ministry*—that is, it is a way in which we serve others in the name of Jesus.

I: Identify Spiritual Understanding Levels

Everyone who comes to Christ brings along a truckload of his or her own learning, experience, biases, concerns, and ideas. Some of those whom you will disciple have already had some Bible training. Others may have little religious background; the things of God will be completely new to them. One of your first tasks will be to assess their spiritual progress to date and to identify the areas in which they need to grow. Consider these three levels of spiritual understanding and a proposed teaching path for people in each of those levels.

Level One: The Pre-believer

With over 4 billion people in the world who are classified as non-Christian, obviously there is a great need to lead people to a decision to follow Jesus Christ. Christ himself taught us about reaching out to people in the scriptural account of the meeting with the Samaritan woman at the well (see John 4:4-30). Pre-believers must be led to look at their condition in relation to the holiness of God and the truth of God's Word. The need of a Savior can't be seen until there is an understanding of the hopelessness of sin (Romans 6:23). We do that in the same way Jesus did—with love and compassion, gently pointing the way out of a sinful lifestyle and into the glorious freedom of grace and forgiveness.

Level Two: The New Believer

The next level of spiritual understanding is seen in the life of one who has recently made a decision to follow Christ. That person may or may not understand who Christ is and what His teachings include.

New believers also face predictable challenges:

- There is a break with the past.
- They often risk broken relationships with family or former friends.
- Their associates may not understand their decision to follow Christ.
- They become a part of a whole new "family."
- They are introduced to a new belief system.
- They are faced with understanding the Scriptures.
- They often have to familiarize themselves with new worship forms.
- They struggle with temptations to revert to their former ways.

Your task as a disciple-maker is to approach the new disciple with a spirit of openness and friendship, letting him or her know that you are concerned about his or her new transition.

Level Three: The Uncommitted Believer

You may need to encourage more established believers to make a next-level commitment. That assignment may be carried out in several settings such as small groups, volunteer ministries, mentoring relationships, or mission trips. You will encourage fellow believers to use their spiritual gifts in ministry to others. You may also be asked to encourage a fellow believer to make a stronger commitment to the local church through church membership. Our task is not only to teach the new disciples the principle of flight but also to encourage them to fly, stretching their wings to become mature, Christlike disciples who can in turn disciple others.

S: Supply a Support System

Encouraging the disciple to a next-level commitment takes a focused and purposeful effort. The time and effort will vary from one person to another, but the basic qualities of commitment, concern, communication, and concentrated training must be present in each discipleship assignment. Those qualities should be present in a support system for your disciple no matter what his or her level of spiritual understanding may be. Here are the basic elements of a support system that a disciple needs.

Bible Study

As a Christlike disciple-maker you are a guide, leading your disciple along the paths of biblical truth. Supply your disciple with a support system of Bible study. A regular (perhaps weekly) Bible study with your disciple is one of the best ways to share the knowledge of God's Word with him or her. Whether you meet in the home, at a restaurant, or on the church property, your faithfulness in teaching the Bible will be reflected in the growth of your disciple.

Accountability

New Christians need to be steady in their walk. They are vulnerable to the influences of the world and need support in developing a changed lifestyle. As a Christlike disciple-maker, you have an opportunity to encourage your disciple to live a life that honors Christ—one that reflects good spiritual coordination. Your disciple may have addictions or habits that are not only psychological but also physiological. A pledge to pray with your disciple about a certain practice is better than chastising him or her. Help your disciple recognize and choose the new lifestyle that Jesus makes possible.

Fellowship

As a newborn develops a response to the affection and affirmation of his or her family, new believers develop responses of affection and affirmation with their new spiritual family. Paul was concerned that disciples understood the depths of commitment and interdependence that come with being a part of God's family. He wanted them to have pure intentions in all matters of the heart. Your disciple has entered a whole new atmosphere of family relationships. Encourage him or her to express his or her affection and affirmation in positive ways. Promote your disciple's involvement in building up the family of God.

C: Contact Regarding Spiritual Progress and Needs

In emergency care there is a window of time known as the "golden hour," in which patients under treatment have the greatest likelihood of survival. In photography the golden hour is the first and last hour of sunlight, when a photographic effect is best achieved. Christlike disciple-makers also have a window of opportunity to give focused care to those whom they are discipling. The golden hour of discipleship is an accumulated sixty minutes of focused contact time each week. Telephone calls, e-mail or text messages, and notes or cards are all excellent ways to capitalize on this golden opportunity. But your best option for keeping in close contact with your disciple is spending time together. Of course, there are many distractions in life. To zero in on personal needs, you will have to be intentional. Don't put off spending face time with your disciple because you are too busy. Make time for this important activity. This is your best opportunity to listen, assess, mentor, and guide this new believer.

You will not have the answer for every question. Your advice will be limited to your own learning and experience. Share what you know of God's Word. Share what God has taught you about your faith journey. Avoid anxiety about your abilities or efforts. God knows your heart, and He will use your obedience and faithfulness to impact others.

I: Incorporate into the Life and Ministry of the Church

New disciples need the life and ministries of a local church (see Hebrews 10:25). Your task as a Christlike disciple-maker also includes incorporating your disciple into the mainstream of a fellowship of believers.

Sacraments

Observances of the sacraments are an opportunity to introduce the new disciple to the life and ministries of the church. Guide your new believer toward the point of receiving baptism and the Lord's Supper. The baptismal service may also be a time of outreach to the disciple's friends and family. The new disciple's first Lord's Supper observance is also an opportune time to incorporate him or her into the life and ministries of the church. The new believer may have received Communion before, but stress the meaning of the event as an act of public witness to his or her new faith commitment.

Worship

A worship event offers a prime opportunity to highlight the disciple's new faith commitment. It not only gives the person a chance to experience worship with a new meaning of its importance but also is a choice time to introduce him or her to other believers. Bring your disciple to worship and help him or her enter fully into the event. Invite the new believer (along with his or her friends and family) to sit with you during worship. Introduce him or her to other attendees (especially age- or interest-related attendees). Explain the various segments of the worship time (singing, preaching, teaching, drama, giving, and so on).

Small Group

Whether a Sunday school class, Bible study, or prayer cell, small groups are an excellent way to include disciples in the church fellowship. The small group becomes a "little church" within a larger church and offers a more personal setting for meeting fellow believers. You may be a small-group teacher or a participant. Either way, make sure your disciple is informed about the group and invited to its meetings.

P: Pray Daily for Spiritual Growth

Disciples need a support team, behind-the-lines "soldiers" who will do battle with the enemy (Satan) on their behalf. A continual communication in prayer for a pre-believer or believer is a weapon of warfare that can be effective in winning people to Christ and supporting new faith commitments. Paul said, "We are not fighting against flesh-and-blood enemies, but against evil rulers and authorities of the unseen world, against mighty powers in this dark world, and against evil spirits in the heavenly places" (Ephesians 6:12, NLT).

Christian living is a team effort. "Confess your sins to each other and pray for each other so that you may be healed. The prayer of a righteous man is powerful and effective" (James 4:16). Of course, each disciple has a personal responsibility to live in obedience to the Word and will of God, but the "family factor" of Christianity provides additional spiritual protection and strength. First Corinthians 12:12 says, "The body is a unit, though it is made up of many parts; and though all its parts are many, they form one body." Various parts of the physical body support the whole physical body. Likewise, individual members of the church body function to support that body.

L: Look for Spiritual Gifts

Who knows what your disciple may become! A pastor? A missionary? A church planter? A denominational leader? A local church leader? An influential layperson? God knows! The seeds of greatness have already been planted in every child of God. Their abilities and personalities are part of His master design that benefits the Kingdom. Your task as a Christlike disciple-maker is to help disciples discover and utilize their spiritual gifts. It is also your task to teach them how the Holy Spirit enables and empowers them to utilize their gifts through sanctification, through being filled with the Holy Spirit (Acts 1:8).

Helping your disciples discover an ability that may be used in Kingdom-building is essential not only to their spiritual growth but also to the growth and health of the local body. Introduce them to a spiritual gifts questionnaire. Point out the abilities that could be used in the church. Make their discovery of their spiritual gifts a matter of mutual prayer. Help them to see how a Spirit-filled life will bring wholeness— and holiness—to their spiritual journey.

E: Enlist in Ministry

Jesus talked about the display of God's graces: "You are the light of the world—like a city on a hilltop that cannot be hidden. No one lights a lamp and then puts it under a basket. Instead, a lamp is placed on a stand, where it gives light to everyone in the house. In the same way, let your good deeds shine out for all to see, so that everyone will praise your heavenly Father" (Matthew 5:14-16, NLT). Nowhere does the "light" of a disciple's life bring a warmer and brighter glow than through ministering to others. Here are some prime opportunities.

Local Church Ministry

Most outside observers of the local church have no idea the depth of cooperation needed to fulfill the church's mission and purpose. To them, church involvement means attending services. Those within the church know that it involves far more. They know that the church is "organizational machinery," which needs both parts and labor. Opportunities for ministry in the local church are many and varied. There is a place for your disciple's interest and ability, such as teaching, prayer ministry, building or vehicle maintenance, childcare, or hospitality. Guide your disciple toward involvement in a ministry that fits his or her spiritual gifts.

Missions Ministry

The church also has a global mission and consequently is in need of disciples who will assist with that mission (Luke 10:1-2). Your spiritual mentoring can encourage your disciple to have a global vision. Teach him or her about Christ's global commission. Share missions publications with him or her. Invite your new disciple to assist with a mission convention. Encourage him or her to participate in a mission trip.

Compassion Ministry

Your disciples must understand that their own community is a mission field. A global vision for missions begins with a vision to minister to people in their immediate area. Enlisting them in compassion ministries is a great place to start. Compassion ministries are, in a biblical sense, holistic. That is, they minister to the whole person—spiritually, physically, emotionally, socially, and financially. A disciple's experience with compassionate ministries may be just the beginning of a wider ministry—including vocational ministry.

Small-group Ministry

Small groups, such as neighborhood Bible studies, Big Brothers/Big Sisters, or prayer cells, are an exciting introduction to ministry. Enlisting your disciple in an organized small group—or launching one—will give him or her the experience and responsibility for various ministries.

No-Limits Discipleship

Do you remember Barnabas? His little-known efforts to introduce Saul (later Paul) to the "way" resulted in a ministry that reaches into eternity. Billions of people have heard the gospel as a result of his faithful ministry. A spiritually blind man received sight. A spiritually troubled man received peace and purpose. A forgiven man received a lifelong direction. When you fulfill the second half of the Church's great commission—to make Christlike disciples—you create Barnabas men and women who will impact the world in ways you cannot now imagine. Your commitment to D-I-S-C-I-P-L-E has no boundaries, because the Christ you serve has no limits!

"Go and make disciples."

Manoj Ingle pastors the New Hope Community Church of the Nazarene in Winnipeg, Manitoba. Where Manoj Ingle is the pastor, people are called into full-time ministry. He is a graduate of Nazarene Bible College with a bachelor of biblical studies degree. In the seven years of Manoj's ministry he has started four new congregations that function as multisite churches of New Hope Community, resulting in an average of three hundred seventy people worshiping God in five venues weekly. He and his wife, Vandana, live in Winnipeg. Mingleco@gmail.com

▪▪ 3 ▪▪
DEVELOPING NEW MINISTRY LEADERS
MANOJ INGLE

In my first week as the pastor at New Hope Community Church of the Nazarene in Winnipeg, one of my tasks was to get my business cards printed. A very interesting conversation took place with my new friends. I was wondering what title I should place on the business card. One friend suggested "senior pastor." I said to my friend that I was not old enough for people to call me a senior pastor. My friend quickly said to me that I should be called a senior pastor because I lead people to become junior pastors for ministry. Another friend suggested, "In that case, your title should be lead pastor, because you're leading people to do ministry."

Reflecting on the matter, I assessed the situation around me, and I realized that neither of these titles made sense. I was the only person who was on the full-time ministry staff at our church. At that time I was not leading any junior pastors for ministry with the intention that they become senior pastors at a church.

As a result of these conversations, this whole idea of leading people into ministry struck me. This was beyond challenging people to get involved in the ministry of the church as laypeople, but I saw the need to lead people to fulfill their calling into full-time ministry and to develop them as leaders. Some people have reservations about the idea of "leadership development." John W. Gardner in his book *On Leadership* talks about this resistance and reservation this way: "Many dismiss the subject with the confident assertion that 'leaders are born, not made.' . . . Most of what leaders have that enables them to lead is learned. Leadership is not a mysterious activity. It is possible to describe the tasks that leaders perform."[1]

One of the top priorities of ministry leaders is to invest in people, so they become leaders. Many times we get caught up in building a church as an organization. Building, money, systems, and many other factors become more important than the real purpose of making followers of Jesus. Jesus tells us in Matthew 16:18 and 28:19 that He will build His Church and that we are to make the disciples (followers). I am convinced as a pastor that the best way I can make a difference is to be involved in making followers of Jesus into ministry leaders, who will in turn make followers of Jesus. It is about people and the mandate Jesus has given us.

Even some of the great business leaders understand that it is about the mandate and the people. Dee Ward Hock, founder and former CEO of the VISA Credit Card Association, said this about an organization:

It surely isn't just a set of bylaws, because I can write a set of bylaws and shove it in a desk drawer, and it just becomes an old moldering piece of paper. And if you really think deeply about it, you discover that every organization and every institution, without exception, has no reality save in your mind. It's not its buildings. Those are manifestations of it. It's not its name, it's not its logo, and it's not some fictional piece of paper called a stock certificate. It's not money. It is a mental concept around which people and resources gather in pursuit of common purpose.[2]

The Church is a living creation from God. Our Heavenly Father is the head of the Church, and He has given us a common purpose: to make fully devoted followers of Jesus Christ. It is not about money, building, name, or logo. It is not about how attractive the business card is or the title on it. It is about introducing people to Christ so that they experience His saving grace, experience forgiveness of their sins, and mature in Christ.

This is a great responsibility and at times can even be overwhelming. The question now is "How do I bring people to Christ? What are the best practices for making disciples of Christ?" As I tried to get answers to these questions, two general principles, or action items, stood out to me very clearly.

Surrender yourself to Christ in all you do. I will not be able to lead people to Christ in my own strength. In fact, it is impossible. The reality is that I have to surrender myself and my ministry to Him. He will lead me in the right direction. So it is never about my title on the business card—it is about Jesus.

Challenge people to act on the call of God on their life for full-time ministry. This is beyond challenging people to get involved in the ministry as laypeople. This means to challenge people to respond to the call of God on their lives for full-time ministry.

One of my favorite authors says,

An organization cannot increase its productivity—but people can! The asset that truly appreciates within any organization is people. Systems become dated. Buildings deteriorate. Machinery wears. But people can grow, develop, and become more effective. . . . Few leaders surround themselves with other leaders, but the ones who do, bring great value to their organizations. And not only is their burden lightened, but their vision is also carried on and enlarged. . . . Great leaders produce other leaders.[3]

As I surrendered myself to Christ and challenged and led people to act on the call of God, this is what took place at New Hope Community Church in the last few years.

- Seven new ministry leaders are processing their call to full-time ministry.
- Three ministry leaders have received a Certificate of Lay Ministry.
- Four new churches have been sponsored by our church, using multiple new church ministry styles with some of these leaders.

As these leaders are committed "to making disciples of Jesus Christ," they are doing so in creative ways. The gospel is being taken to people where they are, meeting their spiritual needs. It is one thing to bring people into the Church, but it is another thing to take the Church to the people. As a result, four satellite church ministries have been sponsored by our church, a congregation that averages fewer than one hundred and forty in weekly worship attendance.

Four New Satellite Ministries

Hecla Summer Church

People are ministered to during summer church on Hecla Island, a place where many people spend their summer. Due to hard winters here in Canada, people are eager to travel away from the city during the summer months.

Den 205 Compassionate Ministry

People find a new spiritual freshness and are accepted unconditionally at a special place called Den 205. Those whose lives are broken and filled with pain are taught to talk to God, so they receive genuine healing, which comes only from Jesus.

Riverton Church

People gather around tables and have fellowship with one another. Not only do they partake in food together, but they also receive a word from God.

South Asian Fellowship

A group of new and old immigrants, along with second-generation immigrants, meet for worship. They enjoy singing songs in their own language and listening to the Word of God. New immigrants find support from people who have been in Canada for a long time.

God's Amazing Results

Children's Ministry

Kids are outside the building even before the start of their service. They are so eager to come to church because they have so much fun, and they learn about God in a fun way. Parents tell our children's director that their kids are excited all week about attending church. They are waiting for Sunday to come. One parent said, "I told my children that if they will not listen and will not do their homework during the week, they will not be able to go to church. This has a positive effect on them, because they simply don't want to miss church."

Increased Conversions

As these ministries are taking place, people are saved. They are accepting Jesus Christ as their personal Savior. In 2006-7, twenty-two people came to Christ. And in the year 2007-8, thirty people came to Christ as compared to other years, when only three to five people accepted Christ. Authentic disciple-making is taking place.

Recruitment

The two keys still remain: surrender yourself to Christ in all you do, and challenge people to act on the call of God for full-time ministry. The following are a few practical principles, concepts, and processes that helped me recruit, develop, and deploy new leaders for ministry.

- *Before asking the "golden question," look for the following.*
  Ministry potential. Look for people who show natural interest in various ministry activities. They have a passion to bring about spiritual change in the lives of people. They may not know how, but they want to introduce people to Jesus.

  Conversations. Listen to them in casual conversation when they are relaxed and speaking from their heart; this may be in a group setting. During these conversations, people will indicate their passion.

  Teachable spirit. We are not looking for people who have everything together and are ready for ministry immediately. Look for people who are willing to learn and have a teachable spirit. It is difficult to take people to the next level of leadership when they think they know everything and there is nothing more they can learn. Do they understand the principle "learning is a continuous process"?

  Varied personality types. It is not necessary that all leaders have an outgoing personality. If we focus only on outgoing type of people, we may lose out on other personality types who are good leaders and have strengths in different areas.

Positive attitude. Skills can be taught, but it is very difficult to change the attitude. Look for positive and cooperative attitudes.

- *Ask the "golden question" privately and personally.* "Have you ever felt God calling you to full-time ministry?" In my experience, many people have a calling but do not know how to express what they are feeling. This could be because of fear, and they may have the question in their mind, "Why would God call a person like me?" Asking the above question helps them understand the call that might be on their lives.

Development

Spend regular and scheduled time with them. Be prepared to spend time with ministry leaders one on one and also in a group to mentor them. This is a time-consuming process, and at times we may feel that we are wasting time and other ministries are suffering, but mentoring is very important, and it takes time. Remember that leaders always create leaders. It is important to keep good notes of every meeting to track the progress. *Coaching Appointment Guides* are a helpful tool to keep good notes during such meetings.[4] (See Appendix 1.)

Use key coaching questions. When you meet, one of the things you do is ask the person key coaching questions. My district superintendent of the Canada West District, Larry Dahl, has developed these questions based on the concept borrowed from Gary Collins.[5] (See Appendix 2.)

Assign simple ministry tasks. It is important that the person does hands-on ministry and experiences the ministry in the real world. To begin, assign simple ministry tasks. If the new leader is faithful in little things, he or she will be faithful in big things.

Assign bigger ministry tasks. Do not be afraid to assign bigger ministry tasks. Allow the person to preach on Sunday mornings a few times a year. Increase the ministry load gradually.

Model the ministry for the new leader. Do not expect the person to always do ministry alone; do ministry along with the person. Model ministry. For example, take the person with you for hospital visitation and when you present the gospel to someone. Always train a new leader.

Evaluate the ministry. During the scheduled meetings, highlight the good things the new leader has done, and indicate the points of improvement from past mistakes. Never correct in front of others.

Give freedom to make mistakes. Let the person know that making mistakes is not bad. We learn valuable lessons from mistakes. When we try new things, we make mistakes. This will take pressure off the new leader and give freedom to try new things.

Make the ministry experience fun and joyful. Let him or her catch your passion to do ministry. Keep it enjoyable by having the new leader serve from his or her strengths.

Learn from them. Learning is a continuous process. As pastors, we are teaching the new leader, but at the same time intentionally learning ourselves. He or she has a lot to offer. Let the person know the things you have been learning from him or her. This will boost confidence.

Encourage formal education. Encourage the new leader to pursue formal education from an approved course-delivery system. This is a requirement for ministerial licensing. It is not always possible for everyone to go to college. Consider options like online education or Nazarene Bible College, or consider starting a Ministry Development Center at your local church.

Deployment

Use a spiritual gifts indicator. It is important to place the person in the right ministry. Use the tools to discover his or her spiritual gifts and talents, and match that to the ministry available.

Listen to their ministry desires. Many times there may not be a ministry available to place the person in. Create ministry opportunity by encouraging him or her to start the ministry he or she feels called to do. Listen to the person's ministry desire. He or she may come up with an out-of-the-box ministry that has not been done before. Listen to those ideas with an open mind. Give the new leader the freedom to start these ministries, and walk with him or her in the process.

Conclusion

I cannot imagine attempting to minister all by myself. Certainly all the church leaders God has called to ministry have helped this church "make fully devoted followers of Jesus Christ." Without their response to God's call on their lives and commitment to ministry, many people would still be looking for freedom in their lives. Hats off to all ministry leaders who have stepped out in faith to minister to people in creative ways. I want to say to all those faithful ministry leaders at New Hope Community Church—thank you for taking the church out of the four walls to the people where they are and meeting their spiritual needs.

Appendix 1
COACHING APPOINTMENT GUIDE

Leader: _____

Ministry: _____ Date: _____

Follow-up items:

Agenda for this session—summary of items discussed:

Key coaching questions:

    Information:

    Awareness:

    Action:

Assignments for leader:

Things I need to do:

Next meeting: Date: _____

Time: _____ Location: _____

Reference: Robert E. Logan and Steven L. Ogne, *Church Planter's Toolkit: A Self-Study Resource Kit for Church Planters and Those Who Supervise Them* (Carol Stream, Ill.: ChurchSmart Resources, 1995), 11-12.

Appendix 2
KEY COACHING QUESTIONS

Wholistic Questions

Questions that demonstrate the value of the person and his or her family—not just for his or her contribution to ministry. Sample questions to use:

1. **Feelings:** How are you feeling about ministry?
   What emotions are you feeling now?

2. **Family:** How is your family?
   Tell me how this affects your family.

3. **Faith:** How are you and God doing?
   What do you think God wants to see?

4. **Focus:** What is important?
   What is urgent?
   What is next?

Strategic Questions

Here is a set of key strategic questions to ask, if appropriate, at each meeting. It follows the acronym **GROW**.

1. **G**oal: What is the goal you are working toward?
   What are you trying to accomplish?

2. **R**eality: What is the reality of the situation today?
   What have you been able to accomplish?

3. **O**ptions: What options do you have?
   Let's brainstorm the options.

4. **W**ill What will you do?
   What are your next steps?

Concept borrowed from Gary R. Collins, *Christian Coaching: Helping Others Turn Potential into Reality* (Colorado Springs: NavPress, 2001).

Sources

Collins, Gary R. *Christian Coaching: Helping Others Turn Potential into Reality*. Colorado Springs: NavPress, 2001.

Gardner, John W. *On Leadership*. New York: Free Press, 1993.

Logan, Robert E., and Steven L. Ogne. *Church Planter's Toolkit: A Self-Study Resource Kit for Church Planters and Those Who Supervise Them*. Carol Stream, Ill.: ChurchSmart Resources, 1995

Maxwell, John. *Developing the Leader Around You: How to Help Others Reach Their Full Potential*. Nashville: Thomas Nelson Publishers, 1995.

WIE: Business Transformation Through Chaos Theory, http://www.wie.org/j22/hock.asp.

Rondy Smith is an ordained elder in the Church of the Nazarene, serving the Hermitage, Tennessee, congregation as community life pastor since 2001. For twelve years prior, she was associate professor of management and graduate program director at Trevecca Nazarene University, Nashville. Rondy is a graduate of Trevecca Nazarene University (BS), University of Kansas (MA), and Vanderbilt University (EdD). Rondy chairs the Nazarene Women Clergy Council for the USA/Canada Region. She and husband, Bobby, have two sons. rondysmith@aol.com

■■ 4 ■■

CREATING A CLIMATE FOR WOMEN IN MINISTRY

RONDY SMITH

"Women hold up half the sky." This Chinese proverb is ironic wisdom from a civilization that has systematically disposed of its daughters for centuries, preferring male children.

Could our church be susceptible to a similar irony? Gender equity has been part of our stated polity since the inception of our denomination. "We recognize the equal right of both men and women to all offices of the Church of the Nazarene, including the ministry."[1] The 1908 organization of the denomination included a gender-neutral statement on ministry. The current *Manual* statement, paragraph 903.5, begins like this: "The Church of the Nazarene supports the right of women to use their God-given spiritual gifts within the church, affirms the historic right of women to be elected and appointed to places of leadership within the Church of the Nazarene, including the offices of both elder and deacon."

Our long-term practice has not proportionately demonstrated that verbal commitment. In 1908, almost 25-five percent of all those ordained in the movement were women. By the time we began paying attention to those statistics again in 1989, only 4.7 percent of the total active clergy in the United States and Canada were women. The latest statistics suggest a steady, though nominal, increase each year since bringing the 2009 female percentage of total active clergy to 15.9 percent.[2] Progress maybe—but not nearly enough.

This paradoxical gap between principle and practice is not only hurting our credibility but also crippling our ability to be maximally missional. If the future viability of our church, as has been argued in this book, is dependent on "recognizing, developing, training, and releasing more passionate leaders with a Wesleyan-Arminian focus," then let us not forget that women hold up half the sky. The secret to unleashing the *full* potential of the church is leadership that reflects the *full* image of God. We need to align our reality with our theology by adopting a clear and comprehensive strategy for the intentional development of women clergy.

The purpose of this chapter is not to offer a scholarly apologetic for the inclusion of women in ministerial leadership. Plenty has been written defending our Wesleyan-Holiness biblical and theological stance on this issue. (Please see the excellent resources suggested at the end of this chapter.) Rather, as we choose to believe that we really mean what we say, the purpose here is to offer a pragmatic strategy for the intentional development of female leaders in the church and to celebrate the ways we are already achieving this in order to encourage others to adopt these benchmarks of excellence.

Celebrate What You Want to See More Of

A time-tested leadership principle is to celebrate what you want to see more of. The year 2004-5 was a banner year for the advancement of women in the leadership structure of the Church of the Nazarene. Three historic elections: Jossie Owens, first female district superintendent in the United States; Corlis McGee, first female Nazarene college president in the United States; and Nina Gunter, first female elected to the highest office, general superintendent. Of her election, Nina Gunter said this in a *New Horizons* interview September 2006: "I pray that my election as a general superintendent will not be anecdotal but will be the opening of the door for inclusive thought and action that becomes the norm."[3]

Capitalizing on the momentum created by these three historic elections, champions began creating opportunities to increase the visibility of women in ministry. Dan Copp, Clergy Development director, formed the first Nazarene Women Clergy Council (NWCC) in 2007. Interestingly, two of his most immediate predecessors had also been active champions of women clergy. Wilbur Brannon, who served in that office from 1982 to 2001, had been instrumental in the founding of the Wesleyan-Holiness Women Clergy association and its premier conference, *Come to the Water*. *New Horizons*, a newsletter for Nazarene clergywomen, was launched under his leadership. Chuck Zink, who held that office briefly before his untimely death in January 2005, had been the district superintendent instrumental in paving the way for the election of Jossie Owens.

The newly appointed Nazarene Women Clergy Council (NWCC) hosted an inaugural event at the M7 conference under the leadership of the initial chair, Carla Sunberg. The entire Board of General Superintendents attended, along with their spouses, to demonstrate their unanimous support of the endeavor. Nina Gunter gave the keynote address and issued a clarion call: A Declaration for Warming the Climate for Women Clergy. Here are her five points of declaration:

1. There is overwhelming evidence that women have a sense of calling from God.

2. God is raising up a generation that recognizes and celebrates the calling of God to women as critical to the definition of the church.

3. Acceptance for women clergy is a sacred biblical and moral response for all Nazarenes.

4. I call for prophetic leadership to support women in their preaching, teaching, and leadership commission.

5. I call for women clergy and leaders to respond to the church in Christian love, not in selfish and demanding ways.[4]

Building upon that solid foundation, the NWCC developed nine strategic initiatives to guide its work:

1. To assure mentoring for called women at all phases of ministry.

2. To develop viable pathways for ministry placement of women clergy.

3. To identify funding sources to support women students and ministers.

4. To lobby for policy and legislation that ensures the systemic support of women clergy.

5. To facilitate the development of networking systems that effectively reach from the general to the regional to the district to the local levels for women in vocational ministry.

6. To promote a culture of value and visibility for the myriad ministry options for women and the excellent ways they are currently serving.

7. To support the production of state-of-the-art educational resources for leadership training on issues of women in ministry.

8. To influence the dialogue regarding a correct Wesleyan biblical and theological view of women in ministry.

9. To utilize all available technology and public venues to market the value of women in ministry.[5]

There are silos of excellence within our denomination where these best practices are happening regularly. In the spirit of celebrating what we want to see more of, I offer a few stories as models or benchmarks.

My Story

My own story is an example of how the church got it right. Ten years ago I was a happy, productive professor at Trevecca Nazarene University with a thriving management consultancy practice—when the Lord interrupted my plans with a radical call. Shocked by what I believed He was speaking into my life, I sought counsel with my beloved pastor, Howard L. Plummer. He was not as shocked, quickly affirming the gifts and graces he saw in me for ministry but recognized the radical nature of God's request and genuinely struggled with me as I counted the cost. We decided together that day that if indeed I was sure the Holy Spirit was speaking, I must obey. Pastor Plummer guaranteed his active support.

I resigned from my position at Trevecca effective May 2001 and began a one-year voluntary assignment as Team Ministries pastor at Hermitage Church of the Nazarene. Pastor Plummer and I crafted a job description together that reflected my unique gifts and graces and matched some very specific needs of our growing congregation. The Spirit blessed, and there was fruit. In November of that year the church board granted me a local minister's license. I will never forget the weightiness on my head of the large hands of my friend and mentor William Greathouse, general superintendent emeritus and a member of my congregation, as he prayed over me at my commissioning service. What a sacred moment!

That voluntary assignment turned into a paid part-time role and eventually became a full-time position as my church continued to grow. In the meantime, I received vital promptings from the Spirit through champions who were investing in my ministry. The late Bob Spear was the first to mention proper credentialing to me. Soon after, I remember a breakfast conversation with Karen Dean Fry when she urged me to seek ordination. I needed the push of these voices of experience. I enrolled in the course of study through the Tennessee District School of Ministry and was ordained at our 2008 District Assembly. What a sacred privilege to have Nina Gunter, our first female general superintendent, preside. She has also been a source of personal inspiration and encouragement to me, along with many other pioneer women clergy I have met during my journey.

It is important for me to share other significant pieces to my development. My local pastor was key. His ability to assimilate me into the deeper life and workings of the church as I made that shift from layman to clergy was critical. He gave me many opportunities to preach and teach, to administer the sacrament of Holy Communion, to baptize, and to engage fully in highly visible ways. He established an environment of true equity on the pastoral staff team for me and my other female colleague, Carol Waller. He championed me on the district through his role on the nominating committee. I kept finding my name on ballots until I was elected!

The district superintendent is also a key player in the intentional development of female clergy members. I am grateful to Bob Broadbooks, who appointed me to the District Studies and Credentials Board after my ordination. I am grateful to Larry Leonard for inviting me to participate in the program at our most recent ordination service. I point these things out because it takes intentionality to assimilate the minority gender into the ranks of the "brotherhood." I am also grateful for the way my peer brothers and elder brothers have received me. Wilbur Brannon is a member of my congregation and makes it a point to find me after every sermon I preach to say, "Pastor, you ministered to me today."

The general superintendents must also be intentional about championing women clergy. I am grateful to Jesse Middendorf for inviting me to participate in a special task force this past year and for appointing me to a general level committee for this quadrennium.

I believe that my story illustrates several significant factors critical to warming the climate for women clergy. Let me point to them by formulating a few questions.

Pastors, Are You—

- Actively looking for women in your congregation who exhibit the gifts and graces for ministry?
- Listening intently to the hearts of women who might be trying to process a call?
- Working diligently to find them a place of service to test the call?
- Publicly championing them in order to lend them your credibility?
- Seeking to hire a competent woman so that you have an active female role model in your congregation?
- Thinking of called women to invite to fill your pulpit on occasion?

District Superintendents, Are You—

- Actively placing women clergy in a variety of positions on your district, including the senior pastorate?
- Proactively educating your church boards on the biblical and theological stance our denomination takes on women in ministry?
- Conscientiously creating gender balanced ballots?

General Superintendents, Are You—

- Using your vast influence to champion the cause of women everywhere in our global denomination?
- Intentionally appointing capable women to all levels of leadership within our denomination?

Recent research by Judith A. Schwanz, professor of Pastoral Care and Counseling at Nazarene Theological Seminary, affirms this anecdotal evidence. Dr. Schwanz conducted over twenty "appreciative inquiry" interviews with successful women in ministry holding various leadership roles within several denominations. She defined success as expressing a call to ministry and having that call confirmed by others by virtue of occupying a place of ministry in which to fulfill that calling. Several trends emerged from these interviews.

One of the clearest trends is that each woman identified three different types of people who influenced her for good in her ministry. First, they all expressed the need for peer support and present-day role models to let them know they are not the "only one" doing what they do. This suggests the importance of networking and making women in leadership today visible so that they can see each other and encourage the younger women who are considering a call. Second, they referred to women in the past who have paved the way, modeling and opening doors for the next generation. We need to tell the stories of those who have gone before us but often don't make it into the history books. Third, they cited the importance of champions in their lives, often men, who encouraged them, prodded them, opened doors, gave positive references, and sometimes stepped out of leadership roles to create open spaces in which they could serve. We need champions to step up.[6]

One such champion is Jon Middendorf, senior pastor of Oklahoma City First Church of the Nazarene. Since fourteen of the twenty-four pastoral staff members at OKC First are women, including the executive pastor and worship ministries pastor, their visibility happens on a regular basis. However, as an added bonus, in November 2009 Pastor Jon initiated an annual Women in Ministry Sunday in order to showcase and celebrate the calling, gifts, and graces of women clergy. He believes this culture of acceptance will cultivate the hearts of young women to answer the call to ministry.[7]

Not Every Story Has a Happy Ending

A few months ago I sat down with a beautiful, vibrant, Spirit-filled, compassionate, educated, articulate, talented, extremely competent woman/wife/ mother/grandmother in her mid-fifties and listened to her heartbreaking story of feeling rejected by her beloved Church of the Nazarene. She had received her call from God in the midst of great success in a corporate career. Her pastor saw gifts and graces for ministry in this dedicated layperson, and he challenged her to pursue the credentialing process while giving her opportunities to serve and test the call. She flourished. There was fruit.

When her pastor became a district superintendent, he intentionally watched for the right assignment in which to place her. She was asked to launch a New Start church. She toiled and toiled, and her efforts were blessed by God. The church thrived and grew. But after five years as the pastor, she felt a strange release. She wondered what God's next assignment would be as she reluctantly but obediently resigned. It was a time of mixed emotions. Why did she have to leave when everything was going so well? Yet she was certain of God's direction. Soon she was asked to join the leadership team in her district office. As the new assignment unfolded, she realized that it was a perfect fit with the experience God had allowed her to gain in the corporate arena. She was helping churches with their strategic and missional planning. Again, God brought fruit from her ministry, but she also hit a few bumps in the road.

A particular church asked the district superintendent not to send "that woman" to assist them. She was dismayed but not deterred as she began to encounter some resistance in certain pockets of the district. All the complaints had something in common—they were not about her competence but about her gender. Though her district superintendent never wavered in his belief regarding her giftedness and calling, it seems the encroachment of a fundamentalist opinion about female ministers was allowed to stifle progress. And then, sadly, the economic downturn hit our nation, and like many churches and districts, budget cuts had to be made, and her position was eliminated. As the supportive district superintendent began to submit her name to churches needing a pastor, he encountered the same gender resistance. After months and months of waiting to be placed, discouragement set in. She knew she was called of God—what now? She found gainful employment in a wonderful secular company, but that was not her calling. Seeking healing during this desert time, she felt that God led her to visit a vibrant United Methodist Church near her home. Through her bittersweet tears, she could hardly explain to me what began to transpire. She did not go looking but was almost immediately approached by leadership at this church regarding ministry opportunities. She felt her heart melting as she sensed that God was tenderly releasing her from her beloved denominational home and providing her a place of service elsewhere in His kingdom.

I know this woman's heart. She told me this story only out of deep concern for the future of our church. The truth is, hers is not an isolated story. I have heard many similar stories, and I share her concern. "Talent bleed," as it is called in organizational leadership literature, is one of the signs of an unhealthy organization. We seem to be suffering talent bleed in the Church of the Nazarene due to placement difficulties, particularly among our female ministers because of the gender bias in a competitive market. Our placement is not keeping up with our talent pool. The good news is that the number of female students in ministerial study continues to rise. The challenge is the expectation of placement opportunities upon graduation.

I read an article in *Newsweek* magazine titled "A Woman's Place Is in the Church," and a particular quote gave me pause:

A young woman looks at the corporate world and sees that she can reach the highest levels of leadership. She is frustrated at the lack of opportunities to live out her leadership in the church. The grave consequence of that is that the church becomes less and less relevant to women. And the consequence of that is that it becomes less and less relevant to her children. . . . If the stories of the women and girls of the Bible aren't told, then mothers and daughters will stop seeing themselves as part of the Body of Christ. They'll walk away. And they'll take their children with them.[8]

Though I do not share quite the pessimism of this author, I am concerned that the church has perhaps unwittingly underserved the female population of our constituency (could that be the majority portion?). Not just by robbing called women of a place to fulfill their calling, but by robbing female parishioners of the value they derive from seeing someone in leadership like them. Reciprocity creates an immediate sense of belonging and connection. There is a lot to be said for same-gender spiritual shepherding or discipleship. I remember being almost overwhelmed early in my ministry by the sheer numbers of women who came out of the woodwork to counsel with me. They each expressed a similar sentiment. They were so happy to finally have a called, biblically and theologically trained leader who also truly understood the female subculture. My perspective as a woman was significant to them. And they are very pleased that their daughters have a positive role model for women serving in ministry. I believe that gender-balanced leadership in the church is good pastoral theology.

One of my favorite management gurus, W. Edwards Deming, said that the number-one job of a leader is to remove obstacles.[9] I wonder if he had been reading the prophet Isaiah? "Build up, build up, prepare the road! Remove the obstacles out of the way of my people" (Isaiah 57:14). Intentional leadership removes the barriers and obstacles to empowerment. Our women clergy need some boulders moved out of their pathway.

Nina Gunter called for "prophetic leadership." In *Prophetic Imagination* Walter Brueggemann says that the main task of a prophet is to give voice to the voiceless, power to the powerless. He suggests that prophets often must criticize in order to reenergize.[10]

One such prophetic voice is Jossie Owens, who has just completed her assignment as superintendent of the New England District. In a recent phone conversation, I asked her to speak on the record about the intentional development of women clergy. She boldly offered these suggestions:

- District superintendents must plow through the resistance to placing women. Male champions will have to sacrifice and suffer for the advancement of women.

- General superintendents must talk with district advisory boards about championing women at district superintendent election time. We must mirror our constituency in nominating boards.

- We must get serious about inclusive language. We need systemic change and formal training in how to talk with one another. She remarked that in many meetings she attends she feels verbally abused by the noninclusive language.

- We need required mentoring relationships and structured programs for leader development.

While there is certainly valid expectation for systemic change within our current institution to warm the climate for our female ministers, I also want to encourage innovation on the part of the women clergy themselves. We need not wait for the perfect opportunity to be handed to us. No minister in the Church of the Nazarene is guaranteed a congregation, a building, a certain position, a salary, or a budget. If we are called of God, then we may need to be willing to preach the gospel from every rooftop, on every street corner, or under every tree. We must engage in outside-the-box thinking regarding ministry roles. The Great Commission is beckoning us to get creative beyond the traditional mix. Get out there and proactively propose new and different ministries. We need motivated self-starters to be paradigm pioneers.

In the book *Execution: The Discipline of Getting Things Done* (2002), authors Larry Bossidy and Ram Charan, experts in senior executive leadership, claim that the execution of strategic plans is the least developed skill in most organizations.[11] We like to plan, but we fail to execute, to follow through and get it done. We have to work hard to see the things we truly value materialize. Intentionality will be the key to creating a climate for the empowerment of women clergy. Let's do it! Let's take action to accomplish the transformation! All of us—together!

Suggested Reading and Resources

Brower, Kent, and C. Jeanne Orjala Serrão. "Reclaiming the Radical Story," *Holiness Today* (May-June 2009).

Green, Tim. "Daughters Who Prophesy: The Way of Pentecost," *Preacher's Magazine* (Pentecost 2008).

Ingersol, Stan. *Nazarene Roots*. Kansas City: Beacon Hill Press of Kansas City, 2009.

Laird, Rebecca. *Ordained Women in the Church of the Nazarene*. Kansas City: Nazarene Publishing House, 1993.

Leclerc, Diane. "A Woman's Place Is Where?" *Holiness Today* (July-August 2006).

Smith, Rondy. "Team-Based Leadership," *Holiness Today* (July-August 2008).

Web site for Wesleyan Holiness Women Clergy—click on "Articles and Booklets" for historic and contemporary literature: www.whwomenclergy.org.

Web site for Wynkoop Center for Women in Ministry, hosted by Nazarene Theological Seminary—click on "Bible Studies" for more detailed information on the biblical aspects of women in leadership: www.wynkoopcenter.org.

Web site for Women Clergy, hosted by Nazarene Clergy Development—click on "Women Clergy": www.nazarenepastor.org.

Dan Copp serves as director of Clergy Development for the Church of the Nazarene. He previously served as district superintendent for the Arizona District and pastored two churches in California. He and his wife, Vicki, are graduates of Point Loma Nazarene University and Nazarene Theological Seminary. They are ordained elders in the Church of the Nazarene. Dan has a doctor of ministry degree from Fuller Theological Seminary. Dan and Vicki live in Kansas City. dcopp@nazarene.org

PREPARING FOR ORDINATION

DAN COPP

The Church of the Nazarene recognizes and insists that all believers have committed to them a dispensation of the gospel that they are to minister to all people. We also recognize and hold that the Head of the Church calls some men and women to the more official and public work of the ministry. As our Lord called to Him whom He would, and chose and ordained His 12 apostles "that they might be with him and that he might send them out to preach" (Mark 3:14), so He still calls and sends out messengers of the gospel. The church, illuminated by the Holy Spirit, will recognize the Lord's call. . . . While affirming the scriptural tenet of the universal priesthood and ministry of all believers, ordination reflects the biblical belief that God calls out and gifts certain men and women for ministerial leadership in His Church. Ordination is the authenticating, authorizing act of the Church, which recognizes and confirms God's call to ministerial leadership as stewards and proclaimers of both the gospel and the Church of Jesus Christ. (*Manual*, 400-401)

This statement provides an inspiring description of God's calling to ministry for all followers of Jesus! It unequivocally affirms the biblical understanding of the priesthood and ministry of all believers and the "ordination" of some called to a more official and public work of ministerial leadership. The Church of the Nazarene embraces the truth that all disciples of Jesus Christ, laity and clergy, are called to be ministers. And while we are committed to equip both laity and clergy for faithfulness to God's calling, the assignment of this chapter is to focus specifically on the calling of clergy and resourcing the process for equipping those called to prepare for ordination and vocational ministry.

These are exciting days in the Church of the Nazarene. God is calling record numbers of women and men into preparation for ordination and vocational ministry. Global Mission Regional Leadership reported nearly 25,000 individuals in the process of preparation toward ordination in the global Church of the Nazarene—and this is in addition to the nearly 16,000 already ordained—for a total of more than 40,000 people ordained or in the process of ordination in the Church of the Nazarene.

The USA/Canada Region is part of this exciting report, experiencing record numbers of people responding to God's call. In 2009 the region reported 2,973 district licensed ministers and 3,604 local licensed ministers, for a total of 6,577 individuals in the process of preparing for ordination. In addition, 324 new elders were ordained in 2009, the highest number ever recorded in the USA/Canada Region.

As God is calling record numbers of people to vocational ministry in the Church of the Nazarene, it is important to ensure that we are properly resourcing the process for preparation and ordination:

> When the church discovers a divine call, the proper steps should be taken for its recognition and endorsement, and all suitable help should be given to open the way for the candidate to enter the ministry. (*Manual*, 400)

The process for ordination and preparation for vocational ministry engages a synergistic partnership that involves the local pastor, the local congregation, the district, the education provider, the denomination, and others. Each of these important partners must be intentionally engaged in a relationship of nurturing and accountability with the person preparing for vocational ministry. It is helpful to understand the importance of these partnerships and the contribution each makes in the process. There are valuable resources on our Clergy Development Web site at www.nazarenepastor.org.

Local Pastor

The local pastor serves most closely with those God is calling to be clergy as they pursue vocational ministry. The local pastor must take primary responsibility for prioritizing a climate in the local congregation where God's calling to clergy ministry is invited, anticipated, and supported. Intentionally included among the list of "the core duties of a pastor" is the pastoral duty "to nurture the call that people feel toward Christian ministry and to mentor such persons as are called. This shall include guiding them toward appropriate preparation for ministry" (*Manual*, 413.10). The pastor must continuously nurture this congregational climate, regularly inviting people to consider God's calling to ministry as clergy. This particular work of ministry is certainly some of the most rewarding and fulfilling for the pastor.

Pastor John recently described the wonderful story of God's calling him to vocational ministry. As a young man, he sensed what he thought may be God's calling. The first person he talked to about this stirring in his spirit was his pastor. John described a deep sense of profound appreciation about how engaged the pastor became in his journey. His pastor intentionally walked alongside him in those important early days, scheduling regular times for them to be together simply to talk or to have John "shadow" him in his pastoral work. Time spent processing with the pastor and seeing firsthand the work of pastoral ministry served to reaffirm for John God's calling to prepare. It was natural for the pastor to invite John to apply for a local minister's license. John is now an ordained elder in the Church of the Nazarene, serving as a local pastor and mentoring in his church a number of young men and women preparing to be among the next generation of pastors.

The story of John and his pastor is similar to that of many of the forty thousand others in the Church of the Nazarene, reminding us that the local pastor has a profound privilege and responsibility to nurture in the life of the local congregation a climate in which God is calling, the called are responding, and the pastor and church readily come alongside in the preparation.

How are you doing, Pastor? Do you live ministry before your congregation in a winsomeness that encourages those watching to ask, "Could God be calling me to be a pastor?" As you journey with your congregation, are you praying and looking for those God may be calling? Do you encourage your congregation to pray and anticipate those God may be calling? In your preaching do you regularly include an invitation to consider God's calling to vocational ministry? As God calls, are you ready to provide the time, equipping, and ministry opportunities needed to support their preparation?

Local Church

The local church is usually the community in which the individual first encounters God's call to vocational ministry and the community that has the opportunity to walk most closely with the clergy-in-training, serving as partners and mentors in the important formation process. A local church can be either a wonderful source of anticipation, encouragement, and help in nurturing those God is calling and preparing for vocational ministry, or a dreadful source of apprehension, discouragement, and obstacle in hindering God's calling. The local congregation must intentionally commit to nurture a climate in which God is calling, the called are responding, and the church readily comes alongside.

The "local minister's license" is granted following the recommendation of the pastor and the review and vote by the local church board. This local license is granted for one year and can be renewed by the same process. The person holding a local license remains a lay member of the church whose board granted the license.

The local license process provides a wonderful opportunity for the local church to participate in the early recognition of God's calling on the person and the important foundational shaping of the minister-in-training. The whole congregation celebrates when the license is presented as part of a worship service recognizing the profound covenant the local church and new local minister enter together.

Each local church can nurture a climate in which God is calling men and women to vocational ministry. Pastor Ray described that during his twenty-five years as pastor with one congregation how one of the most fulfilling aspects of the local church ministry has been participating with God in His calling people to prepare for vocational ministry. He named eight people who began the ministerial preparation process and are now ordained and serving as pastors. Pastor Ray considers it a privilege to have pastored this church of approximately one hundred people for twenty-five years. He knew his church could not do all that larger churches could do, but he participated with his congregation expecting God's call of people to vocational ministry in his church. He went on to describe how God's calling people to ministry in the life of their church has contributed to transforming their rural community and how their church's contributing pastoral leaders for other churches has allowed them to be part of God's transforming work in other communities as well.

Think with me for a moment about Pastor Ray's story. Considering that over 70 percent of our churches in USA/Canada are under one hundred in attendance, could it be that we have a "sleeping giant"? These congregations can have a significant Kingdom impact by partnering with God in His calling and preparing people for vocational ministry. Envision with me: each of our 3,500 churches that are under one hundred in attendance committing to anticipating, praying, and partnering with God in His calling at least one person from their congregation to vocational ministry—and then add a similar commitment in the other 1,500 churches!

How is your local church doing? Do you publicly and privately value your pastor in a way that expresses value for God's calling to vocational ministry and encourages those watching to consider with anticipation, *I wonder if God would be calling me to be a pastor.* As you participate in congregational life, do you anticipate God is calling? Are you praying and looking for those God may be calling? As God calls, are you ready to provide the ministry opportunities and encouragement needed to nurture them and support their preparation?

District

The district offers a broader community to encounter and celebrate God's calling to vocational ministry. The district can keep before its pastors and churches the priority of nurturing a congregational climate in which God is calling and the called are responding. The district can also model this priority in its various gatherings, intentionally leading pastors and people in praying, anticipating, and celebrating God's calling as they plan and prepare for youth camps, camp meetings, and district assemblies,

The district also offers the person preparing for ordination and vocational ministry a broader community of support and accountability. When a person receives the local minister's license, he or she is to begin a validated course of study for ministers under the direction of the District Ministerial Studies Board. The District Ministerial Studies Board is composed of ordained ministers who commit to come alongside those in the course of study to provide encouragement, counsel, guidance, example, and conversation (*Manual*, 230.5). This board is charged with the responsibility to "recommend to the district assembly placement and advancement in and graduation from the various validated courses of study" (*Manual*, 231.3), so they work closely with each person to assure he or she properly navigates the course of study.

When the person preparing for ministry has held a local minister's license for at least one year and has completed approximately one-fourth of a validated course of study, the local pastor and local church board may recommend him or her to the District Ministerial Credentials Board to be considered for the granting of a district minister's license. The District Ministerial Credentials Board's role is "to carefully examine and evaluate all persons who have been properly presented to the district assembly for election to the order of elder, the order of deacon, and for minister's license" (*Manual*, 228.1). The District Ministerial Credentials Board works closely with the District Ministerial Studies Board in this process of considering a candidate for a new or renewed district license (on many districts these two boards have been combined into one board, often called the District Board of Ministry). The ministerial candidate interacts with these district leaders in an annual interview and in a mentoring relationship throughout the year. There is a wonderful opportunity for district leaders to guide and shape the minister in training.

This process has unique expression on each of our USA/Canada districts, including comprehensive ministerial candidate preparation events (some in synergistic partnership with other districts and the regional university), special mentoring relationships, scope and sequence annual interviews, ministry development plans, and so on.

How is your district doing? Do you publicly and privately value your pastors in a way that expresses value for God's calling to vocational ministry and encourages those watching to consider with anticipation, *I wonder if God would be calling me to be a pastor.* As you participate in district life and events, do you anticipate God is calling? Are you praying and looking for those God may be calling? As God calls, are you ready to provide the ministry opportunities and encouragement needed to support their preparation?

Education Provider

The education provider is another important partner in the process of preparing for ordination and vocational ministry. The Church of the Nazarene requires that a candidate for ordination satisfactorily complete a validated course of study before the district board can consider recommending him or her to the district assembly for graduation from the course of study and for ordination. The education provider is the one that provides the validated course of study for the ministerial candidate. Our system of Nazarene higher education continues to serve as our leading education providers for the validated course of study.

The USA/Canada schools serving as our educational providers include—
> Ambrose University College, in Calgary, Alberta, Canada
> Eastern Nazarene College, in Quincy, Massachusetts
> MidAmerica Nazarene University, in Olathe, Kansas
> Mount Vernon Nazarene University, in Mount Vernon, Ohio
> Nazarene Bible College, in Colorado Springs
> Nazarene Theological Seminary, in Kansas City
> Northwest Nazarene University, in Nampa, Idaho
> Olivet Nazarene University, in Bourbonnais, Illinois
> Point Loma Nazarene University, in San Diego
> Southern Nazarene University, in Bethany, Oklahoma
> Trevecca Nazarene University, in Nashville

In addition to the degree programs, a number of our schools provide non-degree classroom extension or on-line certificate programs for completion of a validated course of study. Each of these schools is committed to working closely with the local church and district to assure the minister in training is well prepared.

Although our Nazarene schools are the preferred education provider for preparing Nazarene clergy, the church recognizes the need for alternative education providers under the direction of the appropriate district board. USA/Canada alternative education providers include numerous district training centers, various language-specific training efforts, and select classes or seminars established by the district board.

How is your education provider doing? Do you publicly and privately value the church and pastors in a way that expresses value for God's calling to vocational ministry and encourages those watching to consider with anticipation, *I wonder if God would be calling me to be a pastor?* As you participate in the educational process, do you anticipate God is calling? Are you praying and looking for those God may be calling? As those God calls pursue their educational preparation, are you ready to provide the learning, ministry opportunities, and encouragement needed to support their preparation?

Denomination

The Church of the Nazarene places high priority on resourcing and serving those God is calling to prepare for ordination and vocational ministry. The church specifically lists as one of the duties of the Board of General Superintendents, "To arrange, in conjunction with Clergy Development, ministerial studies for local ministers, licensed ministers, and those serving in ministerial roles, lay or credentialed" (*Manual*, 317.11).

In order to assure fulfillment of educational foundations for ordained ministry, the Church of the Nazarene requires that a candidate for ordination be recommended by the District Ministerial Studies Board to the district assembly for graduation from a validated course of study. Under the direction of the Board of General Superintendents, the Clergy Development Office works with our eight Regional Course of Study Advisory Committees (RCOSAC—Africa, Asia Pacific, Canada, Caribbean, Eurasia, Mexico & Central America, South America, USA) and our International Course of Study Advisory Committee (ICOSAC) to provide an *International Sourcebook on Developmental Standards for Ordination* and *Regional Sourcebooks on Ordination*. Each RCOSAC is comprised of ministry and education leaders from across their region. The ICOSAC includes at least two representatives from each region. These committees and their work are a profound expression of our being a global church. The global perspective represented in the various sourcebooks reflect the educational standards established in the *Manual* and outline the process for reviewing educational programs to consider whether or not the proposed program would conform to the established standards and be approved as a validated course of study.

Any ordination curriculum program submitted by an education provider to be considered for approval as a validated course of study must demonstrate that the program adequately provides the educational foundations for ministry outlined in the *Manual*. The program submission is first reviewed by the RCOSAC of the Global Mission Region. If approved by the RCOSAC, the program is then reviewed by the ICOSAC. If approved by the ICOSAC, the program is then recommended through the Clergy Development Office for adoption by the Board of General Superintendents and the General Board (Global Education and Clergy Development Committee). It is exciting to consider that we now have nearly one hundred programs that have completed this global validation process and are now serving the church as validated courses of study for the nearly 25,000 ministers in training all around the world.

How is your denomination doing? Do you publicly and privately value your pastors in a way that expresses value for God's calling to vocational ministry and encourages those watching to consider with anticipation, *I wonder if God would be calling me to be a pastor?* As you participate in denominational life and events, do you anticipate God is calling? Are you praying and looking for those God may be calling? As God calls, are you ready to provide the education, ministry opportunities, and encouragement needed to support their preparation?

Conclusion

In this brief overview we have been introduced to some of the important partners in this process: the local pastor, the local congregation, the district, the education provider, and the denomination.

The information provided here is intended to outline the process so that all of us as pastors, lay leaders, district leaders, education leaders, and denominational leaders understand enough about the ordination process to assist others who are discerning God's call upon their lives.

While providing some basic information, we are also inspired as we reflect on what God is doing in calling men and women to ordination in the Church of the Nazarene. Record numbers are responding to His calling, including the largest number of people ever on the USA/Canada Region. Reflecting on God's calling inspires each of us to covenant together and do all we can to be faithful stewards of this treasure He is providing the church.

Are you considering God's calling to prepare for ordination and vocational ministry? If you haven't done so already, I encourage you to talk to your pastor and invite him or her to walk with you. You are in for an exciting journey!

Now to him who is able to do immeasurably more than all we ask or imagine, according to his power that is at work within us, to him be glory in the church and in Christ Jesus throughout all generations, for ever and ever! (Ephesians 3:20-21)

For more information visit our Clergy Development Web site at www.nazarenepastor.org.

Strategy No. 2
VIBRANT CHURCH RENEWAL

*We must help each local church
discover new missional life.*

Jesus Christ wants every expression of His body to be healthy and whole. Our world desperately needs vibrant churches that are reaching the lost in creative missional efforts. Paul prayed this for the Colosse church: "We pray this in order that you may live a life worthy of the Lord and may please him in every way: bearing fruit in every good work" (Colossians 1:10). We are intentionally praying that every one of the 5,000 Churches of the Nazarene in the United States and Canada will discover the mission field around them and that God will help them bear much fruit. As Paul suggests, we believe this would "please [the Lord] in every way."

We have a sleeping giant among us. There are 3,500 churches that average fewer than one hundred in attendance. What if just 20 percent of them could discover a new vision and excitement? This would revolutionize our church in the United States and Canada. Many of our churches have not yet discovered how to engage in missional activities. Too many are focused only on just "keeping the doors open." They have ceased healthy outreach and evangelism. Our challenge is to help our churches from being inundated with details and disturbances in order to keep everyone focused on the mission. Our central task must always be finding the lost, winning them to Jesus, and discipling them into Christlikeness. Because of the dynamic presence of the Holy Spirit, there is hope for every one of our churches to experience vibrant church renewal. This section contains four illustrations of local churches that have experienced a fresh movement of the Holy Spirit.

Chapter 6: Keeping a Missional Focus, by Buddy and Gaye Marston

Buddy and Gaye Marston describe how they have kept a missional focus for over fifteen years at Salem Fields Community Church in Fredericksburg, Virginia. It happened by "responding to the passion God placed in our hearts to reach people for Christ by breaking down deeply embedded stereotypes in the hearts and minds of those who were turned off to church—not Jesus so much, just church."

Chapter 7: Discipling as a Journey, by Gene Tanner

Valparaiso Church of the Nazarene has brought in more than one hundred new members by profession of faith in each of the last five years. Renewal has come from a consistent journey of discipleship; an organized plan for taking visitors on a journey to salvation, sanctification, membership, assimilation, and maturity.

Chapter 8: Becoming Missional *and* Traditional, by Dan Newburg

Dan Newburg tells the story of Gardner, Kansas, Church of the Nazarene and reminds us that you can be missional and still be traditional. Renewal is about outward focus and building relationships in the community.

Chapter 9: Fulfilling Missional Purpose: A Tale of Two Brothers, by Daron and Ryan Brown

Daron and Ryan Brown are "as different as oil and water." Yet the Holy Spirit has used their unique personalities and strengths to renew two very different churches.

Buddy and Gaye Marston serve as co-leaders of Salem Fields Community Church of the Nazarene in Fredericksburg, Virginia. They both had previously served together on staff at another Nazarene church. God gave a clear missional vision to the Marstons for Salem Fields. In the fifteen years of their ministry the church has grown from seventy-nine members and ninety-five average worship attendance to almost one thousand members and two thousand average worship attendance. Buddy and Gaye have one daughter. Buddy@SalemFields.com; xberk@aol.com

▪▪ 6 ▪▪
KEEPING A MISSIONAL FOCUS
BUDDY AND GAYE MARSTON

A few years ago we attended the *Rethink* conference in California, where one of the speakers, a dot.com millionaire from Silicon Valley, said that "twenty-somethings" often ask him how they can make millions as he did. He said he quickly tells them that if they set out to make millions, they probably won't. If they focus on doing what they love, most likely the money will be a by-product. It is a simple entrepreneurial principle: it is all about where you place your focus.

That is what happened at Salem Fields Community Church. We did not set out to grow a church—that has been a by-product. We focused on responding to the passion God placed in our hearts to reach people for Christ by breaking down deeply embedded stereotypes in the hearts and minds of those who were turned off to church—not Jesus so much, just church. Over the past fifteen years, sacrifice and steadfast obedience to this all-consuming vision have led us into the experience of living by risky faith.

Not only have we experienced another growth spurt recently, but in the middle of a culture with fiscal fears, God is honoring us financially. We still believe that Salem Fields Community Church has "captured the imagination of God," evidenced by His favor, not only financially but also through the reality of transformed lives.

It is a simple prescription. We keep our eyes focused on the vision He has given us to impact our community and world for Him. We wholeheartedly believe as we *live out* the gospel message, the Holy Spirit woos hearts toward Jesus. We invite people to jump with us into this adventure. As we are experiencing this adventure of faith, we *focus on keeping our commitment*, which produces growth. These two particular commitments seem to be significant.

Radical Generosity

In a culture where nonchurchgoers have become skeptical of the church, SFCC is attempting to break down the mentality that "all the church wants is my money." We give extravagantly to local, national, and global needs. As much as we try, we cannot seem to outgive God, but we keep trying. Not only are we teaching people to take the risk of giving God the first of everything they have, but we are also living out that example as leaders and as a community of faith.

Faith is like walking off the edge of a cliff with the confidence that God will build a bridge under our feet as we go, one foot at a time. That is our philosophy: Faith precedes dollars; faith forges on in spite of obstacles. With each step we have taken, the bridge of God's economy has extended beneath our feet. These are some of the ways we have forged ahead with radical generosity.

In September 2007 we completed a seven-million-dollar building project, intentionally created and designed for people in the surrounding area to connect in nonthreatening ways. The Rubicon Café extends into the community, inviting those who might never step into a church building to come in and relax. Pete's Place bookstore makes finding resources for living easy, and Salem Fields Learning Center is a safe, warm environment that provides childcare as parents provide for their families in the workplace. The building is available free of charge to everyone, from business people, schoolteachers, and leadership conferees to those attending banquets, weddings, and after-prom parties.

Changing a "churched" mentality is difficult, and many of the "feed me" crowd couldn't make the transition to being so others-focused. There was a painful exodus of some, including tithers; however, our target audience increased, and we are reaching people for Jesus. Excitingly, with our monthly mortgage extending from $8,000 a month to $50,000 a month, the obedience of those passionately carrying the vision has brought about God's overwhelming provision. All bills are paid in full, and we have no outstanding debt apart from our mortgage. That alone amazes us as we look at this journey that began fifteen years ago with an incredible amount of faith and nine dollars in the bank!

At our church we have committed that no matter how hard-pressed our finances become, we will pay our denominational budgets in full. We consider budgets our tithe. We are leading the way in what we are teaching—the joy of obedience through tithing and the blessing of going above and beyond. As we look back to the painstaking process endured through the exhausting, lengthy, and overbudget building project, we are amazed at how God provided for all of our financial obligations. Our goal is to continue to stretch until we are giving away 20 percent of our annual income.

When we established a need for a million dollars to offset the cost of the new building, our strategy was risky: "Have a need; plant a seed." Led by a vision to reach people through radical generosity, the church board voted to *give away* one hundred thousand dollars. Checks were given out to well-deserving organizations and ministries around the local region of Fredericksburg and Spotsylvania, as well as extending from coast to coast. It was fun giving money away! We have not received that million-dollar check yet, but we wonder if the blessings we are enjoying right now are because of that risky obedience. We are sure God is blessing us in many unseen ways.

Recently we established a new ministry, GO (Global Outreach). GO is specifically designed to give our resources and ourselves away to serve others locally, nationally, and globally through a wide variety of efforts. All ministry teams (leadership boards, students, children, staff, and so on) spend one day per month in our community in service projects, giving without expecting anything in return. Distributing flowers and doughnuts, washing windows, housecleaning, lawn care, home repairs, and building wheelchair ramps are a few examples. We blitz the community by feeding the homeless, providing back-to-school supplies for underprivileged children, supporting single-parent families, and giving teen moms new hope and skills for the future. Our generosity moves us to send ongoing teams to rebuild homes for Hurricane Katrina victims on the Gulf Coast as well as those affected by tornadoes.

Our generosity extends to other countries. We are meeting needs in Ecuador by bringing hope to children in that country. Salem Fields Port Harcourt, a venue that evolved deep within the bowels of Nigeria, is alive and well. This ministry reaches youth through our Pastors James and Charity Onwah. They carry a passion to reach people through meeting real needs. They take the church to sports fields each week and share the love of Christ in word and action. Many have professed faith in Christ as a result of James and Charity's obedience. Parents are seeing positive changes in their children's lives and are being drawn to Christ. Our church board voted unanimously to buy James and Charity a much-needed automobile and give one hundred thousand dollars to buy land to build a ministry center that will not only meet physical and spiritual needs but also train boys and girls, men and women in vocations that will allow them to rise above their hopeless environment.

Not only do we have faith that God gave this vision of radical generosity to our church, but we also believe He gave a financial vision to support the funding of that vision. We sought Him, and He provided it. We have a strategized giving plan. This plan focuses on three specifically defined offerings a year: those at Thanksgiving, Easter, and Christmas. It cuts out fund-raising; it reduces the number of love offerings by providing for those needs through our general fund; it informs people where every dollar is used through a quarterly newsletter, and it provides a "Ninety-Day Tithe Challenge"—"If God does not bless you in ninety days, we'll give back the total you gave." The stories and testimonies of God's blessing in the lives of people who took the challenge have been overwhelming. We have videoed many of these testimonies and show them in the weekend services to encourage others to catch the vision of being radically generous.

Radical Authenticity and Grace

We have a beautiful pond in front of our building. It attracts geese. On the outside, these creatures are especially beautiful when they land against the backdrop of the sun. But if you know anything about geese, you realize that they make a mess everywhere—on sidewalks, on the asphalt, on the grassy banks. It's stinky and gross. Recently we learned of a clandestine plan to kill the geese so no one would have to deal with the mess again. We quickly intercepted the plan, and it did not take long for a metaphor of life, too often represented by believers, to emerge.

A publication sent out by the general superintendents stated that the church needs to be a "grace community" where people "participate in the grace of hospitality and character formation." That has been our commitment for fifteen years, but it has been messy. It is really all about how you deal with the mess. There is a high personal cost when grace is extended in a faith community; it kicks you out of your comfort zone. We don't hear much about that at conferences or get training in "mess management." Little is discussed about the pain and loss that accompany the creation of a community that extends grace. Seldom do we hear about how leaders overcome doubts, withstand unfair accusations, or dig deep into ongoing introspection, all necessary to create a grace-filled community. Our leadership consultant informed us that God would allow us to carry this vision as far as our tolerance for pain would allow. "Messy" means constant annoyances, frustrations, and nerve-wracking personal challenges. It is the reason we sometimes consider working at Wal-Mart instead of in the local church, but there is a hook that keeps us here. It is the transformed lives, evidence of a supernatural power that has infiltrated our church. God has drawn the "messy" lives of people to us. Our hearts are broken by the messes they have gotten into. We are constantly faced with the effects that sin has had on people of all ages, ethnicity, and gender. It is painful. It would be much easier to shoo them away so we don't have to face the mess and can stay comfortable.

However, character won't have a chance to reform, develop, and restore unless someone or someplace is willing to deal with it. We are so thankful that Jesus tolerated our mess. Our call and our vision are to create an environment where people have permission to bring their "mess" and still be accepted just as they are. An authentic community of grace lowers the barriers that may have hidden Jesus previously. We invite people to relax through laughter, food, and music. Some call that "entertainment," but we see it as reestablishing trust through hospitality and a welcoming, respectful spirit. Everything we do in our weekend services is focused on reaching that person who never went to church, quit because it wasn't relevant, or was turned off because there were too many walls hiding Jesus. We look through those eyes. We listen to those voices, because we remember when we were there. It is in that kind of environment in which people feel safe to hear and respond to the convicting voice of the Holy Spirit.

Voices in the world have found some legitimate hypocrisy that has eroded the credibility of Christians. The unwillingness to throw off our comfy security blankets has covered up the beautiful message of Christ and has dampened the unexplainable joy of a relationship with Him. The only antidote to hypocrisy is transparency and authenticity. It's risky; it's gutsy.

We stopped the plan to get rid of the geese, and we reemphasized that it is our facilities manager's job to see that there is a plan for continual cleanup. We want the geese, so we will have to accept the mess that goes along with their beauty. Salem Fields Community Church will be a place that welcomes the mess, even though we might have to watch out for it, step over it sometimes, or maybe clean it off our shoes when we step in it! The Holy Spirit will gently do His job to woo, infiltrate, and transform hearts. We will carry out our responsibility to teach the truth and love, show grace, and accept people as they are.

We did not strategize all of this so that our church would grow. First, we sought God for His vision for Fredericksburg, Spotsylvania, and the surrounding area, as well as His vision of how to support it. By faith, we have jumped off the cliff. Sometimes fear creeps in and our eyes get distracted; sometimes it seems as though we will crash. We are then reminded of who brought us here and the availability of that bridge beneath our feet. We refocus, step out again, and remember that as leaders we will stand before God and have to answer the question "What did you do with what I gave you?" The reality of that focuses our attention to continue to do our part so that the Holy Spirit is free to do what only He can do—change hearts. It's all about where you place your focus.

Gene Tanner is the pastor at Valparaiso, Indiana, Church of the Nazarene. He has pastored churches in Ohio, Virginia, and Indiana. Gene graduated from Central Michigan University (BA) and Olivet Nazarene University (MA). Valparaiso Church has grown from 527 in average worship attendance in 1994 to 1,364 in 2010. Gene and his wife, Tamra, have two grown children. genet@valponaz.org

DISCIPLING AS A JOURNEY

GENE TANNER

In one sentence our "journey of discipleship" is an organized plan for taking visitors on a journey to salvation—sanctification, membership, assimilation, and maturity. While this seems like an overwhelming task, we have found our journey to be an effective tool. Most people will run on a track if they can see where a track exists. Sometimes we make a mistake of hoping people will run with us, but we fail to show them where to run. We hope our journey of discipleship leaves a clear track. We have based much of our journey on the Rick Warren book *The Purpose-Driven Church*. We have taken Pastor Warren's book and modified it to fit the unique needs and goals of Valparaiso Church. As others consider our journey, I would urge that you also modify our work to fit your needs.

Assimilate Visitors

Our growth has been based on the assimilation of visitors. Not everyone who visits our church desires to come back, but for the ones who show interest, we have a plan to bring them into the body. Once a visitor fills in the connection card available on his or her visit, it opens the door with information for us to follow through. I phone visitors Sunday afternoon to let them know I have received their card and to thank them for visiting. I make a home call on all visitors on Thursday or Friday of that week. I want to see them at the end of the week, so if they promise to return, I have a promise made later in the week as opposed to earlier in the week. I write a report on each home visit. This report goes to our director of adult ministries, Pam Anderson. In the next week, Pam begins a connection with a follow-up phone call. The desire here is to connect and lead them into our journey of discipleship. When I call in the home, if I find the kids are athletic I place this information on the report to Pam. She follows up by telling them about the children's sports programs. If I notice a grand piano in the living room, this is reported, and Pam highlights our music ministries. We use the home call with my report to attract visitors to their interests. Our intent is to guide them into our corporate journey.

Our journey of discipleship is based on the 101-201-301 class model. In our vision statement for the journey we define the entire process: "Sometimes in the journey called life, we can feel all alone. Valparaiso Nazarene Church wants to help you on this spiritual pilgrimage called life. We want to help you discover how to navigate this incredible journey that God has in store for you and for those you travel this road with at VNC."

Course 101

The journey begins with 101. The 101 course is six Wednesdays from 6:30 to 8:00 P.M. As lead pastor, I teach this course. It creates the opportunity for me to connect with new people and helps to build a comfortable relationship. The course is repeated four to five times annually.

The 101 course is mandatory for those desiring membership at VNC. We purposely do the course on Wednesday nights as this is one of our primary nights for children's ministries.

The largest age-group of new people falls between the ages of twenty to forty-five; most have children. They do not need to find babysitting to attend the 101 course—they simply bring their children to our Wednesday programs. This is very important to our design. Once their children have been a part of our ministries on Wednesdays for six weeks, the children want to come back! This is a great tool for encouraging adult attendance.

The setup of the room is very important to the success of the journey. Tables are round and combined to form groups of sixteen. There are seven couples (or singles filling the chairs) plus one couple who is not new. Since most are strangers, we all have name tags. There is one couple at each table who act as "trail guides." The trail guides are established members of VNC; they are there to create a connection among the group and to guide the new people through the six weeks. When the six weeks are over, we continue each group as a small group, meeting at least once per month. After the course, the trail guide transitions into the group leader, setting times and places for continued meetings. Those in 101 have now grown into a small group. Small groups tend to work if everyone begins together and has a shared experience. They all have the shared experience of starting at VNC at approximately the same time, and they have spent six Wednesdays together in class.

The 101 class has the following mission: "Within us there is a longing for a deeper walk with Christ. This is the beginning of the journey. If you were going on a trip, you would always check your supply list to make sure you had the basics for survival. At VNC we offer this six-week class to give you the tools you will need for the journey toward being a fully devoted follower of Christ. This class will teach you about the reality of prayer, Bible study, and service in your relationship with God. It also prepares you to fulfill the Great Commission by living a life of service."

Session One

Each session begins with fifteen minutes of sharing within each group. The connection time is important if we hope to see them evolve from strangers into a small group. The first session begins with the trail guides telling their story. As the six weeks progress, every person or couple will have the chance to tell their story to the group. We begin with the trail guides as they set the tone of openness and vulnerability. The first session covers the history of the Church of the Nazarene, how we came to be. We tell of Pilot Point, Dr. Bresee, and the world mission of our church. From here, we tell the story of VNC, our beginnings in 1924 at the corner of Lafayette and Monroe streets in Valparaiso. The key is to let them know we have a story and that their story is now part of our ongoing story.

We want them to sense ownership early in the sessions. We want them to have a sense of being a part of something bigger than just this church. A sense of history will do this. Next, we explain salvation.

Salvation is explained, no preaching, no clichés, no long stories—just a relationship with Jesus. There is a box in the back of the room. I have three-by-five cards and pens with this promise: "We will be together for six weeks; maybe you came with a question you wanted answered. It would be sad to be here all this time and never have it answered. Write your question on a card, and drop it in the box. At the last session, I will answer the questions." At the end of the first session I say, "If anyone prayed the prayer of salvation, write on a card, 'I prayed the prayer.'" I have never had a 101 class without people coming to Christ in this first session.

Session Two

In the second session we begin to share some strategy. We unveil our mission statement—"Helping you become fully devoted followers of Jesus." We talk about execution. Without execution our mission statement is merely a slogan. Our execution is based on something we call worship+2. Our church is very good at worship; now let's focus on +2. Our two other parts of the puzzle are growth and service. If worship is the only thing you do at VNC, you are seeing only one-third of the picture of what God has for you. We also explain our goals for outreach. Here we use Pastor Warren's definitions of "community," "crowd," "congregation," "committed," and "core." We end this session by defining "worship." As worship is part of our execution in worship+2, we must define our terms. We make clear that worship is what we give God, not what God gives to us. The elements are (1) celebration (Psalm 122:1), (2) inspiration (Isaiah 40:31), (3) preparation (Ephesians 4:12), (4) communication of God's Word (Ephesians 3:10), (5) witness (Acts 1:8), and (6) maturity (Hebrews 6:1). All these elements help you become a fully devoted follower of Jesus. We end the session with our core values.

Session Three

The third session takes us back to theology. We teach the core beliefs and focus on free agency and sanctification. Prayer and developing our walk by allowing the Word into our hearts are themes here. We pray the prayer of sanctification at the conclusion of this class. While I do not repeat the "I prayed the prayer" activity on a three-by-five card, I have had great feedback from those who prayed the prayer of sanctification.

Session Four

The fourth session is building on where we have been. How cute to see a baby, but if the baby looks the same in a year, something is very wrong. Nourishment and connection are vital for a baby to grow. It is the same for us spiritually. We begin to talk about taking our tables of sixteen people and changing them to small groups.

Once the 101 class is over, there is a class specifically designed for growth meeting on Wednesdays in this time slot. (The kids are already locked in— why pull them out just because 101 ended?) If the participants are not planning on being a part of the next sessions, we ask that they share specific plans on how they are going to grow. Remember—our mission is to help the convert become a fully devoted follower of Jesus. There are other options of connection and growth at VNC, and I explain the ministries available to them and talk about participation.

We stress that growth is not an accident. Growth is always a decision and is purposeful. We explain, "The church cannot grow you—you must grow you." We conclude by coming back to the execution of worship+2.

Session Five

Session five is designed to teach God's plan for the church. Every Christian is to be a part of a church family, or else he or she is an orphan. Unity is a key here. We are all different but unified, much like an orchestra is made up of different instruments but plays the same song.

A church has a skeleton. As we can't grow beyond our skeleton, a church will not grow beyond its skeleton. The skeleton is composed of fellowship (Acts 2:42). We are fellows on a ship. We are rowing together. We partner together and with God in what He has for VNC. Our story is your story. The second piece of our skeleton is family (1 Peter 3:8). Blood is thick. Jesus' blood paid a price I could not pay, and as blood brothers and sisters, we function in this divine family relationship with one another. We forgive each other, we lift each other up, and we encourage each other. The requirement of a pastor in 1 Timothy is that he manages his family. We are a family, not an organization. The third part of our skeleton is body. We are a body not a business (Romans 12:4-6). Each part is important, and you are important. Everyone has a gift that God expects us to use. Our execution is worship+2 grow and serve. No one on the sidelines! Why did God bring you to this church? What does He want you to bring to this body? The fourth and final part of our skeleton is flock (John 21:16). Let us flock around you. No one should laugh alone or cry alone. As you are part of VNC, we want to flock around you. I give examples of the church meeting individual families' needs (no names are given).

Session Six

Session six concludes by discussing the difference between a guest and a homeowner. A guest can sit on the furniture and watch television. The homeowner must vacuum and make the beds. There are guests in the church, but our desire is that they become owners. The key here is service. Ministry opportunities are discussed, and an interest survey is taken to help place new members in areas of meaningful service. If they desire, we want them involved immediately. This session also discusses financing the vision. We explain that tithe is not strictly a Nazarene concept, but we walk through the biblical teaching and blessing. We detail the tithe envelope with its unique lines for faith promise and our building pledges. Time is spent on membership, and application forms are passed out.

Completing the course does not guarantee membership. I am sure to deal with any concerns or red flags from the application privately. Time is also spent with the trail guides in designing their first group meeting for the next month. If anyone has not told his or her life story, this is also completed. I end by answering any questions left in the box.

Finally, the staff makes a contact with the class members to help assimilate new members into the ministry of interest.

Course 201

Once the 101 class is complete, the class members automatically progress into 201. The mission statement of 201 is "So what happens next? You have traveled the journey for a few weeks, picked up some supplies, gained some knowledge about the lay of the land, and met some great people who are heading in the same direction. Some of us are wired to be around people. Some of us are not. For those who need more time in relationships, we encourage you to continue your spiritual growth and get involved in a connection group. Your connection group will include a trail guide and a group of people you can meet with periodically to discuss life and God. You'll also be able to live life together."

The 201 is the continuation of the group that met for six weeks in 101. It is an important step. It keeps them together. The log out of the fire is the first to burn out no matter how hot it was in the fire. We set 201 to keep everyone in the fire. The small connection group is our strategy to accomplish this.

Course 301

We then go straight to 301. The mission statement for 301 is "In the marketplace, many of us have to continue in our education to 'keep up.' In our journey, we need ongoing education to grow in our faith. Our relationships grow and deepen as we get to know each other more intimately. In our relationship with God, He has given us a great resource to know Him more, the Bible. The core is designed to keep you growing as a follower of Christ. In these different classes, you will be challenged to go deeper and discover a continuing maturity as you walk with Christ."

The 301 is the class we really desire our 101 graduates to attend. It is on Wednesday and is scheduled around the 101 schedule. When the 101 class is completed, there is a new 301 class beginning the next Wednesday night. The 301 class is taught by staff and covers such subjects as the Book of John. As their children are in our Wednesday night programs, this becomes a natural step for our new believers.

As we have stayed faithful to this intentional disciple-making plan, it has been blessed by God. For the past five years, VNC has brought in more than 100 new members by profession of faith each year.

Dan Newburg is the pastor of Gardner, Kansas, Church of the Nazarene. Gardner is Dan's first church after graduating from Nazarene Theological Seminary with an MDiv degree. Gardner has grown in the fifteen years of Dan's ministry from 46 to 131 in average worship attendance. He and his wife, Denise, live in Gardner with their four teenagers. gardner_nazarene@yahoo.com

▪▪ 8 ▪▪
BECOMING MISSIONAL
AND TRADITIONAL

DAN NEWBURG

I began attending Sunday services shortly following my birth, and according to older family members, I hardly ever missed. On my way to my expected seat, I would pass my grandparents, great-aunts and great-uncles, and aunts and uncles. I would find seated on the front row my siblings: Steve, Tom, Connie, and Jim. As I would look into the choir loft, I would see my dad, Jerry, and at the organ my mom, Marilyn.

The holy seasons of Advent and Lent had a powerful impact on my formation. I would watch each week as the Advent candles were lit, leading to that blessed night when we commemorated Jesus' birth. As an adult, I recognize that each of the Advent candles has a spiritual significance. However, as a child, I found that the anticipation would grow stronger as each successive candle was lit. I remember thinking, *Only three more weeks until Christmas; only two more weeks until Christmas; only one more week until Christmas.* At midnight on Christmas Eve, I would think, *Tomorrow morning I finally get to open presents!* The traditions of the church created the memories; it was the church that created the sense of anticipation.

The same impact continued into the Lent-Easter season. Each Wednesday night of Lent was made more special knowing that all my relatives would be coming to our house for sandwiches, coffee, and dessert. After most services my Great-aunt Eva would state, "Oh, Marilyn, we don't want to impose. You have all those kids, and they have school tomorrow." My mom would reply, "Don't be silly. The coffee is on, and the sandwiches are made." At this Aunt Eva would instruct Uncle Hoyt, "Well, in that case, Bussy, run down to the car and get those rolls I baked."

On Palm Sunday we would enter the sanctuary waving our Palm branches to the congregation's singing of "All Glory, Laud, and Honor." On Thursday of Holy Week, Maundy Thursday, we would receive Communion. On Good Friday morning we would observe the community-wide service, and that evening we would participate in the Tenebrae service. Holy Week would reach its grand conclusion as we celebrated the resurrection of Jesus Christ on Easter Sunday. Indeed, the traditions of the Church are clearly etched in my memory.

In the early months of 1989 I was called into pastoral ministry and moved to Kansas City to attend Nazarene Theological Seminary. The comments of numerous professors and chapel speakers challenged me. For instance, Stan Toler suggested in one service, "If I had to do it all over again, I would be back at the church where I began my ministry." Gary Henecke added, "The problem with the Church of the Nazarene is just about the time the local community learns the name of the Nazarene pastor, he or she leaves." These statements had a profound impact on my ministry. Through them, God was shaping my view of mission in the local church and the importance of pastoral longevity in building long-term relationships in order for the church to be missional.

When I left Nazarene Theological Seminary, my commitment was to follow God's leading to a church—and stay. It was never my intent to serve at one location while looking to the next opportunity. I vowed I would never serve a congregation with the intent to move to a new assignment.

Gardner Church Journey

When I accepted the call to pastor the Gardner, Kansas, church, it was a church in crisis. Two years prior to my arrival, the church suffered a split. Conditions at the church had become very serious; the decision was made by the district leadership to close the church. The remaining twenty-five members refused to believe that the church doors should be locked. They were hurting, but in their pain they clearly stated their belief that God had a reason for His church to be in Gardner.

Keith Wright, Kansas City district superintendent, asked if I would be interested in interviewing for the position. "Dan, they're hurting. What they need is for someone to come in and just love them." An interview was arranged. They elected me as their pastor, and I began a love affair with a group of people and the community of Gardner, Kansas, that continues after fifteen years.

Our Relational Journey

In the church of my youth, Pastor Carl Eliason was the one constant. In every way he represented stability for the community of faith. When new building projects brought change to the church facility, Pastor Eliason was the one constant. When issues of polity were discussed, he led the congregation through the difficult process. When my grandparents died, he cried while officiating at their funerals. When my siblings and I were baptized, he held each of us in his arms. When my parents lost a child, he mourned with them. Our pastor was always present. I never wondered if he would leave. He was there, in the good times as well as the bad. It never occurred to me that it could be any other way.

I believe that it takes a period of three to five years before a pastor begins to know and be known by a congregation. It takes time for the pastor's strengths and weaknesses to be known. It also takes time for the pastor to know the congregation. Who fills the role of patriarch or matriarch? Who has been hurt, and how? Who struggles to offer grace? Who finds it difficult to receive grace? Who is able to handle a pastor's openness and honesty, strengths and weaknesses, and who cannot?

Long-term ministry means to become vulnerable, sometimes to the point that the pastor can be hurt. Based on the frequency of moving pastors, it appears the idea of being known is a challenge that is difficult for some to handle. However, when the pastor and congregation express openness toward one another, then strengths and weaknesses are known, the pastor and congregation choose to love each other, to live redemptively together, and real community exists.

This is what the Church should be. We must live in such a way that, in spite of our differences, in spite of our weaknesses, in spite of the fact that we sometimes hurt each other, we still choose to love each other and live together in community. How can this happen if the pastor leaves every three years?

I once heard Jeren Rowell say, "I tell my people that I'm on a journey, and they are invited to join me." Through relationships that developed over time, I have been invited into their lives.

Eldon and Audrey were two of the twenty-five who fought to keep the church open. Their daughter, Gloria, her husband, John, and their children, Krista and Greg, were a part of the original twenty-five. They were all kind to me, but none of them really trusted me. The unspoken question seemed to be, "How long will you stay before you leave?" Fifteen years later, we are extremely close because of the relational journey we have been on together.

Two years after I arrived, Eldon was diagnosed with brain cancer. I offered pastoral care, visiting him on many occasions. I was asked to officiate at his funeral, my first. Six years later, I officiated at Audrey's funeral.

Greg was married two weeks after we arrived. Several years later, he and his wife were blessed with a beautiful little girl. Before her first birthday, she was diagnosed with leukemia. After a long, hard battle, her cancer went into remission, and after five years she was declared cancer-free.

Many times Krista told me she wondered if she would ever meet "Mr. Right." She did, and at her wedding her little niece was the flower girl. Unwilling to walk down the aisle by herself, Greg carried his three-year-old daughter to the front of the church. As I watched, God gave me a vision into the future, a vision of the same daddy and little girl walking down the aisle on the young lady's wedding day.

I was there when Krista informed the family that she was pregnant with twins. I was there when she told the family she had lost them. I was there for the memorial service, releasing balloons for the twins and two other babies she miscarried. I was also there when Jack was born, and I was there when she recently announced that another baby was on the way. I was there when Greg announced that his wife was pregnant, even though they had thought they were unable to conceive again.

I have been their pastor. I was with them through the good times and the bad times. I officiated at funerals, crying with them as we stood together next to a casket. I officiated at weddings, rejoicing with them at one of the most sacred times of life. I celebrated new arrivals and held their children as they were dedicated to the Lord. I know their strengths and weaknesses, and they know mine. We choose daily to love each other, to live redemptively with each other. Others notice, and they want to be a part of this community of faith.

Our Traditional Journey

The rich traditions of the church have become a key component to the growth and stability of the Gardner church. Believing there would be a positive impact, I decided to implement some of the same traditional elements of worship that I experienced growing up. The congregation seemed to embrace these traditions wholeheartedly. In the midst of a church culture that continually wrestles with style, method, and a host of other issues, we discovered and accepted the fact that it was okay to identify ourselves as "the traditional alternative."

We sing hymns, have frequent Communion, "pass the peace," and pray the Lord's Prayer every Sunday. We meet together for Sunday school, Sunday morning and Sunday evening worship services, and Wednesday night prayer meeting.

We began to use the church calendar, the major seasons of the church year, to make our own memories. The most significant of these seasons has become the time from the first Sunday of Advent through Easter. We used the Advent wreath, lighting the first four candles as symbols of expectation, proclamation, joy, and purity. The celebration reaches its conclusion on Christmas Eve. During this service, the Christ candle is lit in honor of His birth, at the same time anticipating His second advent.

Rather than pack the Christ candle into a box, along with the other Christmas decorations, we have chosen to display it in a prominent place in the sanctuary, continuing to light it each Sunday as a part of the service. The symbolic power of this candle became clear one Sunday when we simply forgot to light it. In the middle of the service an usher came to me with this message, "Kip wanted to let you know that the Christ candle is not lit." What amazed me was that the person who noticed was not a believer. Could it be this simple symbol has evangelistic potential?

We continue to light the Christ candle every Sunday through the season of Lent. The only exception to this is on Good Friday at our Tenebrae service. As the passion narrative is read, recalling the suffering and death of our Savior, the candle is extinguished when the words are spoken, "Then Jesus, having uttered a loud cry, breathed his last breath."[1] The congregation is left sitting in a dark, silent sanctuary to consider the price Jesus paid. While the symbolic power of darkness on Good Friday is overwhelming, it cannot surpass the impact made on the congregation on Easter Sunday when the darkness is broken by the light of the relit Christ candle. Carried into a darkened sanctuary, the light of this candle reminds us that the light of Christ has overcome the darkness of sin and death.

Our Missional Journey

Gardner church knows my faults and weaknesses, and they love me. The congregation lives with that same assurance. We function as a redemptive community; we live as a community that reflects the love of Christ, and it causes us to be missional.

As the "love of Christ reflecting redemptive community," we are on a missional journey touching lives of thousands of people annually who do not yet know Jesus as their Savior. In 1995 the Gardner church met on Sunday mornings but had no Sunday evening service, Wednesday evening service, or other ministries. Since 1995 we have intentionally focused outward, missionally. And we have experienced steady growth as new believers have been attracted and become involved in our "traditional *and* missional" journey. The remnant of twenty-five members has become 145 members and an average of 130 to 150 in our morning worship service. Recently I was asked to relate how many missional ministries we were involved in. I had to think for a while to compile the list. There were twenty-six outwardly focused missional ministries that we could identify. We know others are occurring, because being missional is who we are. It's not a program but a redemptive community relational journey; relation with God, with one another and with the community where God has placed us. Yes we are traditional—*and* we are missional!

Ministry	Description
1. Angel Food	Half cost monthly food distribution
2. Mobile Food Pantry	Free monthly fresh food distribution of dairy, vegetables, bakery, and so on
3. Local Food Pantry	As needed at the church
4. Backpack	Food into backpacks on Friday for at-risk kids for weekend at two local schools
5. HUGS Program	Hats, Underwear, Gloves, and Socks (kids at elementary school)

6. Public Servant Appreciation   Provided baked goods for police, fire and city workers; cookies and breads

7. Trunk or Treat/ Hallelujah   Halloween alternative

8. Thanksgiving Dinner   Free community-wide Thanksgiving dinner at the church

9. Big Tent Event   Concert, food, games, free school supplies

10. VBS   Week-long outreach to community, culminating in the Big Tent Event

11. Free Family Counseling   Professional marriage and family counseling

12. LMNOP   Love Meeting Needs of People (raking, cleaning, shopping, minor repairs)

13. Prayer Shawl   Ladies knit comfort shawls and give to hospitalized and bereaved

14. Juvenile Detention Center   Sunday morning Bible studies at the detention center

15. Christmas Eve Memoirs Service   Service of remembrance for those in the community who have lost loved ones

16. Soccer Camp   Teens provide a camp for area children

17. Foster Families   Various families in the church provide foster care for children

18. Annual Mission Trip   Work and Witness week-long trip

19. Local Missions   Support of other churches with painting, heating system, materials, repairs

20. Tapestry   Women's ministries; food for bereavement, support; women supporting women

21. DMG   Disorganized Men's Group (fun outings for all men)

22. China Showcase   Women; fancy banquet with speaker, sponsored tables, fun and fellowship

23. Women's Retreat   Spiritual renewal for friends and members

24. Nursing Home Ministries   Provide worship services for three care centers

25. Pathway to Hope   Mental health ministry with intervention and professional counseling

26. Gardner Serve Day   In partnership with eight other area churches, roadside and city parks beautification

Daron Brown, the older brother of this pair, is the pastor of Waverly, Tennessee, Church of the Nazarene. This is his first church since graduating from Trevecca Nazarene University and Nazarene Theological Seminary with an MDiv degree. In his nine years as pastor, Waverly has grown from sixty-eight in average morning worship attendance to just a little under two hundred. Daron and wife, Katie, have three little ones living with them in Waverly. pastordaron@waverlynazarene.net

Ryan Brown, the younger brother of this dynamic duo, is the pastor of Hendersonville, Tennessee, Church of the Nazarene. This is also his first church, where he has pastored for three years. The church has rebounded from a low of fifty-five in worship when Ryan arrived to 134 average attendance in 2010. Ryan is completing his ordination educational requirements through the District Ministry Training School. Ryan and wife, Jamie, live with their two children in Hendersonville. pastorryanbrown@yahoo.com

·· 9 ··
FULFILLING MISSIONAL PURPOSE
A TALE OF TWO BROTHERS
DARON AND RYAN BROWN

Night and day. Oil and water. Daron and Ryan. We have parents in common. But not much else. Our story is Cain and Abel or Jacob and Esau without all the drama. We were born two years apart in the mid-1970s in Clarksville, Tennessee. Daron was dark-haired, small framed, and bookish. Ryan was blonde with a big build and an aversion to school. Daron was the introvert who looked for reasons not to speak. Ryan was the extrovert who spent several years in the sales industry. Daron is organized and deliberate. Ryan is, well—not so much. In fact, it's a minor miracle we managed to collaborate on this writing project. If you saw us, you would not guess we are brothers. And if you get to know us, you would be less convinced that we're related. Our personalities and interests vary. Some people might say that Daron was the "good sheep" while Ryan was the "black sheep." The truth is that Daron was never as good as many people thought. And Ryan was never as bad as many people thought. Nevertheless, we are both God's sheep. And it is good to know that God loves and welcomes and calls all kinds of sheep.

Early Years

We were ages ten and eight when our parents divorced. Our sister, Laura, was five. We were a fragmented family in more ways than one. Our fragile single-parent household craved completion. We found ourselves vulnerable emotionally, spiritually, and financially. Looking back, we know that our young lives could have taken any number of wrong directions.

In 1985 our single-parent mom began searching for a church family for the four of us. We were in and out of some fine churches that didn't seem to fit. When we entered the doors of Clarksville First Church of the Nazarene, we found our home. We were quickly and warmly received by the church. Several older couples took an interest in us. They saw a family in need of stability and support. They invested in us and loved us. This connection was one of the turning points in the life of our family. We like to think that, in a way, the church saved us before we even knew Jesus.

If our story has a hero (besides God), it would be our mother—a single mom who raised three children. She worked two and sometimes three jobs to keep bills paid and bellies full. After the divorce, we moved into a small two-bedroom apartment. Laura had a room to herself. We shared the other room. For years mom slept on a pullout sofa bed in the living room. To this day she has back problems to prove it. We witnessed in our mother a true self-giving spirit. She modeled one of our most important life lessons: love means sacrifice. Her constant willingness to put her own interests on the back burner for our sakes was not lost on us. It was mom who prompted us to receive God's salvation at the altar during a Sunday night service in 1987. She has been our greatest cheerleader throughout our lives. Her wide smile and nurturing spirit have been graces of God at work in us.

Our later childhood and teenage years were lived at church. We attended church camps, played church league sports, went on church mission trips, and took part in every other church activity. Seeds were planted. Some of them took root immediately. Others took years to germinate.

Divergence: Daron's Path

During our teenage years our paths diverged. I (Daron) continued to grow deeper into the life of the church. My relationship with God strengthened. My faith grew. One of the turning points of my journey was a hot summer morning. Our youth pastor asked me to "go get a Coke" with him. I remember thinking "A Coke? Are you serious? I have Coke in my fridge." The two of us drove around and talked. We ended up in a parking lot at Governor's Square Mall. I remember his telling me that I could be a leader. In that moment something changed in me. I walked away from that conversation with a newfound confidence that I could be a leader of others. It was as if I had no choice in the matter. I saw myself as a leader, and I *was* a leader. Not that I've always been a good one. But since that day I have known that I *am* one.

I can trace my call to ministry back into my early childhood years. The signposts were all there pointing me to a life of vocational ministry. I didn't always see them at the time, but in hindsight they are clear. Throughout my teen years I ignored my call. Stricken with severe stage fright, I did not give it much thought. Several people told me that I would be a preacher one day, which only increased my resistance.

When high school graduation came, I did not have to think about where to attend college. I applied to one school, Trevecca Nazarene University. During my first semester, I continued to struggle with my call. God would not call someone who cannot speak—surely He's never done that before! I painfully recall the day I was to stand in front of my speech class. It wasn't even a speech. I was just supposed to act out one word. My word was "amused." I stood before the class and froze. People began guessing my word: "Confused."

"Scared." "Embarrassed." After an awkward eternity, all I could say was, "I can't do this." And I sat down. Later, I buried my face in my pillow and cried like a baby. "God, You can't be calling *me* to preach!"

During the fall revival on campus God continued His relentless work. On Thursday night, He wooed me to the altar. Conversation ensued:

"I'm calling you."

"You can't be."

"I am."

"I can't."

"I'll be with you."

That night the struggle ended. I answered God's call, still unsure of how it would work. My submission to God's call was my moment of entire sanctification. It was the last unyielded part of my life. There have been many times since then that I've questioned *why* God has called me. But since that day, I have never questioned *that* God has called me.

I received my bachelor of arts degree in pastoral ministry at Trevecca before moving to Kansas City to pursue my master of divinity degree at Nazarene Theological Seminary. Needless to say, my educational path was the classic, prescribed journey for one called in the Church of the Nazarene. I cherish my education. Both institutions gave me solid theological footing for a life of pastoral ministry.

Divergence: Ryan's Path

In my (Ryan's) later teen years, I drifted away from the Lord. My older brother chose to be "the older brother." He opted for obedience. Knowing that I didn't want to be like him, I set off for the distant country. I began hanging around the wrong crowds and making bad choices. It was a classic story of teenage rebellion: smoking, alcohol, and sex. When I started college, my major was wild living. I soon left school to pursue my major with more vigor.

In my teens and twenties, I had about a dozen different careers. I drove a truck, managed a few restaurants, owned my own restaurant, and sold insurance. With the memory of a relationship with God, my life had become aimless and unsettled.

I met and in less than ten months married the love of my life. And God gave us two beautiful children. Even though I was a family man, I continued to live unhappy and unsettled. After a few years, my selfishness began to jeopardize my marriage. Thinking that my wife was the problem, I desperately returned to Clarksville First Church of the Nazarene so God would "fix" her. Instead, He changed me.

It was Jamie's first exposure to Jesus and to church life. Our whole family was hungry for God. And we took every opportunity to satisfy that hunger.

We enrolled in discipleship courses and began serving in every way we could. God had called the younger brother home.

On a summer evening when I was in my late twenties, God called me to preach. I was at home. No public altar call. No fanfare. I was blindsided and scared. No one had ever pulled me aside and told me that I would be a preacher. I didn't have the chorus of voices directing me to the pulpit as Daron had. Just one voice—God's voice. He was clear. For the first time in my life, I became settled and focused.

While serving as a lay leader at Clarksville First Church, I began preparing for ministry in the district course of study. I was grateful to be surrounded by pastors and mentors who coached me forward.

Two Cities and Two Churches

The cities of Waverly and Hendersonville, Tennessee, are as different as Daron and Ryan. Waverly is a small factory town in middle Tennessee. Many of the residents have lived there their whole lives. In some ways Waverly is your classic Mayberry: music on the court square on Saturday nights, a quaint, historic downtown area, a place where people know people. But in other ways, Waverly experiences the realities of a broken world such as sizeable rates of alcoholism, methamphetamine production and use, and fragmented families. To be sure, Waverly is a mission field.

The Church of the Nazarene in Waverly has a deep-rooted sixty-year history of health. It has been a springboard of sorts for green pastors. It has been a solid church that has offered a safe, beginning place for young people who are starting ministry. With a healthy core of lay leaders and a lineup of faithful pastors, it has a rich history of stability and devotion to Christ.

In the spring of 2001, while I was finishing my (Daron's) seminary education, Katie and I interviewed at Waverly. From the first moment, the people and I felt a genuine connection. We reached consensus. God was calling me to be their pastor. The church was a traditional, small-town church. They were looking for someone to put down roots. I was looking for a place to put down roots.

Hendersonville is one of the fastest growing cities in Tennessee. Twenty miles from Nashville on Old Hickory Lake, Hendersonville serves as a bedroom community for many who commute to the metro area of Nashville for work. Expanding suburbs and life on the lake tell the story of Hendersonville. As the city swells, so does the need for mission.

Hendersonville Church of the Nazarene began in 1964 in the middle of a neighborhood. The church has rich history with many wonderful leaders. In recent years that history had become less stable. With large facilities and large debt, the congregation was diminishing. When given the opportunity to welcome a young man with no experience and very little education, they probably didn't feel they had much of a choice.

Vibrant Church Renewal

The noteworthy story here is God's work (sometimes through us and often despite us) to bring vibrant renewal to two established churches. While we can count endless differences between us and our places of ministry, we also see commonalities in how God has brought renewal to the Churches of the Nazarene in Waverly and Hendersonville.

Vibrant Church Renewal: Powered by Prayer

Both pastors and both churches have made intentional commitments to prayer. We desire for prayer to be more than another program or activity of the church that is tacked onto an already frenzied calendar. Instead, prayer is the very lifeblood of the Body of Christ. The Early Church was powered by prayer. You can open the Book of Acts to any page and find the Church either praying or moving in response to answered prayer.

When the Waverly church interviewed Daron, they expressed their desire that the pastor be a praying pastor. And the pastor has expressed his desire that the people be a praying people. Visit our board meetings, and you might just think you are attending a prayer meeting. While the Hendersonville church was searching for a pastor, they regularly met at the altar asking God to ready the right person to come and lead them. Both churches have active prayer chains. People outside the churches and communities often call upon the prayer chains because of their reputation for being praying churches. Both churches have initiated Prayer & Care Groups. Each week these groups meet to make cards for people who are sick, grieving, or have other needs. Then we spend time praying for those needs. Small groups/Sunday school classes in both churches are saturated with prayer. Prayer has become our first order of business. Prayer keeps us on track and in tune. Our corporate emphasis on prayer has become the starting point for vibrant renewal.

Vibrant Church Renewal: Missional Hearts (That Lead to Missional Hands)

Another common thread to the renewal of both churches is the emphasis on missional living. Michael Frost and Alan Hirsch tell us that "the missional church disassembles itself and seeps into the cracks and crevices of a society in order to be Christ to those who don't yet know him."[1] The Church belongs in "the cracks and crevices," because Jesus spent His ministry in "the cracks and crevices." And today the Holy Spirit lives in the cracks and crevices. We can hear Him calling to us, "Church, over here! Come be a part of what I'm doing!"

We find nothing wrong with the attractional model of doing church, unless attractional is at the expense of missional. It is good and fine to embrace both models. Interestingly, we have learned in our short tenures in ministry that missional *is* attractional. People hunger for opportunities to touch broken people in a broken world in ways that God has gifted them.

Waverly church adopted a local elementary school. We donate food and stuff backpacks for needy children on Friday afternoons. We receive offerings and budget funds to help teachers purchase supplies for their classrooms that they would normally purchase themselves. Several of our members greet at the doors of the school each morning. We pray for employees, send cards of encouragement, share gifts, and prepare meals for them. In addition, the administration of the school knows to let us know about special needs. They know we are here to serve them.

Waverly church also initiated a dynamic jail ministry to ladies. Several of our ladies meet with ladies in the jail to listen to them, to lead them to Jesus, and to disciple them. When one of these ladies accepts Christ, the sheriff and deputies bring them (wrists and ankles in shackles) to the church to receive the sacrament of baptism. They are greeted by our church family with encouragement. After a time of sharing and prayer, the ladies are immersed, chains and all. As they step out of the water, praise erupts from the people. The discipleship journey continues for these ladies. We keep track of them when they are released—that is when the hard work begins.

Ryan walked into a loving church at the Hendersonville church and has helped them focus that love outward. They, too, have begun an active jail ministry. They have provided school supplies for needy children in a couple of schools. With their eyes on the community, they have served their local fire department, Girl Scout and Boy Scout troops, the U.S. Navy, local preschools, and city league sports teams.

The most significant missional work done through Hendersonville church has been their sponsorship of New Start churches. Each year they partner with an inner-city New Start congregation on the district. They supply those churches with worship instruments and resources, furniture, discipleship curriculum, coats and groceries for people in the surrounding community, and cash. At one church, they assisted in building a halfway house for women released from prison. The church quickly realized that God brings renewal and revival to us when we help other churches become healthy and stable. Seeing God work in these new churches has brought energy and inspiration to the congregation.

Ryan's journey away from God has allowed him to connect with many unchurched people in Hendersonville. The church is led by a pastor with a recent memory of living lost. With that understanding, Ryan has brought a fresh, missional perspective to the church. Almost all of Hendersonville church's growth has come from people who have little or no church background.

In addition to intentional church-wide missional efforts, both of us equip people to live missionally through our preaching, teaching, and relationship-building. Our call and passion are to make disciples who become disciple-makers—to empower people to engage others for Christ in their homes, workplaces, neighborhoods, and communities.

Vibrant Church Renewal: Permission-Giving Lay Leadership

Another common key to the renewal of both churches has been permission-giving lay leadership. Both Waverly and Hendersonville churches are blessed with key leaders whose lives are focused on serving Christ and others. Their hearts beat in unison for the mission of God. They freely give permission for new ministries, new leaders, and necessary changes. Our leaders have opened the door for new worship structures and styles. They have not only embraced new staff members, but they have also let those staff members "loose" to serve the community. For example, Waverly church's children's pastor gives eight to ten hours per week volunteering at the local elementary school (on the clock for the church, of course). When presented with new ideas, instead of standing in the way or thinking of reasons it can't be done, our leaders often respond with "Why not?" and "Let's do it!"

When differences of opinion come to light, it is not uncommon to see board members in the minority on a certain issue say something like "I don't know about this. But I trust our pastor, and I trust the rest of you." Such a spirit is indicative of maturity of character that can be explained only by holiness of heart and life. Both churches are blessed with lay leaders who are tuned into the big picture of God's mission in the world instead of being distracted by mundane minutia. The leadership of both churches is filled with "armor bearers" who lift us up in prayer, support us with encouragement, and model God's vision for our churches.

God is yearning to breathe new life into established churches. The question is—Are people willing? Sadly, lay leaders sometimes become gatekeepers instead of armor-bearers. Territorial mind-sets and personal agendas bring ruin to work that is done in the name of Jesus. We have witnessed the opposite. We have seen the core leadership of two established churches live in submission to the Lordship of Christ. Their faithfulness to God, their willingness to do whatever it takes, and their spirit of humility and personal sacrifice have yielded great results for the kingdom of God. Not everyone in a church has to be on the same page. But we are convinced—if the core leaders are unified and missional, the church becomes a mighty tool in the hands of a mighty God.

Vibrant Church Renewal: Authentic Pastoral Leadership

We see similarity in our authenticity as pastors. Neither of us is very slick. We don't ooze smooth, velvety voices and we don't think we always look the part. And even though we're relatively young, we're not overly hip. In fact, we're not hip at all. There isn't much glimmer to our leadership styles. We believe that people hunger for authentic, Spirit-filled leaders. People in our churches and in our communities are smart enough to sniff out something that isn't genuine. That is good, because genuine is what we want to be. We are the same in the pulpit and in the post office and on the porches of our homes. Our prayers, sermons, training sessions, and one-on-one connections are consistently authentic.

When seeking to build authentic disciples of Jesus, the leader must be authentic. Gimmicks fizzle, and "hip" has an expiration date. We seek to make real disciples by being real disciples.

Conclusion

Throughout the Bible, God makes a habit of calling the unlikely and unusual. Our story is nothing new. God called a backward bookworm and a black sheep—both from a broken, "bedraggled, beat-up, and burnt-out"[2] family. One of us took a mostly straight path. The other one took a winding, roundabout journey. Both have come to the place where we are fulfilling God's call upon our lives. The apostle Paul could have easily been speaking of us:

Take a good look, friends, at who you were when you got called into this life. I don't see many of "the brightest and the best" among you, not many influential, not many from high-society families. Isn't it obvious that God deliberately chose men and women that the culture overlooks and exploits and abuses, chose these "nobodies" to expose the hollow pretensions of the "somebodies"? That makes it quite clear that none of you can get by with blowing your own horn before God. Everything that we have—right thinking and right living, a clean slate and a fresh start—comes from God by way of Jesus Christ. That's why we have the saying, "If you're going to blow a horn, blow a trumpet for God." (1 Corinthians 1:26-31, TM)

We celebrate God's work in Waverly and Hendersonville. He is bringing vibrant renewal to two established churches. And we, who know a thing or two about being renewed, are blessed to be part of the action.

Strategy No. 3
Clear and Coherent Theological Identity

*We must facilitate communication and collaboration
between the Global Ministry Center, educational
regions, educational institutions, and our ministers
and laity through print, electronic media,
civil conversation, and clear preaching.*

There seems to be an increased contentiousness in the marketplace today. Must that contention bleed into the Church? Paul prayed for the Philippian Christians—"This is my prayer: that your love may abound more and more in knowledge and depth of insight, so that you may be able to discern what is best and may be pure and blameless until the day of Christ, filled with the fruit of righteousness that comes through Jesus Christ—to the glory and praise of God" (Philippians 1:9-11). We are praying with Paul that the Church of the Nazarene in the United States and Canada will abound in the fruit of righteousness and that we will live and work together in unity and civility.

We need to facilitate conversation between our educational institutions and our leaders so that we can work together more effectively to reach our world. There is great potential for partnerships among our districts, our schools, our churches, and the Global Ministry Center departments. We have decided as Holiness people that we will lovingly dwell together under the banner of "Holiness unto the Lord." This conversation continues through the following chapters.

Chapter 10: Celebrating Our Wesleyan Theological Heritage, by Tom Noble

Tom Noble helps us to celebrate our Wesleyan theological heritage of justification and sanctification. His chapter's portion on entire sanctification describes five fundamental areas of substantial agreement between Wesley and later teachers in the Holiness Movement.

Chapter 11: Living Holiness: The Gospel in Word *and* Deed, by Dan Boone

Dan Boone declares that evangelism *and* social action go together like milk and cookies, flesh and blood. Dan asks, "Cannot both be right? Can there be a draw, or even a partnership, between the two rather than a fight?"

Chapter 12: Thinking Cross-Culturally, by Oliver Phillips

Oliver Phillips states, "There is no greater cross-cultural thinker than Jesus." True disciples of Jesus will consciously seek to be culturally intelligent so that ministry across cultures can be wholesome.

Chapter 13: Making Disciples: A Biblical Theology of Mission, by Bill Wiesman

Bill Wiesman develops a biblical theology of making disciples utilizing four statements of Jesus as a framework: (1) "I will build my church" (Matthew 16:18), (2) "Look at the fields" (John 4:35), (3) "Go and make disciples" (Matthew 28:19), and (4) "Sanctify them" (John 17:17).

Tom Noble's grandparents were charter members of the first Nazarene church in Britain, founded in 1906. He is a graduate of Glasgow and Edinburgh Universities, taught theology at Nazarene Theological College, Manchester, 1976-96, and since then has been a professor of theology at Nazarene Theological Seminary in Kansas City. He also supervises PhD research at Nazarene Theological College, Manchester. The Nobles have four daughters and six grandchildren. Tanoble@nts.edu

CELEBRATING OUR WESLEYAN THEOLOGICAL HERITAGE

TOM NOBLE

Christian theology is not just an abstract study of doctrine. It is our expression together of our personal knowledge of the living God. In the Wesleyan tradition, that means that it is about *holiness,* for the living God is the holy God. And it also means that it is *missional* theology, for the living God is the one who is engaged in mission to a lost and dying world.

For all Christians, theology begins with Christ, the only way to the Father. We come to know God only as we follow Jesus on the road, becoming *Christlike disciples.*

And it is also about the Holy Spirit who alone opens our minds to confess, "Jesus Christ is Lord" and so to cry, "Abba, Father." Wesleyans therefore, along with all true Christians, confess that by faith we have come to know not abstract doctrine but the living God—Father, Son, and Holy Spirit.

What, then, are the particular emphases of Wesleyans within the family of the worldwide Christian Church? Wesley strongly adhered to the creeds and the doctrines of the Reformation as set out in the Thirty-nine Articles of the Church of England. But he said that his particular concern was to revive the Church by emphasizing "repentance, faith, and holiness."[1] In short, it was a matter of becoming Christlike disciples. This is sometimes called "the doctrine of the Christian life," and according to H. Ray Dunning, it has "two foci"—justification and sanctification.[2]

Justified in Christ

The preaching of John Wesley began with the evangel, the good news, the gospel of sins forgiven. Justification, said Wesley, means pardon. All have sinned, individually *and corporately.* And we cannot earn or merit forgiveness: it comes by God's free grace, His incredible *generosity.*

But although pardon is free to us, it was costly to Christ. It cost Him His life. Therefore, justification cannot be separated from the Atonement, and particularly the Cross. We have to repent and believe, but it is not our repentance and faith that merit forgiveness. Nor is it attempting to be Christlike disciples in our own strength. Not even our act of faith saves us but rather the One in whom we put our faith. We have personal assurance of salvation only when we put our faith in Christ.

John Wesley was a clergyman of the Church of England who had been trying to be a Christlike disciple by his own self-discipline. But he had no assurance of forgiveness until he went to a meeting in Aldersgate Street in the old City of London on May 24, 1738. He tells us in his journal that he heard someone reading from Luther's preface to the epistle to the Romans, and then he writes, "I felt that I did trust Christ, Christ alone for salvation."

That was when he received the assurance of sins forgiven and famously said that his heart was "strangely warmed." From Luther he had grasped the Reformation message that salvation was by *Christ alone*.[3]

For Wesley, as one scholar has said, the Atonement was therefore "the burning focus of faith."[4] It is only because Christ "bore our sins in His own body on the tree" (1 Peter 2:24, NKJV) that, when we place our faith in "Christ crucified," we can know that we are pardoned, forgiven—justified! It is not merely believing an abstract doctrine. Nor is it merely some kind of cold commercial or judicial transaction. It is entering into a personal relationship, trusting the One "who loved me and gave himself for me" (Galatians 2:20).[5]

However, a *personal* relationship is not merely an *individualistic* one. Wesley's evangelistic preaching was to bring people to personal faith in Christ and so to justification. But his pastoral practice was strongly *corporate*. He gathered his people into classes and bands to confess to each other and encourage each other as members of the Body of Christ.

The important theological point is that we are not just saved *by* Christ, but we are saved *in* Christ. And to be in Christ is to be in His Body, the Church. We are not in Christ because we are justified, but rather we are justified because we are in Christ. "There is therefore now no condemnation," Paul writes, "for those who are in Christ Jesus" (Romans 8:1). Being justified or "vindicated" is being united to Him so that as members of His Body we share in *His* vindication. He "was raised for our justification" (Romans 4:25).

Wesleyans therefore preach the gospel of "justification by faith," but that faith must be a personal trust in Jesus Christ. We are thus *incorporated* into His Body: we are in Christ.

Sanctified by the Spirit

We must not stop there, however. Some seem to think that the gospel is only about pardon and justification, but Wesleyans are convinced that there is more. The incredible generosity (grace) of God not only pardons us but also transforms us! We have to go on to speak of sanctification.

The first thing to note is that we do not achieve our own sanctification by a disciplined obedience to the law or by trying to be Christlike disciples in our own strength. There is a need for disciplined obedience, of course, but that does not merit or achieve our sanctification. Rather, it is the consequence of the work of the Holy Spirit within us. Sanctification too is by the grace or generosity of God.

And again, as the Holy Spirit gives us assurance of sins forgiven (justification) by uniting us to Christ, so too we are sanctified by the Spirit because we are in Christ. That means that here too our sanctification is the fruit of His atonement. We often concentrate on justification as a result of the Cross. But Wesleyans want to emphasize that "Christ crucified" is not only the source of our justification or pardon, but even more miraculously, the source of our *sanctification*. It was "to sanctify the people by his own blood" that Jesus "suffered outside the city gate" (Hebrews 13:12). And the Atonement cannot be separated from the Incarnation. As Paul writes,

God has done what the law, weakened by the flesh, could not do: by sending his own Son in the likeness of sinful flesh, and to deal with sin, he condemned sin in the flesh, so that the just requirement of the law might be fulfilled in us, who walk not according to the flesh but according to the Spirit. (Romans 8:3-4)

Mark pictures this walk as the journey of *discipleship* in which we take up our cross and follow Jesus (Mark 8:34). And for Wesleyans this has to be seen as a journey. Initial sanctification comes in the form of regeneration, the new birth. But that has to be followed by what Wesley called "the gradual work" of sanctification.[6] That leads in turn to entire sanctification, after which the gradual work continues.

Regeneration: Initial Sanctification

According to Wesley, *entire* sanctification was subsequent to justification. But that was the culmination of sanctification, not the whole story. The beginning of that growth in grace, which led to entire sanctification, was in regeneration. The point is that justification is not merely a legal fiction by which our sins are pardoned while we remain unchanged as sinners. As Wesleyans, we believe that the transformation begins immediately with our regeneration. We are not only justified—at the same moment we are born again. Justification and sanctification may be distinguished, but they cannot be separated!

The transformation of regeneration is *within*, in what the Bible calls "the heart"—the center of our thinking, feeling, and willing. Paul writes that "God's love has been poured into our hearts through the Holy Spirit that has been given to us" (Romans 5:5). As soon as we are born again, we are motivated by a new love for God. But again, that is not merely individualistic. We have been embraced by the love of the Christian fellowship. Within the Body of Christ, we have come to know the love of God that passes understanding. So we are now able not just to love our neighbors as ourselves (previously hard enough!), but to experience the "new" commandment: "This is my commandment, that you love one another as I have loved you" (John 15:12). That is an infinitely greater measurement of love. This, then, is *corporate* love, a quality of love found within the fellowship of believers and nowhere else on earth. But as yet, the newly born-again are novices and infants in the practice of love.

The change *within* also means a change *without*, that is, in our behavior. Wesley strongly emphasized 1 John 3:9[7]: "Those who have been born of God do not sin." That may seem a terrifying text! Can any one of us say, then, that we are born again? It was to meet that question that Wesley adopted his famous definition of an act of sin: "a voluntary transgression of a known law." All Christians fall short in that we fail to be what we could be, unintentionally offend or mistreat people, fail to understand what we ought to do, and generally err and fall short. We ought to confess daily our faults and failings. That is the humility that is essential for Christian holiness. But no truly born-again Christian, according to Wesley, deliberately in outward action flouts the known, written law of God. In other words, regenerate Christians do not lie, steal, cheat, deceive, commit adultery, blaspheme, murder, embezzle, or otherwise break the known law of God. If a child of God *does* deliberately commit any obvious outward sins, "We have an advocate with the Father" (1 John 2:1). But deep, serious, and grieving repentance is necessary to repair the damage to the relationship with God.

Sometimes it is thought that it is *entire* sanctification that gives us victory over voluntary sinning, but that is "Keswick," not Wesleyan, doctrine. Wesley stood by the teaching of 1 John that the regenerate do not intentionally sin in open, deliberate ways. Sometimes people think when they have a new experience of victory at this level that they are entirely sanctified—when actually all that has happened is that for the first time they are truly regenerate!

"The Gradual Work of Sanctification"

Of course, this is only *initial* sanctification: it is by no means complete. Those who are born again are now motivated by a new love for God, for the fellowship, and for the lost. But that love for God and neighbor is still in tension with the old mind-set, what Paul calls setting "the mind on the flesh" (Romans 8:6). That does not mean merely sensuality but could be paraphrased as "the mind set on human goals and values." It is pride, idolatry, and self-centeredness. It is the disposition to live for self-gratification or self-promotion. Strangely, it can even take negative forms of self-obsession such as self-denigration or subjecting oneself to some idol. It is indeed spiritual sickness.

There is therefore still a tension between "the mind that is set on the flesh" and the mind set "on the Spirit" (Romans 8:7, 6). The old disposition to live for human goals and values is in tension with the new disposition to live for God and others. And once again, this is not merely individualistic. We all belong to corporate interest groups—families and social groups and parties and nations—all affected by corporate human sin. These, too, sometimes want to claim our idolatrous allegiance.

There is also another dimension. We all still live in the fallen human body with its natural desires and psychological drives based in our physiology. These are legitimate human desires, part of creation and so not evil in themselves. But in the fallen body they become occasions for temptation.

John Wesley often based his understanding of the gradual work of sanctification on 1 John 2:12-14.[8] Even the children, the newly born again, know that their sins are forgiven, but it is those who have grown up and become "young people" who "have conquered the evil one." In other words, like athletes in training, they have developed their spiritual muscles precisely through wrestling. It is consistent victory in temptation that has led to increasing maturity. In the power of the Spirit they have learned to discipline their bodily desires, they have increasing victory over sinful thoughts, and they have experienced increasing victory over "the mind that is set on the flesh," that is, the tendency or bent to live for themselves. They are progressing on the road of *Christlike discipleship*.

This, too, should be corporate and not a lonely, individualistic fight. That was why Wesley gathered his converts into classes and bands, accountability groups to confess and testify to each other and pray together. Wesley was one of the Church's greatest practitioners of spiritual formation. Paul's picture of spiritual growth toward perfection is a *corporate* one:

> Speaking the truth in love, we must grow up in every way into him who is the head, into Christ, from whom the whole body, joined and knit together by every ligament with which it is equipped, as each part is working properly, promotes the body's growth in building itself up in love. (Ephesians 4:15-16)

Not only justification then, but sanctification, including both initial sanctification and gradual sanctification, is a matter of being corporately in Christ by the Spirit. That corporate love is enacted as we participate in the one loaf of the Holy Communion (*koinonia*), that *corporate* expression of the love of the fellowship (*koinonia*) that (Wesley taught) is essential to the gradual work of sanctification in the members.

But Wesley insisted that love should flow out from the corporate fellowship of believers into the world. That was why one could not be a member of a Methodist society without face-to-face service to the poor. In order to grow in sanctification toward entire sanctification, one had to keep the commandments zealously—not only enjoying victory over sin but also positively engaging in active love to everyone.[9] That characterizes the truly Christlike disciple. The world will dismiss as sheer hypocrisy any claims to holiness that are based on private religious experiences and are not embodied in practical action on behalf of the poor and needy.

Within the nineteenth-century Holiness Movement, William and Catherine Booth and the Salvation Army were the greatest exemplars of that. Hospitals and other health work, disaster relief, and all forms of compassionate ministry are part of those "works of mercy" that Wesley saw as essential for our growth in Christian holiness. For without that growing Christlike life of outgoing love, there was no hope of entire sanctification.

Entire Sanctification

According to Wesleyan theology, it is the gradual work of sanctification that prepares the Christian for entire sanctification. The two are interlinked. Without a true and real hope of entire sanctification, the gradual work languishes. But without genuine progress in the life of outgoing love, Wesley taught, entire sanctification is forever out of reach.

Later teachers in the Holiness Movement have added their interpretation, and sometimes these have been thought to be in conflict with Wesley. But actually, if we see the development of the Wesleyan tradition in perspective, the differences are minor. There is in fact fundamental agreement. We may safely say that Wesley and later Holiness teachers substantially agree on the following points in the doctrine of entire sanctification.[10]

Perfect Love

First, the heart of this doctrine is that it is all about Christian "perfection," which is perfection in *love*. Wesley was often challenged about this word "perfection": surely no one can be perfect in this life! It is true that the word "perfection" can be very misleading. But Wesley insisted that the word was in the Bible and had been used right down through the seventeen centuries of the Church. What we must understand is that it does not mean absolute perfection, Adamic perfection, or angelic perfection—in other words, "sinless" perfection. Within this life the Christian can become "perfect" in one way only—perfect in love. This is how Wesley explained the doctrine again and again when he was challenged to explain what he meant by "Christian perfection." It meant the fulfilling of the great commandments, to love God with all the heart, soul, mind, and strength, and to love our neighbors as ourselves. All Wesleyan theologians and teachers agree on that.

While it is *personal*, it can never be *individualistic*, but always *corporate*. Isolated individuals can only selfishly love themselves, and that is the very nature of sin! Love is impossible without interpersonal relationships in a community. And it is the community or communion (*koinonia*) of the Holy Trinity that is the origin and fountain of all interpersonal love. It is that Trinitarian *perfect love*, the fellowship (*koinonia*) between the Father and the Son in the Holy Spirit, that we are invited to share! "Truly our fellowship is with the Father and with his Son Jesus Christ . . . And by this we know that he abides in us, by the Spirit that he has given us" (1 John 1:3; 3:24).

An Instantaneous Work

Second, Wesley and the later nineteenth-century teachers in the Holiness Movement all agree that "perfect love" results from "entire sanctification," which occurs in an instant and is subsequent to regeneration.[11] Perfect love is the end; entire sanctification is the means. The Christian is not entirely sanctified to enjoy the private blessing of feeling pure or to enjoy great waves of joyous emotion. The Christian is entirely sanctified so that he or she can love God passionately and supremely, can love the brothers and sisters in the fellowship, and can get out there and love the neighbors out in the world just as Christ has loved him or her. That is the point of it all—perfect, wholehearted, undivided, unadulterated, unreserved love.

Wesley and later teachers in the Holiness Movement also agree that this entire sanctification comes about in an instant. It is true that the later Holiness preachers made much more of this. Nineteenth-century revivalism more often saw this as a great emotional, dramatic, public moment. They even called it a "crisis." Neither Wesley nor the Bible calls it a crisis, and Wesley was prepared to grant that there might not *appear* to be such a moment, that the coming of perfect love might *appear* to be gradual. But he was convinced that there actually was always an instant when entire sanctification took place. He reasoned like this: that if once I did not love God with all my heart, but now I do, there must have been a moment (whether I was conscious of it or not) when that became true. But what mattered, he insisted, is not whether I can remember the exact moment, but whether I do actually *now* love God with all my heart, mind, soul, and strength, and my neighbor as myself.[12] It was not the event or happening that mattered but the consequence—the love of God filling my heart.

Filled with the Holy Spirit

Third, Wesley and all the teachers of the later Holiness Movement agree that this is the work of the Holy Spirit. Of course, every aspect of sanctification is the work of the Spirit. By uniting us to Christ, He begins our sanctification in the new birth. We are "born of the Spirit." By His continuing work, we abide in Christ and grow in love and in holiness and, as He gives us more light in different areas of our lives, so we have increasing victory over more subtle temptations. So when we are *filled* with the Spirit of Christ, the Spirit who is love, our hearts are filled with love to God and neighbor.

Whether it is biblically correct to call that the "baptism of the Spirit" or exactly what happened on the day of Pentecost is more controversial. The use of that phrase to refer to entire sanctification was not part of Wesley's teaching but was the teaching of the non-Wesleyans, such as Charles Finney and Asa Mahan, and was accepted by some Wesleyans.[13] It depends on what is meant by the phrase. If the word "baptism" simply means a dipping or immersion in the Spirit, then that is presumably the same as being filled with the Holy Spirit. But if the word "baptism" takes on the idea of *initiation* (since baptism is the sacrament marking our initiation into Christ), then it can convey the erroneous idea that the Holy Spirit comes to the Christian only at *entire* sanctification. That is clearly wrong, for "anyone who does not have the Spirit of Christ does not belong to him" (Romans 8:9).

What all can agree on is that on the historic day of Pentecost, the ascended Lord baptized His gathered Church in His Holy Spirit and ever since, because the Spirit has been poured out on all flesh, each Christian today can be filled with the Spirit of Christ.[14] That is why disciples today can be so wholly sanctified as to love God in a full and wholehearted and undivided way. That is the secret of being Christlike. The Comforter has come!

The Nullifying of "the Mind Set on the Flesh"

Fourth, Wesley and all the teachers of the later Wesleyan-Holiness Movement agree that *entire* sanctification brings about a "death to sin" in a very specific sense. They all used a phrase from the King James Version of Romans 8:7, "the carnal mind," but we must understand what that means. The word "carnal" here does not mean what it sometimes means in the English language— "sensual." And despite the translation in the NIV, "sinful nature," neither the word for "sinful" nor the word for "nature" is there in the Greek text. A literal, word-for-word translation then is: "the mind of the flesh," and the NRSV gives an excellent interpretation of this: "the mind that is set on the flesh." Since "the flesh" basically means "the human" in the Bible, we can paraphrase this as "the mind set on merely human goals and values." Pride, self-centeredness, and idolatry are really a twisted form of corporate self-worship.

It is this mind-set, "sin that dwells within me" (Romans 7:17), which has been in tension with the "mind on the Spirit" ever since the new birth. The new love for God that began then has been increasingly victorious, but it has always been opposed by the old habitual self-centered mind-set. Now when the heart is filled with the Spirit of Christ, the Spirit of love, the motives and desires are united in this holistic consecration. The old divided mind is ended, not by my willpower but by the Spirit filling me with His love. Full consecration is now possible, not in my strength but in the power of the Holy

Spirit. As Christ was "full of the Spirit" (Luke 4:1), so His disciples may be Spirit-filled.

The Gradual Work Both Precedes and Continues After Entire Sanctification

Fifth, it is true that there have been some writers in the Holiness Movement who have denied any gradual sanctification and have narrowed the meaning of the word "sanctification" to mean *only* entire sanctification. That is true neither to Wesley nor to the New Testament. The mainstream of the Holiness Movement has always agreed that there is the gradual growth in grace, not only *before* entire sanctification but also *after it*. It is important to realize that in 1 Thessalonians 5:23, the word translated "entirely" or "wholly" (RSV) does not apply to the verb "sanctify" but to the persons Paul is praying for. He is not praying that their sanctification may come to an end! He is praying that they may be sanctified *as a whole*. It is a prayer for "holistic" sanctification.

But although he prays that they may be sanctified "through and through" (NIV), he does not expect them to be given their resurrection bodies right away! They will still be in the old mortal bodies. Wesley understood this to mean that for want of better bodily organs (especially their "disordered brains"!) and not for want of perfect love, they will continue to err and do things wrong and say the wrong things, to offend people and fall short of what they could be.[15] As long as we live, even the holiest among us must continue to grow in grace and be increasingly enlightened by the Spirit and recognize our faults and failings and continue to climb "higher every day."

But what a revolutionary gospel this is! It proclaims not only complete pardon for sinful actions and thoughts but also cleansing from that inner pride, self-centeredness, and idolatry that are (metaphorically) the "root" of sin. Put more positively, it means that the Church *corporately* is to be such a fellowship of love in the power of the Holy Spirit that it can move out in effective reconciling and redemptive mission to a sad, twisted, and lost world.

It is by the love and generosity of the Father, by the incarnation and self-sacrifice of the Son, and by the giving gift of the Holy Spirit uniting us in Christ that we may become truly *Christlike disciples*.

Dan Boone is president of Trevecca Nazarene University. He has served as a pastor, university and seminary teacher, writer, and college administrator. He holds a DMin degree from McCormick Theological Seminary and an MDiv degree from Nazarene Theological Seminary. He is a proud graduate of Trevecca Nazarene University. He and his wife, Denise, live in Nashville, where they enjoy life with their three married children and four grandchildren. dboone@Trevecca.edu

▪▪ ǁ ▪▪
LIVING HOLINESS
THE GOSPEL IN WORD AND DEED
DAN BOONE

One of the long-running debates in the Christian world pits evangelism against social action. Like boxers squaring off in a ring, only one will be left standing. One is the true champion, the other only a contender.

Those in the evangelism corner declare that one's eternity is the true goal and that getting one saved, forgiven of sin, and headed for the afterlife in heaven is the true work of the Church. Social action is peripheral to this endeavor and should not overshadow evangelism, the gospel in word.

Those in the social action corner declare that any gospel that goes only word-deep and does not result in deeds is a truncated gospel and does not reflect the full ministry of Jesus. Social action is interested in the here and now of salvation, experienced as life transformation for the good of the person.

Cannot both be right? Can there be a draw, or even a partnership between the two, rather than a fight? Like milk *and* cookies, sun *and* rain, flesh *and* blood, can we not do evangelism *and* social action?

The declaration of Jesus in the Nazareth synagogue seems to blend the two as one.

The Spirit of the Lord is upon me,
because he has anointed me to bring good news to the poor.
He has sent me to proclaim release to the captives
and recovery of sight to the blind,
to let the oppressed go free,
to proclaim the year of the Lord's favor. (Luke 4:18-19, NRSV)

From this announcement, Jesus went forth teaching, preaching, healing, feeding, empowering, and challenging the social structures that oppressed the poor, exposing the misuse of power, and refusing to submit the kingdom of God to earthly governance. The announcement of Jesus was straight from the Old Testament prophet Isaiah, who, along with his fellow prophets, spoke mostly of the kind of action that defined the people of God. But we must not forget that the path to right action was found in right worship—the confession and forgiveness of sins and the cleansing of the heart to love what God loves and do what God does. The Church of the Nazarene has been about holiness of "heart *and* life" her entire existence. To drive a wedge between evangelism and biblical justice is to forget who and whose we are.

Our Heritage

We are the theological heirs of a man named John Wesley. He spent years at Oxford studying the Scriptures and being formed by the theology of the Anglicans. His roots were deep it the ancient Holiness traditions. He experienced God as holy love expelling sin, thereby enabling him to be restored in the likeness of Jesus. This profound experience caused him to saddle a horse and ride into the world. He traveled with his Bible open on his lap, reading as he went. He interpreted his world through the lens of Scripture. He believed the God of love he experienced had gone into the world ahead of him and was calling him to follow. This God was not hiding in doctrines or waiting behind closed church doors to be discovered and debated. This God was en route to redeem His creation from sin. Wesley was given the eyes of God to see children in factories needing education, the poor needing food and shelter, the debtors in prisons needing money, the sick needing good medical care. Wesley saw the broken world through the eyes of a loving God. He preached in the coal mines, the open fields, and the town squares. Preaching was so essential to his work that he raised up an army of Methodist ministers and gave them sample sermons to preach. He taught his people to bear witness to their experience with God. Wesley's gospel was one that found its best home in the world. He was not afraid of the world or its ideas, even when it rejected and attacked his God. He was a curious lifelong learner. He wrote about health, money, estate gifts, economic theory, personal grooming, literature, politics, science, and the arts. He made friends among those who had differing Christian theologies, offering his hand of fellowship in a catholic spirit. Wesley did not think God in need of human defense but did think humans in need of godly help. His life of loving service caused people to be interested in his doctrine of entire sanctification. They wanted to know about the God who could do this kind of thing in a human heart and prompt such a life of service. Wesley ministered in word and deed.

This heritage calls us to a unique ministry. We believe in a transforming experience that occurs when faith is born by hearing of the Word of God. The proclamation of the good news of Jesus' death and resurrection is accompanied by the inspiration of the Holy Spirit, who bears witness to us that we are the sons and daughters of God. Remove the proclamation of the Word, and our faith rests on the presence of moral good deeds to ignite saving faith. Evangelism is critical to the experience of God that humans are made capable of.

My favorite definition of evangelism is "telling someone into a better story." We all have a story. Evangelism is love in action, listening to their story until we can name God into that story, enabling them to see the hand of God reaching toward them even before they knew it. Their story merges with the story of God, rooting them into a saving reality that began in the creation of the world. Through conversion, they now belong to a people, a family, a church.

But this Church is not formed to sit around and wait for the heavenly bus to make a pit stop at their address. This Church is the hands and feet of Jesus in the world, going where He goes, doing what He does, empowered by the Spirit of the risen Jesus dwelling in the gathered/scattered community of servants.

And what does this "word *and* deed," "evangelism *and* Christian compassion" church look like? I invite you to browse a photo album of congregations I've been privileged to serve.

The Birth of a Family

God has blessed the congregation with strong, solid marriages. Each week they gather for worship. But the statistics reveal that these homes are a fading reality in a world of rampant divorce, marital infidelity, and family chaos. God places a burden on the Church for the marriages of the community. (Note that most ministries of impact do not begin by copying what was seen at a high-powered megachurch conference but by listening to God. God sees each community and calls specific congregations to hear the cry of His heart for broken people.)

The congregation prays for guidance. Concerned people gather for a holy conversation about the status of marriage in their community. The resulting strategy is to connect with young engaged couples at the beginning of their journey and to befriend them. The church, old and quaint, restores its chapel as a beautiful space for weddings and offers it as a gift to the community. In a town where a wedding chapel costs $500 to $1,000, this church offers their facility free. The only stipulation is that they be willing to go through a premarriage counseling program.

The exemplary couples of the church spend time learning the Prepare/Enrich program (now called Life Innovations). They are trained as premarital counselors and offer themselves to the young couples in the community. The six-session program includes a get-acquainted meal with the engaged couple in the home of the mentors. Over the course of the program, a professional inventory is administered, family origins are discussed, and the role of faith in the home is explained. The mentoring couple shares their own faith and the difference Christ makes in their marriage.

To attract nonchurched couples to the program, winsome people in the church read the weekly newspaper section featuring engaged couples and make a phone call inviting them to use the church sanctuary and be enriched by the free premarital counseling program. The church also hosts a dinner for the leading wedding planners and directors in the city, shows them the church, and explains the premarriage program. The church trains its own wedding directors as one more touch in these lives.

Over time, this program results in the beginning of new young-married Sunday school classes dealing with topics on the first years of marriage. The nursery begins to grow. Infant dedications and baptisms become large crowd events as the young parents are given church-printed invitations to share with their family and friends. Many couples who disappeared for a while after the wedding make their way back to the church for the dedication of their first child. The church has one more critical touch in the life of this couple.

From a burden for homes in the community, this congregation finds a way to be face-to-face with lost people, share the gospel in the context of their need, and begin a relationship that may result in conversion and membership in the community of God.

Immigrant Outreach

Jerry runs a cleaning service and hires Laotian immigrants. They work hard and are dependable. His business prospers, and he is moved to find ways to deepen his relationship with them. As he explores the process by which Laotians come to the States, he discovers several needs being addressed by World Vision. In his visit to World Vision he discovers several needs that the members of his local church could meet. (Again, the best ministries are not copies of what a megachurch might be doing but simply the result of Christians paying attention to God as they go about their daily work. It's like following a trail of bread crumbs to the source. God is leading us to places of service.)

In time, Jerry's church offers Word Vision office space in the local church, and through lay involvement, one of the local church members, a former missionary, Lee, becomes the head of World Vision in the city. The concentration of Laotians becomes significant enough that the church hires a Laotian pastor and launches a Laotian congregation. The local church provides aid to incoming immigrants, English as a Second Language (ESL) classes, jobs via Jerry's company, and a congregation where the adults can worship in their own language while their children interface with English-speaking children in Sunday school.

As new immigrant groups come to the city, the church sponsors short-term housing, jobs, and settlement aid. A Russian Sunday school class begins, which later becomes a small congregation.

Because a businessman listened to God, the entire immigrant Laotian population in a large city is introduced to the compassion of Christ, hears the gospel preached in their own language, and is given tools to begin a new chapter in a strange land among friends.

Gardening for God

Chris is the biology professor at a Christian university. His university is located near a public housing community where some of the poorest residents of the city live. They have one grocery store in the community, which carries overpriced food and very little produce. One of his students, Jason, has caught the vision of the way the produce of the land is connected to the story of God.

For the people of God, having land was a primary gift. The current-day Middle East conflict is over land. The people of Israel cling to it as a gift from God. Their faith was formed as they lived among the worshipers of Baal and dealt with pagan rituals of crop fertilization as an expression of religion. The Jewish understanding of food production connected them to the story of their deliverance from Egypt and the gift of a land flowing with milk and honey. The poor were people who had no land. They were dependent on others for food.

Chris and Jason believed they could restore dignity and profit to a community through food production. They searched for land partners where organic gardens could be planted. They created community gardens, using the labor of university volunteers, the compost of university paper and food scraps, and land redeemed from dumping by the cleanup efforts of the university. They taught the elderly and youth to garden. Extra produce was shared with neighbors or sold to the local grocery store. A community farmer's market is in the near future. People who once paid too high a price for canned food now produce their own and experience the freedom of self-provision.

The stories of witness that come from the gardening families are remarkable. Relationships between differing ages, races, economic levels, and educational levels that would never have occurred on the public street now happen in a garden. Two graduates of the university have started a church in the community. Several graduates have moved into the community. A blighted area of the city is becoming a garden, a family, and a place of grace.

Now these farmers are offering to teach bi-vocational pastors to raise rare herbs and plants in their backyards as a way of funding their ministry. They've even added a tilapia fish tank to the equation as a means of providing fertilizer while multiplying high-protein fish. The poor have good news preached to them. Who ever thought it would be in a garden?

Global Connectedness

World evangelism seemed miles away to this congregation. They were faithful in paying their yearly world missions budget, hosting the drive-by sermons of furloughed missionaries, and hawking the yearly reading books. But their feel-it, touch-it, know-it, experience-it culture wanted a deeper connection to the people and places their money was going.

The ethnic cleansing in Rwanda that saw the massacre of thousands had come to an end. The report of the bloody battle between the Hutu and Tutsi tribes had been headline news for more than a year. The Church of the Nazarene was preparing to reenter the country with four missionary couples.

A retired medical missionary was in the local church. Juanita wanted to return following the bloodshed, but her age and health would not allow it. She had served the refugees on the border of Rwanda until forced to leave by the violence. (As her pastor, I can testify that they were wrong about her health. She outworked every layperson in the church for ten years following her retirement.) Juanita kept the crisis alive in the heart of her church by her constant prayers, updates, and conversations.

As the congregation was considering its Faith Promise campaign, she suggested that the local congregation adopt the new work in Rwanda. The cost of reopening the work was the equivalent of the world missions budget of the local church. With permission from the denomination, the local congregation shouldered the task of getting the new missionaries to the field. They invited the missionary families to come to their city, live in their homes, and do their groundwork planning together. The congregation provided daily meals, watched their children, and provided for their needs as they planned their ministry. Each missionary was assigned to a Sunday school class and met with them once a week to update the class on strategy.

When the missionaries left for the field, the correspondence was daily, personal, and productive. Classes provided money for guitars, generators, suits, Bibles, and other needs. The congregation provided a JESUS Film team for village evangelism and $25,000 to build the First Church of the Nazarene in Kigali, the capital city of Rwanda. It was the first congregation in the country comprised of Hutu and Tutsi tribe members worshiping together. Communication between Rwanda and the local church was no longer secondhand or in a reading book, but by e-mail and phone call between laypersons and missionaries. Friendships developed. A congregation developed a worldview that exposed American materialism for its shallowness and emptiness. The great joy of the church was to build six more churches in Rwanda and celebrate the work of God in the most bloody, violent land of that decade.

Evangelism *and* social action walked hand in hand into a place that had broken the heart of God. And it all began with a retired missionary who had a burden.

King's Kids

Kim taught in an inner-city school. She was tough enough to do it, and Christian enough to care beyond Friday at 3:00 P.M. She began to bring her school kids to church on Sunday morning. They filled the family car, so her husband drove the other car. Then they started recruiting their friends to drive. A part of the city so violent that it was called Little Viet Nam saw a caravan of middle-class white folks driving through the neighborhood collecting children for church on Sunday morning. Soon the church had to buy a bus. A church with 80 percent of its offering going to the building payment found its ministry to people even more strapped.

Julie and Scott began to work for the church. Julie was paid as a one-eighth-time university pastor, about $35 a week. Scott was paid the same as a one-eighth-time children's pastor. Julie established a weekday ministry called King's Kids. It wed the people of the church, the students of a Christian university, and the residents of a retirement community to the children of the inner city. At King's Kids a child could get help with homework, eat, play, hear a Bible story, or create something with his or her own hands. Scott began a Sunday morning children's church and a great musical choir/drama program. His children's choir was one-third Laotian, one-third African-American, and one-third Anglo. Some called it the Rainbow Coalition. Parents came to the performances. A few began to attend church.

Over the years (more than twenty now), this congregation has been connected to the public housing project. The church has provided tutoring that helped the local elementary school get off the No Child Left Behind failure list. A drug recovery ministry has grown out of the effort and is now in partnership with the city's drug court. Counseling, food, jobs, and hope flow from the deeds of this compassionate congregation. Rarely does a baptism service occur without the testimony of a former prostitute, drug addict, or alcoholic.

This church could have preached the gospel inside its doors for decades and never known the name of a child or adult in a broken community. Now they sit together in Sunday worship and plot the next ministry and converts. It started with a school teacher, a couple of young adults who worked hard for pennies, and a congregation who believed that our Holiness DNA has evangelism *and* social action in it.

Now It's Your Turn

The doctrine of creation does not end with Genesis 1. Our God is still creating. He is at work making all things new. He does it in odd ways. Upward Basketball. A food distribution center. Hurricane relief. Habitat for Humanity. The Red Cross. The Salvation Army. The local crisis pregnancy center.

Alcoholics Anonymous. Drug recovery. Grief help. Hospital chaplains. Police ride-along partners. Student mentors. Prison recovery. Jail preaching.

We are the theological heirs of John Wesley. His experience of God as holy love expelling sin restored him in the likeness of Jesus. This profound experience caused him to saddle a horse and ride into the world. He traveled with his Bible open on his lap, reading as he went. He believed the God of love he experienced had gone into the world ahead of him and was calling him to follow. This God was not hiding in doctrines or waiting behind closed church doors to be discovered and debated. This God was en route to redeem His creation from sin.

Are you?

Oliver Phillips serves as the director for Mission Support in the USA and Canada Region Church of the Nazarene. Oliver gives leadership in the areas of compassionate, multicultural, and urban ministries. Phillips is certified to conduct training seminars in cultural intelligence. Prior to his current position, Oliver pastored in Maryland and Washington, D.C. He is a graduate of Caribbean Nazarene College, Howard University School of Divinity (MDiv), and International Bible College and Seminary (DMin). He and his wife, Jean, live in Olathe, Kansas. ophillips@nazarene.org

■■ 12 ■■
THINKING CROSS-CULTURALLY
OLIVER PHILLIPS

Undoubtedly, there is no greater cross-cultural thinker than Jesus. His jour-ney from the portals of heaven to incarnation was the result of cross-cultural thinking. What Jesus demonstrated for us was a lesson in cultural intelli-gence.

Our Cultural intelligence Quotient (CQ) is the level of our ability to function effectively in a variety of cultural contexts. True disciples of Jesus will consciously seek to be culturally intelligent so that ministry across cul-tures can be wholesome. The heralded practitioners of cross-cultural thinking have been missionaries who for centuries have perfected the art and science of this discipline. On the other hand, CQ is a relatively new model grounded in the fields of anthropology, sociology, and psychology as well as experiential research from the fields of business, education, and missions.

Consider for a moment these USA/Canada estimates:

- By 2050 the Hispanic population will double to 24 percent of the US population, while the majority of non-Hispanic whites will drop to 52 percent.
- According to the United States Census Bureau, between 2005 and 2010 the white population grew by only 3.2 percent, while the Hispan-ic population grew at a rate of 14.4 percent, Asian Americans/Pacific Islanders at 15.4 percent, and African-Americans at 6.3 percent. The growth rate for the overall population during that timeframe was 4.2 percent.
- According to the 2000 Census, there were over 30 million immigrants in the United States, representing 11 percent of the total population.[1]
- Between 1970 and 2000 the naturalized citizen population increased by 71 percent.[2]

Toolkit for Improving CQ

Cross-cultural leaders with high CQs understand how to encounter new cultural situations, judge what goes on in them, and make appropriate adjust-ments to behave effectively in those otherwise disorienting circumstances. They have repertoires of strategies and behaviors for orienting themselves when they encounter unfamiliar behaviors and perspectives so they can discern whether an unfamiliar behavior is explained by culture or is unique to a particular person or group. Such discernment is critical in, for instance, sponsoring new congregations, understanding new cultural opportunities, unifying dispersed leadership teams, and developing strategic plans for missions.

The four factors of CQ—motivation, cognition, metacognition, and behavior—can be further expanded in terms of how one enhances one's CQ. Let me unpack these factors in greater detail.

CQ Drive (Motivation)

Effective cross-cultural thinking goes beyond the collection of knowledge about a particular culture. CQ drive has more to do with the mental conditioning necessary to pursue a cross-cultural assignment when things don't seem to be going right. What is it about the assignment that will motivate us to persevere? Answering an informal set of questions can help us to be honest with ourselves:

- Do I like cross-cultural interactions that are new to me?
- Do I prefer to stay with locals when I travel cross-culturally, rather than in a hotel by myself?
- Do I prefer eating local foods when I go to a new place?
- Do I enjoy spending time with people who don't embrace Christianity as their worldview?
- Am I confident I would be effective in cross-cultural ministry?[3]

Here are some pointers that can help one improve CQ drive in cross-cultural thinking and the experience of ministry:

- Be honest with yourself. Be aware of the challenges that surface, and take inventory of the discomfort you are experiencing.
- Examine your confidence level. Do you have enough confidence that you can be successful and fruitful in this assignment if you continue?
- Eat and socialize. Share meals in both formal and informal settings. It takes a lot of motivation to eat unfamiliar foods, but learning to like some of those foods can be of value, even if your prayer is "Dear God, help me to keep it down!"
- Count the perks. Don't take the collateral benefits that are serendipitously revealed on the journey for granted, as they serve as excellent motivators for a weary traveler.
- Become passionate about the bottom line. The challenge for all who become involved in cross-cultural thinking is to be anchored to the bottom line. What difference would it make if you fail in this assignment? What difference would it make if you succeed?

Key question: What's your level of confidence and motivation for this cross-cultural assignment? If it's lacking, what can you do to increase it?

For successful adaptation to a new culture, a person must be sufficiently motivated to want to associate with those who are part of that culture and be more than willing to go the extra mile in seeking opportunities for meaningful interaction.

CQ Knowledge (Cognition)

The single most powerful word in cross-cultural thinking is "understand." Cognition CQ is the quest to understand what culture is and how it shapes us. Here are some initial questions that can reveal whether we currently have the driving force to acquire more knowledge about cultures other than our own and what we must do to acquire it:

- Am I fluent in a language other than English?
- Do I know the ways other cultures approach conflict? Do I know the different role expectations of men and women in other cultures?
- Do I know the basic cultural values of several cultures?
- Do I understand the primary ways Christians differ in their beliefs and practices in different cultural settings?[4]

The first step in understanding cultural differences is to understand one's own culture. Ignoring the need to understand one's own culture—or assuming that one has already mastered it simply because he or she has lived in the culture for decades—is probably just as disastrous as ignoring the shades and nuances of another culture. An educated contrast between one's own culture and that of another will take effort, energy, and inquisitiveness. American culture, after all, is not a monolith: consider the difficult task of defining the "average American."

Going Below the Surface

Some definitions of culture may be helpful at this point:

- Culture is "a pattern of thinking, feeling, and reacting to various situations and actions."[5]
- Culture is the shared understandings people use within a society to align their actions. "While culture is defined, created, and transmitted through interaction, it is not interaction itself, but the content, meanings, and topics of interaction."[6]
- Culture is the collective programming of the mind that distinguishes the members of one group from another. It is the software behind how we operate.[7]
- Culture is the way a group of people solve problems and reconcile dilemmas.[8]

Five Important Cultural Values

A sure way to exegete another's culture is to undertake a careful study of the cultural values that seem to be present in all cultures. These five values stem from the long-standing literature on how people from every culture deal with their environments.

Please note as we review these cultural values that they reflect only an individual's personal emphasis and preferences. Being low or high on a specific cultural value has no built-in meaning; it is not better to be low or high. Individual cultural value orientations are simply descriptions of preferences.

Event Time vs. Clock Time. In cultures that focus on event time, events begin and end when all the participants feel the time is right rather than artificially imposing clock time. This value is probably the cause of most misunderstandings among immigrant cultures in the United States and Canada. Clock time is a precious commodity in developed industrial countries where punctuality and strict adherence to a schedule is important, but event time is the accepted mode of operations in developing countries, where relationships take precedence over schedules. When working with groups from other countries, one should pay close attention to these clues.

I am witness to the fact that most Anglo congregations who give worship space to a group from another culture are sometimes not sensitive about this area, as the other culture may or may not take up exactly the ten minutes (or fifteen or five) they're given in the order of service. As a naturalized American citizen from another culture, I have never really understood Americans' infatuation with time, although I have come to appreciate the consistency. Sadly, most Americans believe that "punctuality is a virtue and have never thought about other ways of being on time, other than noting 'clock time.'"[9]

High Context vs. Low Context. In high-context cultures, people have significant history together, so a great deal of mutual understanding can be assumed. In high-context cultures, communication is indirect and emphasizes implicit roles and understanding. A low-context culture is one in which, because there is not a long, detailed history of existence together, much attention is placed on communication and nothing is left to a guessing game.

How we behave in church services on Sunday mornings is an example of high context at work in a negative way. For the most part, it is assumed that the church family knows the rules and protocols for behavior. When a visitor enters the building, it is a strange land without clues or signs because the members assume that everyone knows how to behave and knows the difference between the Old and New Testaments. Notice how often Scripture is cited in sermons with chapter and verse, as though the visitor understands the references. The Church of today exists in a very high context.

An effort to enhance one's CQ knowledge should involve the study of the context in which cultures exist.

Individualism vs. Collectivism. Some cultures are largely governed by a commitment to do what's best for the individual. Studies have shown that the United States scores higher than any other nation in individualism. People from individualistic cultures treasure self-reliance and tend to retain functional, relatively tenuous bonds with others. On the other end of the continuum is China, which scored the highest in collectivism. In collectivist cultures the needs of the group are more important than the needs of the individual, so collectivist cultures emphasize families, work groups, communities, and other groups above the individual. Most Asian cultures are collectivist, as are most Latin American and African cultures.

The point to remember is that individualism orientation emphasizes "I" and individual identity and prefers individual decisions and working alone, while collectivism orientation emphasizes "We" and group identity and prefers group decisions and working with others.

Low vs. High Power Distance. A narrative account of low vs. high power is probably the best way to tell this story. American manager John Potts operates a maquiladora just inside Arizona's border with Mexico. His American employees have always considered him to be sympathetic and sensitive to their needs. As a way to get to know his Mexican workforce better, Potts arranged a dinner at his house and invited three of his Mexican managers. After refusing the invitation several times, the managers agreed to take him up on the offer. From his perspective, the dinner went well, and he felt that the experience opened new doors of communication.

One week after the dinner two of the managers quit. Potts was disheartened. What signals had he missed? What might he have said that offended the managers? What protocols did he violate in inviting them to his home? What was it about the food that he and his wife served?

Later, Potts learned that it was nothing that he had said. However, the dinner lowered the power distance between him and these managers; the act of socializing with them ran counter to the cultural work environment, and the managers feared that they might be expected to do the same with their workers, and that doing so would make it difficult for them to demand the respect and loyalty from them that they felt they deserved. Removal of the power distance was alien to the men's culture, and Potts's invitation destroyed an element that was an essential tool for effective management in that culture. While he was seen as an empathetic boss in his own culture, in the Mexican managers' culture he was seen as weak. He missed the cues that should have alerted him of these significant differences.

Low vs. High Uncertainty Avoidance. Uncertainty avoidance is the extent to which the culture feels comfortable with risk. Low uncertainty avoidance cultures prefer few rules, less structure, and fewer guidelines and tolerate unstructured and unpredictable situations well. High uncertainty avoidance cultures prefer written rules, structure, and guidelines and are uncomfortable with unstructured or unpredictable situations. Research has shown that Britain, Jamaica, and Sweden lead the way in low uncertainty. Those of us from the Caribbean would attest to the reality that Jamaicans are, by and large, an expeditious and risk-taking people.

Thinking cross-culturally means paying attention to a culture's attitude toward risk, for it will determine the level of detail at which a strategy should be communicated.

Key question: What cultural understanding do you need for this cross-cultural assignment?

CQ Strategy (Metacognition)

Thinking cross-culturally involves not only the collection of knowledge about another culture but also a strategy of engagement for the interaction. Determining a strategy of engagement is a little like deciding whether to use the cruise control when one drives. Driving in an unfamiliar environment requires a different set of skills, including being acutely aware of the intersections, signs, pedestrians, and signals. Under these circumstances, one would not be advised to use cruise control.

As a frequent speaker in churches with members from other cultures, I have often found myself in a situation in which it is easy to ignore the cultural setting in which the sermon is being presented. Preaching to an African-American audience is different from preaching to people from any other culture. The call and response genre that is an interactive cue within African-American congregations and that may incite a continuous sense of movement and crescendo may be absent in other congregations. To ignore the difference in the culture of the group for which the sermon is being preached could ruin an opportunity to bring good tidings to weary travelers.

The real challenge of developing CQ strategy is learning how to apply knowledge about the intended target culture to other situations. Thinking cross-culturally involves mapping out the strategy of engagement using the knowledge acquired. Before I meet with one of the more than twenty ethnic strategic readiness teams, I must take the time to readjust my thinking about the values and assumptions of the group, as well as the behaviors that might differ fundamentally from mine. Strategic mapping may give me the answers to some basic questions such as—

- How does this group regard the importance of this meeting?
- How much time should I spend in introductory "casual talk"?
- What is an appropriate segue into the actual purpose of the meeting?
- How much interaction does this group expect?

Key question: What do you need to plan in order to do this cross-cultural assignment successfully?

CQ Action (Behavior)

CQ action (behavior) is where everything we've learned about drive, knowledge, and strategy is finally realized. Behavior is the only measurable outcome that can indicate whether one is maturing in terms of CQ.

If there is one word that describes CQ action, it is "communication." CQ action is the extent to which we can manage our verbal and nonverbal actions in our relationships with other cultures to ensure that they are appropriate. If the other areas of CQ have contributed to the toolkit in thinking cross-culturally, then what takes place in our behavior will be a transformation from within rather than a change of behavior on the outside. CQ action is the cumulative effect of our drive, knowledge, and strategy.

In his book *Leading with Cultural Intelligence*, David Livermore suggests a threefold path to developing effective communication: (1) "adapt your communication," (2) "negotiate differently," and (3) "know when to flex and when not to flex."[10]

Adapt Your Communication. Every culture receives information on different radio wavelengths and frequencies. Because of the different contexts in which all cultures interpret what is being said or not said, communicating effectively probably means changing one's mode or style of communication. For example, the same speech or lecture that creates enthusiasm and vision when presented to one culture might instill lack of confidence and distrust in another, leading to alienation and a breakdown in future efforts to communicate.

Negotiate Differently. When a sponsoring congregation enters a relationship with a daughter church, negotiations take place that could lead to disharmony. Cross-cultural negotiations should take into account the motivations of both congregations, as well as the manner in which each congregation interprets its mission and vision for the community. Cultures view negotiations differently; in some cultures negotiations take place only after social friendships are developed and levels of trust are established, and in others they are handled as business transactions alone.

Know When to Flex. This area is delicate, because it is sometimes the expectation of the host culture that visitors act like those in the host culture. It is difficult to determine how much alteration in our actions is necessary to be accepted in a culture. When is it okay to refuse to eat something that does not appear to suit one's culinary taste? This exercise requires drawing extensively on CQ knowledge and CQ strategy to anticipate what people from other cultures expect from us. On a visit to Kenya, a country with whose culture I was not remotely familiar, I had to be constantly aware of people's expectations. I was there with Nazarene leaders from eight African countries, each with its own cultural uniqueness. How do these Nazarenes expect me to act, knowing that I am from the United States? How do they expect me to act, knowing I am African-American? How should their expectation affect my behavior? My answers to these questions undoubtedly affected my stay in Kenya.

A warning must be sounded here. Some level of adaptation within a culture is viewed positively, but a too-high level of adaptation could be viewed as mimicry and send a negative message. We need to adapt based on our CQ knowledge, drive, and strategy.

Here are some suggestions for effective behavior-monitoring:

1. Be aware of your own assumptions, ideas, and emotions as you engage cross-culturally.
2. Look for ways to discover the assumptions of others through their words and behavior.
3. Use all your senses to read a situation, rather than only hearing the words or only seeing the nonverbals.
4. Use an open mind to view every situation from different perspectives.
5. Create new paradigms/categories for seeing things.
6. Seek out fresh information to confirm or deconfirm new categories of experience.
7. Use empathy to try to identify.[11]

Key question: What behaviors should you adapt for this cross-cultural assignment?

Conclusion

In his book *Cultural Intelligence: Improving Your CQ to Engage Our Multicultural World*, David Livermore suggests ways for improving CQ thinking for ministry in a diverse world. Here are a few salient suggestions:

1. Start the anthropological dig in your own soul. There must be a relentless commitment to reaching across to seek the welfare of the other.
2. Root your view of the other in the image of God. It is difficult to be entirely appalled by someone who reflects God.
3. Seek first the kingdom of God. CQ cannot be compartmentalized. We do not embark on this journey to be politically correct; we are concerned about thinking cross-culturally because we, the Body of Christ, are the language of God today.
4. Live up close. We are designed to live in relationship with those who see the world differently than we do, not to cloister ourselves with those who look, think, and act like us.[12]

Bill Wiesman serves as the director of Evangelism Ministries and New Church Development for the USA and Canada Region of the Church of the Nazarene. Prior to his present position, he served in Tennessee and Alabama with district responsibilities for new churches and church health. Bill is the founding pastor/planter of four Nazarene churches, the sponsoring church pastor for four new churches, and has coached over fifty additional churches through the birthing process. Bill is a graduate of Johns Hopkins University, Nazarene Theological Seminary (MDiv), and Fuller Theological Seminary (DMin). Bill has five children. He and wife, Sharon, live in Gardner, Kansas. bwiesman@nazarene.org

▪▪ 13 ▪▪
MAKING DISCIPLES
A BIBLICAL THEOLOGY OF MISSION
BILL WIESMAN

The Church of the Nazarene has one unifying mission: To make Christlike disciples in the nations. This mission is built on the core values of being Christian, holiness, and missional.[1] Shortly after Jesus found me through the Bellflower Church of the Nazarene, I read through the New Testament beginning with the Book of John. The words of Jesus were in red. I paid particular attention to those words. I still do today. My theology begins with Christ, the only way to the Father. A biblical theology of making disciples can be developed utilizing four statements of Jesus as a framework: (1) "I will build my church" (Matthew 16:18), (2) "Look at the fields" (John 4:35), (3) "Go and make disciples" (Matthew 28:19), and (4) "Sanctify them" (John 17:17).

Jesus Said, "I Will Build My Church" (Matthew 16:18)

God's Plan and Initiative

The sovereign Lord Jesus has declared emphatically that He is the one who will build His Church. It is His Church, and He is its Head. The Church came into being at a finite point in time as God the Father sent the Son to live, die, rise from the dead, ascend into heaven, and pour out the Holy Spirit.

Acts 2 describes the day of Pentecost. That small group of praying believers who were huddled together in the Upper Room was changed instantly as they were filled with the Holy Spirit.

Once filled with fear and anxiety, they were now filled with the Holy Spirit and power. Once marked by denial and betrayal, they now poured out of that little room into the streets of Jerusalem to communicate the gospel.

Once characterized by factions, strife, and envy, their hearts were now purified by faith through the cleansing presence of the Holy Spirit. Jesus was building His Church, and the early disciples would never be the same!

The Church for which Christ died is God's sovereign plan. He has no plan B. What happened on that Jewish festival day of Pentecost 2,000 years ago originated in the mind of God before the beginning of recorded time. When

Jesus proclaimed, "I will build my church," He clearly proclaimed God's plan and initiative to reconcile a lost world to himself.

This reality saves us from taking the growth of the church into our hands as if it is all our doing. It roots the work of pastoral ministry in the initiative of God. Before we get up, God is already building His Church. Our role is to recognize what God is doing and to participate in it.

The Church and Making Disciples

The church consists of those "called-out ones" (*ecclesia*) and is made up of the "divinely adopted sons of God. It is not, therefore, merely a human organization."[2]

The incarnate Jesus was divine-human. So the Church on earth, as an extension of His incarnation, is also divine-human. Christ is the Head. "From Him it receives its life through the indwelling Spirit."[3] The Church is His Body, composed of the different members as He has called them and joined them together.[4] Those who have responded to His call and have received Him (John 1:12) are the Church.

The Church is the divine-human means through which the sovereign Head of the Church has chosen to extend His call to all people (2 Corinthians 5:20). Those who respond and receive Him by grace through faith (Ephesians 2:8-9) become a part of His Church, and disciple-making occurs. The Book of Acts is the history of early disciple-making. Three thousand were added to the Church after Peter's sermon on the day of Pentecost, and that was only the beginning. Soon the young church and its leaders were accused of turning the whole world upside down as more members were added and local churches were multiplied (Acts 9:31; 17:6).

It is God's will and purpose for His Church to expand, to reach to the uttermost ends of the earth (Acts 1:8). He works through His Church to expand and extend His Church. Jesus said, "I will build my church." Therefore, He is vitally and intimately involved in fulfilling that mission.

Scripture is filled with examples of the importance of counting and of numerical increase. The shepherd would never have known that one sheep was missing had he not counted the ninety-nine (Luke 15:4). We are informed that 3,000 were added on the day of Pentecost (Acts 2:41). We are informed also that our Heavenly Father even knows the number of the hairs on our heads (Matthew 10:30). When we count members, attendance, and so on, it is because each one counted represents an individual for whom Christ died. Those who are missed must be sought and brought into the safety of the fold. As the Body of Christ, it is expected that the Church will grow, as does every healthy living organism.

Quantitative and Qualitative Growth

The building of the Church of Jesus Christ cannot be less, but it is certainly more than merely increased numbers of members and congregations. Ephesians 4:10-12 clearly points out the maturing, growing process necessary for all believers. This, too, is disciple-making. It is growing in Christlikeness, a maturing in character that goes beyond the destiny-changing new-birth experience and the purifying, empowering experience of entire sanctification. It is the privilege and responsibility of every believer to grow in grace, to experience qualitative growth in his or her relational experience with Christ. This growth in grace is a maturing process as God's grace leads to increased knowledge and wisdom in discerning His will.

Measuring qualitative growth is more difficult than measuring numerical growth. The evidences of qualitative growth are seen in an increasing conformity to the example of Jesus in devotion and service.

Making Disciples and Human Participation

The key to human participation in making disciples is discerning what God is doing and getting in step with Him. God is sovereignly and faithfully at work in building His Church through Spirit-led members of His Church. Programs, methods, procedures, and correct goals are all important. But none of these things can guarantee making more and more disciples. Paul declares, "Neither he who plants nor he who waters is anything, but only God, who makes things grow. The man who plants and the man who waters have one purpose" (1 Corinthians 3:7-8).

It is God who causes growth, but He works through "planters," "waterers," "reapers," and so on. Paul had declared earlier in that same portion of Scripture that he and Apollos were "only servants, through whom you came to believe—as the Lord has assigned to each his task " (v. 5).

Human participation is essential to the building of His Church. God has chosen to work through human beings with all of the imperfections and frailties to bring about disciple-making. Each member of Jesus' Church has an important task to perform in accomplishing His overall task to build His Church. The Holy Spirit has given spiritual gifts to each person as He had determined in order to accomplish His mission (12:1-11).

The Church and the Kingdom of God

Purkiser, Taylor, and Taylor have pointed out that "the more than 70 instances of the phrase 'the kingdom of God' (*basileia tou theou*) . . . in the Gospels [have] led modern scholarship to conclude quite unanimously that the Kingdom of God was the central message of Jesus."[5]

However, modern scholarship is anything but unanimous in its conclusion on the relationship of the Church and the kingdom of God. Peter Wagner draws upon an address by Andrew Kirk at the Lausanne Congress on World Evangelization to clarify how "a few authors make a complete identification, a large number make a partial identification, and a small group makes a radical separation between the two."[6]

I agree with the "partial identification" group. The true universal Church of Jesus as a divine-human extension of the Incarnation is part of the kingdom of God. "Wherever hearts render obeisance to God as King"[7] is where the kingdom of God exists. This is also where the Church exists. However, "The kingdom of God" as used by Jesus designates not only "the kingly rule of God" in the hearts of men made possible through relationship to himself but also the new order which He was establishing with all its blessings.[8] Kingdom growth also includes an increase in freedom from oppression. It includes liberation from that which would prevent God's creation from becoming all that He would want it to be. Kingdom growth includes, but is not limited to, a local church growing.

Jesus said, "I will build my church." But some apparent growth is not always Kingdom growth. It is possible for a local church to receive fifty new members by transfer from another local church. Because we do not have the "overall big picture," we might measure that increase as Kingdom growth. In reality, the Kingdom did not grow at all. One local church added fifty members, but another lost fifty members—yielding a net Kingdom growth of zero. It is important to distinguish the type of growth that is occurring.

If the Church is seen merely as a corrupt human institution, then certainly a sharp distinction would be required between the Church and the kingdom of God. But if our theology of the Church sees the Church as an extension of the Incarnation, then such a *sharp* distinction is not necessary. A distinction is necessary, though. The Church and the kingdom of God as they exist today in the world are only samples of what one day will be. Both have the frailties of humanity as inherent characteristics.

Jesus Said, "Look at the Fields" (John 4:35)

One of the most important tenets of making disciples is the *doctrine of the harvest*, as given by Jesus in John 4:35; Luke 10:2; and Matthew 9:37-38.

Focus

Jesus commands His disciples to open their eyes and look at the fields. We could translate this phrase as "Open your eyes and *focus intently* on the fields." This is not the look of casual vision (*eido*) or voluntary observation (*blepo*) or a watching from a distance (*skopeo*) but rather an intense, earnest, close examination (*theaomai*).[9]

Disciples are to "focus intently" on the fields. If we will look as He commands, then we will begin to perceive people as Jesus does. Arndt and Gingrich list three major meanings for *theaomai* (look). The first is quite literally in the physical sense—to see. The third meaning is where the perception is wholly supernatural, such as, "He perceived much error in us." The second meaning fits best in John 4:35. The second meaning is "to behold literally with physical eyes, but in such a way that supernatural impression is gained." Other examples are found in John 1:32, where John sees the dove and becomes aware that it is the Spirit. We also see this meaning in John 1:14, "where we saw the person and work of Jesus and perceived in them the divine glory."[10] If we will open our eyes and focus intently on the fields, then the Holy Spirit will enable us to perceive the people we see as Jesus does. We look, focus, and study. He supernaturally gives significance to our perceptions.

Jesus commands His disciples to open their eyes and look at the fields. This implies that the disciples had their eyes closed or were focused in the wrong direction. The Church continually runs the risk of becoming inward focused. The Church does not exist for itself or by itself. The Church exists to be the means through whose members Jesus makes His appeal in the power of the Holy Spirit to all people to be reconciled with the Father (2 Corinthians 5:18-20). The ministry of reconciliation provides the framework in which the Holy Spirit sets the agenda for the Church of Jesus Christ. The agenda set by the Holy Spirit for the Church will keep an outward focus on the fields.

The Harvest Fields—

Are Ripe. If we will open our eyes and focus intently on the fields, then the Holy Spirit will enable us to see people as Jesus does. Jesus tells us that the fields "are ripe for harvest" (John 4:35) and that "the harvest is plentiful" (Luke 10:2). God's prevenient grace is already at work, drawing all people to himself. Many people are ready to receive Christ and His life-changing, destiny-changing gospel. According to the Lord of the harvest, there is a large number of receptive persons that He likens to a ready harvest field. They have not been harvested, but they could be—if harvesters would go into the fields to harvest.

Are Lost. Jesus had compassion on the crowds, "because they were harassed and helpless, like sheep without a shepherd" (Matthew 9:36). People without Jesus really are lost. "Salvation is found in no one else, for there is no other name under heaven given to men by which we must be saved" (Acts 4:12). People with the appearance of worldly success and happiness need the Savior, in the same way that people in poverty and pain need the Savior. He is the common denominator for all who are saved. He is "the way and the truth and the life. No one comes to the Father except through [Him]" (John 14:6). Thousands of persons alive today would make life-changing responses to the freely offered grace of God. Those who have not responded are condemned to spend an eternity apart from God in hell. People without Jesus really are lost.

Are Different. When we open our eyes and focus intently on the fields, we discover that people are different from each other. In John 4, Jesus is talking to a Samaritan woman when He uses the opportunity to teach the disciples about the harvest. The perceived differences between Jews and Samaritans were so great that it was surprising to the Samaritan woman that Jesus would even talk to her. People really are different.

A Labor Shortage

Jesus said, "The harvest is plentiful, but the workers are few" (Luke 10:2). According to Jesus, the only reason for not harvesting is a labor shortage.

Human Excuses Not Acceptable. In the same manner in which God initiates and sets the conditions for salvation by grace through faith in Jesus, so He sovereignly declares the harvest to be plentiful and ready. The only reason for not harvesting is a lack of workers. Any other human reasoning is an *excuse,* and human excuses are not acceptable to the Lord of the harvest.

One common but unacceptable excuse is to "blame" the harvest field. This excuse goes something like this: "I will offend people if I ask them to receive Jesus." The truth is that there is an "offense" to the gospel. People confronted with a real opportunity to receive Jesus must confront their own sinfulness. But we are "not ashamed of the gospel, because it is the power of God for the salvation of everyone who believes" (Romans 1:16). The offense of the gospel will cause some to turn away, while others receive gladly the salvation of God.

Paul describes how the same gospel can cause life or death. "We are to God the aroma of Christ among those who are being saved and those who are perishing. To the one we are the smell of death; to the other, the fragrance of life" (2 Corinthians 2:15-16). The only reason for not harvesting is a labor shortage.

Pray

Jesus gives us the solution to the labor shortage when He declares: "Ask the Lord of the harvest, therefore, to send out workers into his harvest field" (Luke 10:2).

Cannot Overemphasize. Overemphasizing the importance of prayer is not possible. We affirm that people without Jesus are lost, that God wants the lost found, that there is a greater harvest than the present harvesters can reap. God has placed the responsibility upon the Church to exercise faith, to pray and ask the Lord of the harvest to send out workers into His harvest field. "More laborers" are the key to increased harvest, and prayer is the key to "more laborers."

A Close Communion. John Miley calls prayer "a means of grace of very large value." It is this close communion with God that yields "an assurance of the divine fullness and love, which enlarges our petitions and inspires petitions and inspires the confidence of a gracious answer from our Heavenly Father." Miley goes on to point out that sincerity, contrition, and consecration are essentials to effective prayer. These must be accompanied by faith, "faith in the form of confidence that our petitions will be granted."[11]

Power in Prayer. It is this close communion with God, this close relationship that provides power in prayer. This power is evidenced by the fervency or effectiveness of James 5:16 and the total dependence upon the Holy Spirit as described in Romans 8:26-27. That "the Spirit intercedes for the saints in accordance with God's will" (Romans 8:27) gives us the confidence to pray knowing that God will hear and answer prayer. He has asked us to pray; He helps us to pray; He answers our prayers. Ask the Lord of the harvest, therefore, to send out workers into His harvest field!

Jesus said, "Go and Make Disciples" (Matthew 28:19)

Michael Green lists three evangelistic motives of the Early Church: a sense of gratitude, a sense of responsibility and a sense of concern.[12] Charles Shaver affirms two primary motives: the Holy Spirit within and the love of Christ.[13]

The Great Commission

Jesus commanded His disciples to "go." Christianity is active, advancing, going into the entire world. Elmer Towns sees the Great Commission as being given at five different times in separate locations. On each occasion the Lord added to the previous command. Towns provides a great outline for understanding the full implication of the Great Commission. His outline is (1) John 20:22—Commission: I am sending you; (2) Mark 16:15—Recipient: Go to all the world and preach to every person; (3) Matthew 28:18-20—Strategy: Disciple all "peoples," and then baptize and teach; (4) Luke 24:46-48—Content: Preach repentance and forgiveness of sins based on the resurrection of Christ; and (5) Acts 1:8—Geography: Jerusalem and to the uttermost parts of the earth.[14]

The Great Commission is not the "great option." It is given to us as an imperative. We could call it "the great commandment" except that we have already coined that phrase for Jesus' imperative to "love God supremely and to love one another." Those who profess to being "lovers of God" and to being filled with His Spirit cannot help but be compelled (2 Corinthians 5:14) to respond to the command of Jesus to "go and make disciples."

Church Planting in the Great Commission

Matthew 28 includes two aspects of strategy. The first is to "go to every person and evangelize them personally." The second aspect is to go to all peoples by the planting of churches, where they may be baptized, disciple, and taught to obey all things.[15]

Virgil Gerber helps to clarify how "evangelism in the New Testament does not stop with reaching people with the Gospel, nor with the proclamation of the Gospel, nor even with relating them to the church through baptism and teaching." Gerber goes on to affirm that "the ultimate evangelistic goal in the New Testament is two-fold: (1) to make responsible, reproducing Christians, and (2) responsible reproducing churches."[16]

God Wants the Lost Found

Jesus said: "Go and make disciples." He did not say, "Go and try to make disciples, and that will be sufficient." It is the Holy Spirit who convicts, convinces, forgives, regenerates and adopts those who will receive Jesus. He is already at work in many ways to bring people to a place of saving faith in Christ. Jesus said, "Go and make disciples," with the full expectation that His disciples would go and that disciples would be made. He was not asking them to merely try to do something. What He commanded them to do, He expected them to accomplish.

Yet in communities filled with lost persons, there are many churches that no longer go out and *find* anyone. This is not pleasing to God. He expects the lost to be found. When Jesus tells the parables of the lost in Luke's Gospel, the rejoicing and celebration occur when the lost sheep (Luke 15:6), the lost coin (v. 9), and the lost son (v. 24) are found.

Why do I spend so much time in discussing this area? It is possible for a type of "seeking mentality" to subtly become a part of our theology. This "search theology" excuses the Church from finding the lost.[17] We can become content to merely *proclaim* the gospel without *persuasion* or, worse yet, to merely be a *presence* for Christ with only occasionally proclaiming or even *not* proclaiming His gospel. "Results" is not a theological "bad word." The strategies developed and the methods utilized based upon a theology of *finding*, of going and *making* disciples, should produce measurable results. Deep within the heart of our Heavenly Father is the desire for the lost to be found. He has made known no other plan to us except for His Church to "go and make disciples."

Jesus' Prayer, "Sanctify Them" (John 17:17)

In this high priestly prayer Jesus is praying for the entire scope of sanctification, both initial and entire sanctification. Initial sanctification occurs at the new birth and represents a cleansing by the Holy Spirit of the new believer from the acts of sin or acquired depravity. Entire sanctification is distinct from initial sanctification. J. Kenneth Grider called entire sanctification "Wesleyanism's most distinctive doctrine."[18] We shall consider here this distinctive doctrine of entire sanctification and its implications for disciple-making.

Entire Sanctification Defined

Grider defines entire sanctification as "essentially an instantaneous cleansing from Adamic sin, and an empowerment, which Christian believers may receive, by faith, through the baptism with the Holy Spirit."[19] The *Manual* of the Church of the Nazarene defines entire sanctification as follows:

We believe that entire sanctification is that act of God, subsequent to regeneration, by which believers are made free from original sin, or depravity, and brought into a state of entire devotion to God, and the holy obedience of love made perfect.

It is wrought by the baptism with *or infilling of* the Holy Spirit, and comprehends in one experience the cleansing of the heart from sin and the abiding, indwelling presence of the Holy Spirit, empowering the believer for life and service.

Entire sanctification is provided by the blood of Jesus, is wrought instantaneously by *grace through* faith, preceded by entire consecration; and to this work and state of grace the Holy Spirit bears witness.

This experience is also known by various terms representing its different phases, such as "Christian perfection," "perfect love," "heart purity," "the baptism with *or infilling of* the Holy Spirit," "the fullness of the blessing," and "Christian holiness."[20]

Perfect Love

In "entire sanctification" or "perfect love" the Spirit of God fills the consecrated, obedient believer with love and awakens love in return. Hence, Paul declares, "God has poured out his love into our hearts by the Holy Spirit, whom he has given us" (Romans 5:5). And Peter declares, "Now that you have purified yourselves by obeying the truth so that you *have* sincere love for your brothers, love one another deeply, from the heart" (1 Peter 1:22, emphasis added). Paul's statement is of a purification that removes from the heart everything that is contrary to the outflow of perfect love.[21]

"This is the full life of love, made perfect in the heart by the agency of the Holy Spirit. Pure love reigns supreme without the antagonism of sin. Love is the spring of every activity."[22] John writes to his "little children": "In this way, love is made complete among us so that we will have confidence on the day of judgment, because in this world we are like him" (1 John 4:17). How are we like Him in this world? In love made complete (or perfect).

An Important Distinction

An important distinction must be made to guard against error. We must distinguish between purity and maturity. Purity occurs instantaneously when the heart is cleansed of inbred sin and filled with perfect love. Maturity takes a lifetime of growth in grace.

Everyone's Privilege

This experience of entire sanctification or perfect love is not only obtainable in this life but "is the normal experience of all those who live in the fullness of the new covenant."[23] It is the privilege of every born-again believer to be entirely sanctified.

In 1907 the Southern California District of the Church of the Nazarene was organized by Phineas Bresee with fourteen churches and 2,074 in membership. In that first district assembly, which began on Wednesday, September 4, 1907, "Dr. Bresee spoke briefly as to the distinctive work of the Church of the Nazarene, to preach holiness, and impressed upon the Assembly the necessity of sticking to our job."[24] Robert Pierce, district assembly secretary, quotes Bresee as going on to say, "We should be a people filled with the thrilling, anointing power of the Holy Ghost and be all aglow with the love of God."[25]

Implications for Disciple-Making

Jesus prayed, "Sanctify them." His prayer was answered on that first Pentecost for one hundred twenty believers as recorded in Acts 2. His prayer has continued to be answered for those who have believed through the centuries.[26]

The implications of the doctrine of entire sanctification for disciple-making are twofold. First, it is the empowering. Second, it is the denominational distinctive.

Empowering for Service. Acts 2 records three supernatural phenomena on the day of Pentecost: "sound like the blowing of a violent wind," "tongues of fire," and that they "began to speak in other tongues" (Acts 2:2-4).

The "tongues of fire" represent the purifying cleansing of the heart that Peter describes in Acts 15:8-9. He is describing the similarities between what happened to the first believers with what happened to the newer Gentile believers. "God, who knows the heart, showed that he accepted them by giving the Holy Spirit to them, just as he did to us. He made no distinction between us and them, for he purified their hearts by faith."

This is the answer to Jesus' prayer—"sanctify them" (John 17:17)—for the Gentiles. Their hearts were *purified* by faith. "Wesley was clear on the matter that God cleanses us from original sin radically."[27] Wesley "spoke of love filling in the heart, expelling (not just suppressing) pride, anger, desire, self-will."[28]

This heart-purifying is foretold by John the Baptist in Matthew 3:11-12. He describes the baptism by Jesus with the Holy Spirit as a baptism with fire that would burn up the chaff with unquenchable fire. The heart where pride, envy, self-will, and carnality no longer dwell becomes a clean channel for God's love and power to flow through.

The "sound like the blowing of a violent wind" represents the power of the Holy Spirit. Jesus said, "You will receive power when the Holy Spirit comes on you" (Acts 1:8). The Holy Spirit came at Pentecost just as Jesus promised He would, and the believers were filled with God's power. Where once there had been fear and cowardice, now there was the power of the Holy Spirit. This was the empowering for service by God's Holy Spirit that in just a short period of time caused those in Thessalonica to declare that they "have caused trouble all over the world" (Acts 17:6). By this power of the Holy Spirit Christianity exploded rapidly throughout the known world. The power at work in and through Spirit-filled believers is the only possible explanation. Once the believers' hearts were cleansed, they became the clean vessels through whom God could work. When pride, envy, and self-will are cleansed, then and only then will His power flow through the willing channel to change the world. God's method for making disciples is by the power of His Holy Spirit flowing through purified hearts to bring others to the saving, sanctifying relationship in Jesus.

That they "began to speak in other tongues" or languages represents the proclamation of the gospel to all people. All the different "ethne" heard in their own heart languages. Communication at this level in any language is possible only by the Holy Spirit.

The Holy Spirit cleanses in order to empower and in order to communicate. The Early Church grew as ordinary people, baptized-with-the-Holy-Spirit people, entirely sanctified people went everywhere telling everyone about the gospel of Jesus.

Denominational Distinctive. The first implication of the doctrine of entire sanctification for making Christlike disciples is empowering for service. The second is that entire sanctification is our denominational distinctive.

Phineas Bresee was convinced that God had raised up the people called Nazarenes to spread scriptural holiness. The Bible teaches that the key to Kingdom expansion is the Holy Spirit working through entirely sanctified believers. Nazarenes stand squarely in the mainstream of the movement of the Holy Spirit with the truth of the key to the Kingdom.

Disciple-making does occur where holiness is not emphasized or taught, but how much more would the Holy Spirit be able to do if the channels were cleansed? How much more would the Holy Spirit be able to do if the message of entire sanctification were received and experienced by all believers? The importance of spreading scriptural holiness cannot be overemphasized.

Those who need to hear are not only the unsaved. Sincere, godly believers in existing churches want to do what is right but are beset by "the sin [condition inside] that so easily entangles" (Hebrews 12:1). Spiritual energy is drained by a war of internal maintenance. The full good news is that Jesus "suffered outside the city gate" even for our sanctification (13:12). God has provided the answer for the hearts of humanity. As the psalmist prays, "Give me an undivided heart, that I may fear your name" (86:11).

The implications of the doctrine of entire sanctification for disciple-making may be summarized in two statements: (1) God has made clear the key to disciple-making: the Spirit-filled, entirely sanctified believer—the clean, empowered channel through whom He can work; and (2) God has raised up the Church of the Nazarene to spread scriptural holiness.

Mrs. C. P. Lampher, president of the Nazarene Women's Foreign Missionary Society in 1907, affirmed that the "Church of the Nazarene will not come short we are sure. Holiness must be planted in every land."[29]

Strategy No. 4
Passionate Missional Outreach

We must release and encourage our people to
embrace with open arms and hearts both the needy
and the new people groups among us.

The gripping question for the Church of the Nazarene in the United States and Canada is "Will we love them here as we love them there?" Paul said to the Colosse Christians, "Devote yourselves to prayer, being watchful and thankful. . . . Be wise in the way you act toward outsiders; make the most of every opportunity" (Colossians 4:2, 5). There are needy people and new people groups all around our churches. We are praying that God will show us how to effectively "make the most of every opportunity."

Will we reach them? If each church would make an assessment of the hurting and needy near their building, they would find some. What are they doing to meet those needs? This is what Jesus would have done. He left the building and walked among the people. Too often we exist as Christians only when we are gathering to worship. It is said that Jesus had one hundred twenty-two conversations in the New Testament and that only eight of them happened inside the Temple. There are needy among us, and they need compassion. But there are also many new people groups near us, and they afford us a rich opportunity for ministry. If our churches will open their eyes, they will discover the thrill and excitement that new people can bring to the family. The Church of the Nazarene is now ministering in one hundred fifty-six world areas. It is estimated that representatives of 80 percent of the people groups to whom we have sent missionaries are presently residing within the borders of the United States and Canada. God has brought the mission field to us. Will we seize this opportunity?

Chapter 14: Taking It to the Streets: From Marginal to Missional, by Mark Bane

Mark Bane describes the joys and dangers of intentionally moving an existing church from "marginal to missional." Using his church as a master illustration, Mark asks probing questions and gives some practical guidelines.

Chapter 15: Multiplying Ministries Where People Live, by Carol Anne Eby with McArthur and Millie Jackson

McArthur and Millie Jackson relate their own transformation story and how God has helped them to minister to the drug addicts, the homeless, and the downtrodden in Memphis. Retired Missionary Carol Anne Eby adds how Trevecca Community Church is using its building and a vast number of volunteers from the church and Trevecca Nazarene University to bring hope and a future to recovering addicts, disenfranchised children, the homeless, and the incarcerated.

Chapter 16: Following the Leader, by Matt Friedeman

Matt Friedeman shares the important lesson of being willing to say with Paul, "Follow my example, as I follow the example of Christ" (1 Corinthians 11:1). Being a leader means following Jesus and being willing to ask others to follow us.

Chapter 17: Making Christlike Hispanic Disciples, by Roberto Hodgson and Walter Argueta

Roberto Hodgson challenges us to reach out to the vast number of Spanish-speaking people in the United States and Canada who need to experience the love of Jesus. Walter Argueta gives us a great illustration of making Christlike Hispanic disciples. His church in Owings Mills, Maryland, has found ways to minister to the new and needy people groups around the church who speak Spanish.

Mark Bane is the pastor of Sandia Church of the Nazarene in Albuquerque, New Mexico. Mark previously was the pastor of churches in Arkansas and Missouri. He is a graduate of Trevecca Nazarene University (BA degree) and Nazarene Theological Seminary (MRE degree). In 1997, when Mark arrived at Sandia Church, the membership was 371, and the worship attendance was 284. In 2010 the membership was 928, and the worship attendance was 925. Mark and his wife, Cheryl, live in Albuquerque. They have two grown children. Pastor@gracepointe.com

■■ 14 ■■
TAKING IT TO THE STREETS
FROM MARGINAL TO MISSIONAL
MARK BANE

The Marginal Church

From marginal to missional is the best way I know to describe our story. Fourteen years ago Sandia Church of the Nazarene was much like many average churches anywhere in the United States or Canada. We had a nice facility in a middle-income community. The members were predominantly middle-income Caucasian. There was a peaceful feeling among the people. Everyone knew everyone, and everyone generally liked everyone. The same people had pie together each week after worship. The reason we were marginal is that we had a marginal impact on the surrounding community. We asked ourselves the following eight questions and failed the test.

1. If your church disappeared tomorrow, would there be a risk of someone starving as a result?
2. If your church disappeared tomorrow, would there be a risk of someone going without clothing as a result?
3. Are more than 25 percent of the congregation's resources spent on those outside the congregation?
4. Does your church bring into membership (by profession of faith) at least 10 percent of the previous year's worship attendance?
5. If your church disappeared tomorrow, would it impact significantly anyone other than those attending and their families?
6. If your church disappeared tomorrow, would there be risk of someone being homeless as a result?
7. Are staff members hired primarily for the needs of those not yet in the church?
8. Are the people of your congregation more concerned about what happens to those outside the walls of the church than they are those who are inside the walls of the church?

If your answer is no to any one of these questions, your church might be a marginal church. We were.

Sandia was a marginal church. As a result of experiences and the conversations early in my ministry at Sandia, I made a decision to embrace and teach the following principles:

1. To train every believer at Sandia to be a disciple-maker. "He made us to be a kingdom of priests" (Revelation 1:6, NCV).

2. To take seriously the admonitions presented by Christ in Matthew 25:31-46—to care for "the least of these," such as the marginalized, the disenfranchised, and the oppressed.

3. To set a goal that within five years we would spend fifty percent of our total income on those not yet part of the church. "Each of you should look not only to your own interests, but also to the interests of others" (Philippians 2:4).

4. To develop ministries so vital to the community that it would be difficult for the community to have a healthy existence without those ministries in the future (Matthew 5:13-16).

5. To embrace the concept of "responsible compassion," that is, we would insist that everyone we gave a cup of water to would also hear a simple message about the love of Jesus (John 4:10).

The decision was to become a mission outpost. I came across a document compiled by Carl Bangs titled "P. F. Bresee: Man of Christian Compassion."
Phineas Franklin Bresee (1838-1915) ministered where people were uprooted and dislocated—on the Iowa frontier, in burgeoning Los Angeles, and across North America. His parish was the world of needy people caught in the poverty and confusion of new cities with their economic and moral anarchy.

Bresee was touched by the sorrow of Jesus over Jerusalem. Jesus wept over Jerusalem. If we say we love Jesus we must ask, "Do I love His passion for people? If people are poor and needy, does it demand my loving sympathy? Do I seek them because my Lord died for them? Or do I want a little club or clique of men who are rich in this world's goods and given to filling up their souls with worldly gain?"

"The Church of the Nazarene," said Bresee, "has a divinely-appointed mission." It is especially raised up to preach that we are to be sanctified wholly in this life, and to fulfill that evidence of its possession, the preaching of the gospel to the poor." This mission "was not taken up of our own accord, nor for our convenience. We went into it at the call of God."[1]

I was reminded that these principles not only were biblical but also were clearly at the root of our movement. At that point the Sandia church was one facility with Sunday morning worship and a plan to end the evening worship service because of lack of interest. The next twelve years took us on a journey of outreach, compassion, evangelism, and discipleship that not only has completely changed the ministry of our church but has also in many ways impacted significantly the city of Albuquerque.

The Transitional Church

I learned that transitioning a church from marginal to missional is nearly an impossible task. When we changed our ministry focus from those inside the church to those outside, we went directly to the Bible for our direction and to prayer for our power. We started all-night prayer vigils; we initiated Bible studies that were directly from the Bible. We began ministries for those not yet churched. To my surprise, some existing church members did not like these transitions. They felt threatened. We had shifted our focus from maintenance ministries to missional ministries. The atmosphere became combative and filled with strife. Most pastors can relate to the tensions felt when attempting to move a congregation through a process of change.

There are three frequently asked questions about our transition.

1. What made the transition so difficult?
2. Did we lose people in the transition?
3. What were the keys to making it through and ultimately becoming a missional church?

1. What Made the Transition So Difficult?

The short answer is almost everything. A church committed to move from marginal to missional finds itself right in the middle between a memory of the past and a vision for the future. In a marginal church there is a sense of peace and quiet, because everyone knows everyone else, and every activity has been going on for some time. Everyone enjoys everyone, and the only people who feel disconnected are the visitors.

The Comfort Level of the Existing Members. We decided to continue all the existing ministries of the church to minimize the discomfort experienced by the existing members. I was not interested in causing discomfort. We did everything the church had been doing while developing new ministries focused on those outside the church.

When some of the good folk began leaving our church in those transitioning years, they would comment, "Pastor, I love the church and the ministries we are doing, but I simply want to go to church on Sunday morning and pay my tithes."

The Culture of the Church Changed. Previously if someone came to church on Sunday morning and paid his or her tithes, he or she would be elected to serve on the board, asked to teach classes, and be considered an all-around good, committed Christian. After the transition began to set in, the level of commitment required for those positions had been elevated. We had young, excited, new Christians who were winning others to Christ, bringing new people into the church, giving above the previous norm of "a tithe," and doing it with great attitudes and humble hearts. When those who had been in leadership in the marginal years were no longer elevated to positions of leadership, they felt disenfranchised and marginalized. As a result, they moved to other churches whose culture demanded less. It is important to note the change in culture was a move of the Spirit, not a decision of the pastor or church board. This cultural change happened because new people simply had a deeper fire and energy for ministry. They had a higher commitment, because their faith was vibrant and new.

Financial Problems. Why? We decided to continue the existing ministries *and* to start new ones. I stopped taking a salary for five years. I became a bi-vocational pastor of a church that eventually was raising nearly a million dollars a year and averaging 600 to 800 in weekly worship. It seemed crazy to many, but the cost had to be paid. Laypeople at Sandia made and continue to make great sacrifices to see the mission accomplished. One of our saints said, "I had to let my dreams of home ownership and other normal American dreams die in order to pursue the mission and dreams that God had for our church." I believe that this was the norm in the New Testament church. To have the same impact on the world and have the same power as the New Testament church, we had to be willing to pay the cost.

Pursuing the Great Commission at a More Accelerated Level Is Hard for Some to Take. One of the greatest challenges to making the complete transition is recognizing this potential problem and making every effort to help the old guard to stay plugged in. This problem created such strife between the new and the more seasoned believers that at times it felt almost wrong to emphasize the Great Commission for fear of these types of conflicts.

2. Did We Lose People in the Transition?

When a marginal church begins to focus outward, a reaction occurs. Those focused inwardly become very uncomfortable when the center of attention moves outward. I believe it is possible to keep most of the marginal minded folk if there is an intensive effort to do so. However, all the energy used to do so will take away from the energy needed for the transition. I believe the reason some churches stop short of becoming an authentically missional church is that they are more concerned about the feelings, relationships, and emotions of their existing friends than they are the eternally lost souls. The problem in many marginally minded churches is not being willing to lose a few to win many.

I will never forget the night that I drove to the top of the Sandia Mountains and began to weep over the families I was sure would leave our church if I pursued the call to become a missional church. I began to point out to God the lights that glowed representing the some seventy-five families who were so accustomed to inward-focused ministries. I wept over each one and told God that I didn't want one of them to leave. I told God to let me leave and let them stay. I argued with God for hours that night at my home. It wasn't until the neighbor whose yard was adjacent to my "prayer perch" called the police to shoo me away for fear that I was up to no good that I got His answer. It was almost funny when the officer knocked on my window around midnight only to find a weeping preacher pleading for "His flock."

I asked the officer, through my sobs and tears, if I could have just a few minutes to compose myself, because I could hardly see through the tears. Those few minutes were life-changing, church-shaking, and city-impacting minutes. For when the officer left, I began again to point out to God those homes. God interrupted me with a vision. He asked me if those seventy-five families were more important than the 800,000 people who surrounded them. I argued again and reminded God that those seventy-five were people He called me to shepherd. He reminded me that He had called me to equip those seventy-five to win the 800,000. Suddenly the tears began to change. I began weeping for the 800,000. I began to hear the cries of the 800,000 who didn't know Jesus, such as the family who had a dying loved one and didn't have the Holy Spirit as a counselor or a pastor as a prayer support. I began to weep for the thousands of homeless who had no home and no food and no clothes and no family and no God and no support. I began to weep over the drug addicts who were concerned about where they would get their next hit. I began to weep over the families who were about to go through the horror and pain of a divorce. I began to weep over their children who would have to decide to which parent they would pledge their allegiance. God made one profound statement: "Who is weeping over those who are not yet in the church? Trust me with the seventy-five (they are, by the way, Mine), and join Me in the lonely tears I have been shedding over the 800,000. Give me the church, and I will give you access to the city!"

Well, we lost people, lots of them, but never more than we won. God has kept the promises He made to me that night. The people who left went to other churches. The city now knows about our church. We have had the opportunity to preach the gospel of Jesus and the message of holiness to over 500,000 people. We have seen desperately lost drug addicts find deliverance. Marriages have been saved and families healed. We have fed and found housing for thousands of homeless. Was it worth the releasing of some families? As painful as it was, it wasn't nearly as painful as it might have been if I had to stand before God and realize that I let Him weep alone for the masses while I cared for the few.

3. What Were the Keys to Making It Through and Ultimately Becoming a Missional Church?

The answer is threefold: *faith, hope,* and *love.*

I have heard myself say many times: "We are doing the right thing, we are doing the biblical thing, and we are doing the God thing." The times when we ran out of money—we knew we were doing the biblical thing. When some left the church—we knew we were doing the right thing. When other pastors accused us of doing the wrong thing—we knew we were doing the God thing. *Faith* is being sure you are doing what God wants you to do. The writer to the Hebrews reminds us that "Faith is the substance of things hoped for, the evidence of things not seen" (11:1, KJV). Faith is the foundational key to transitioning a church from marginal to missional. Faith gives assurance that this is exactly what God wants us to do. If we are certain that God wants us to be a missional church, we will be willing to do whatever it takes. If we have the faith that God has truly called us to make the move from marginal to missional, it can never cost too much, take too long, or be too difficult. If we know it is God's will, we will exhaust the resources, spend the time, and pay the price.

In this context the word "hope" can be interchangeable with the word "vision." *Hope* is "to expect with confidence." Sounds like vision, doesn't it?—the kind that comes from a deep passion of the soul to see the world around us saved. God will help the process of creating a plan to move to the next level. The leader must have a clear vision of what the new missional model looks like. It must be clearer than any obstacle, accusation, hardship, or trial. Only hope can conquer the challenges that will face a pastor who decides to transition from marginal to missional. I had to recommit to the vision almost daily in order to keep the vision above the circumstances. This hope and vision will require hours of prayer, thousands of dollars, and dealing with opposition. The enemy of the souls of humanity will make certain that the cost of this type of vision is very high.

Love is the final key to making it through the transition. Do I love God and His plans for the world more than I love mine? Do I love those who are lost and headed for hell more than I love my luxuries, leisure, and conveniences? Jesus didn't say, "Come, follow me, and I will make you great churchmen." He didn't say, "Come, follow me, and I will make you great planners." He didn't say, "Come, follow me, and I will help you to fulfill the American dream." No, His words are clear: "Come, follow me, . . . and I will make you fishers of men" (Matthew 4:19). If we are going to take our churches to the level of missional impact, we will have to love Him and the lost of this world more than we love our world. In 1 John 3:16-18 we read—

This is how we know what love is: Jesus Christ laid down his life for us. And we ought to lay down our lives for our brothers. If anyone has material possessions and sees his brother in need but has no pity on him, how can the love of God be in him? Dear children, let us not love with words or tongue but with actions and in truth.

As leaders we can demonstrate the kind of faith that trusts God regardless of the cost and consequences, the kind of hope that is bigger than the obstacles that oppose it, and the kind of love that causes us to forget about ourselves. If we do, we will change our world.

The Missional Church

After hearing from God so clearly, we decided to expand into the places most Christians never go. Sandia church began branching out all across the city with a variety of outreach and compassionate ministry efforts. We started fourteen years ago with two acres of property, 17,000 square feet of floor space, ministering to two hundred fifty people at one location. Currently we have expanded to twenty-six points of ministry, four separate church congregations and facilities, thirty acres of property, 150,000 square feet of floor space, ministering the gospel of compassion and holiness to some 50,000 different people annually through a variety of missional programs and events. It would be impossible to share all the various points of light and ministry. I will highlight four categories of missional ministry outreach: (1) Major outreach events, (2) compassionate ministries, (3) taking-it-to-the-streets outreach, and (4) ministry to the incarcerated.

1. Major Outreach Events

The original event that got it all started was the "Big Back-to-School Bash." We gathered three hundred backpacks, mailed the bulk rate mailer invitations, and completed the event. As a result, we had eleven hundred mostly unsaved people attend. Over two hundred came forward to accept Christ. We ran out of backpacks. The last family to leave following the event included a woman driving a small '70s Nissan pickup filled with eight kids. She approached me and asked if she could come back for a regular service. She continued by sharing they had not received backpacks but loved the service and would be back. Of course, I asked her to return on Wednesday night and I would have backpacks for all the kids. She returned and continued to attend regularly. After a few months, one of our older laymen, in his late sixties, developed a burden for the area of her residence. It turns out she lived in an area about twenty some miles from Albuquerque called the Pajerito Mesa. This community was composed of mostly Hispanic families with questionable paperwork proving ownership of property. There was no water, electricity, or other utilities in the community. The layman began small group Bible studies in the community. He spoke little Spanish while most of the attendees spoke little or no English. His burden grew, and so did the Bible study. One night I received a call: "Pastor, God is calling me into ministry." I was amazed. Larry pursued his calling and today is an ordained elder in the church. He has acquired a ten-acre property and has built a church, parsonage, and water well to help the community. He is training leaders to carry on the ministry in the future.

The best part of the "Big Back-to-School Bash" story is that it inspired the people at Sandia to dream about other events. Now we conduct five major outreach events, preaching the gospel to over 25,000 unsaved people annually. We estimate that the total impact of the outreach events over the years has resulted in over 300,000 hearing the gospel in Albuquerque.

2. Compassionate Ministries

Our compassionate ministries began with food distribution to the poor following our midweek services. We discovered that there were many homeless people in Albuquerque who needed a meal on Sunday morning, so we added Sunday morning breakfast and later a Saturday night meal. After a few months, we began distributing food boxes a few times weekly. At that point we were probably feeding three hundred to four hundred mouths a week. Things were going fine until items from the local food bank showed up before the midweek meal. My associate pastor asked those present to join in prayer. At that moment the emissary said, "You can't pray for this food—it is food bank food." The associate prayed for the food anyway. Two days later I received a letter from the food bank stating that we were no longer invited to receive food from them. We began to pray that God would provide an answer so that we would not have to turn away hungry people who needed a meal and desperately needed Jesus. The next day an *Albuquerque Journal* front-page headline read, "Church cut off by food bank because of prayer." Immediately we began receiving calls from food wholesalers and supermarkets who had previously supplied the local food bank. They each asked if it was true. Many promised to begin supplying us with food. The beauty of it was that we had been paying from fifteen to eighty cents a pound for the same food from the food bank. Now we had more food than we could give away—and it was absolutely free. Today we feed some 75,000 hungry people annually at no cost. As a result of our food distribution ministry, we have planted one church, thousands have heard the gospel, and over a hundred homeless receive a meal and hear the gospel weekly.

The food bank ministry has now led to the opening of a thrift store to help those who have need for clothing and appliances. The Thrift Store Ministry has developed into one of our most fruitful ministries both in resourcing the ministry and in touching thousands of needy families and the city of Albuquerque (Matthew 25:31-46).

3. Taking-It-to-the-Streets Outreach

It was Tuesday about 6:30 P.M. The sun had just disappeared in the west valley, and the beautiful soft watermelon red color on the Sandia Mountains had drifted into darkness. The normally car-cluttered streets of Central Avenue (old Route 66) are now filled with street walkers— slurring, staggering, or passed-out intoxicated souls and drug addicts looking to find the next fix. The Taking-It-to-the-Streets Ministry team begins to assemble. Their stories are marvelous.

There was Jenee, a young Hispanic woman who just six years earlier was a hustling crack addict working the streets and the system, evading incarceration at all possible cost. Now Jenee is on staff, teaching small groups, and is our pastor of Restoration and Recovery. Her husband, Stevie, is the Men's Ministries director at Sandia Valley Church. She is also the leader of the Thursday night Taking-It-to-the-Streets Ministry. How good is our God to transform lives so completely?

There was Shawn, a Native American woman who was a meth addict most of her life. She had been converted some years back and wanted to give back to others. When she and her husband, Johnny, were first converted, they made a pledge of $500 to help fund one of our outreach events. They would bring a sock of change each Sunday morning and Wednesday night before the services. I really didn't know how they got the change, but I thanked God for the effort. The first was $56; the next was $70. Then one day just before Christmas the final amount was $500 and not a penny less. How did they do it? Shawn had baked cupcakes. For many Saturday mornings she and Johnny went to the local supermarket and sold them. Today Shawn is one of our most faithful Christians and is working as a pharmacy assistant. She serves on our church board. Her husband, Johnny, has recently been called to ministry and is serving on staff as our Spanish ministries pastor for the Valley church.

There was Pricilla, a single Hispanic twenty-something single mom with a handsome young son. Her life has been radically changed by God's grace. Now she wants to give a little back.

There was Cheryl, the pastor's wife. Cheryl is an Anglo woman who was raised in a heavily sheltered Christian home. She grew up with backyard swimming pools, tennis courts, Mercedes-Benz, and Porsches. Although she had lived her life in relative safety, this ministry grabbed her heart and moved her to take risks that she had previously thought absurd and unsafe. These and many others have taken to the streets in this unique ministry.

After holding hands in a circle of prayer, they headed into the dark "war zone" of Albuquerque's streets armed with bags filled with hygiene items for the hurting, abused prostitutes, hearts of love to touch those who most avoid and with faith that the average Christian would call foolishness. After many months of "taking it to the streets," this past Wednesday, D. J. (a cross-dress-ing male prostitute) and Shirley (an alcoholic prostitute) showed up for our midweek meal and stayed for church. Who knows what will happen as God continues to work through this precious group of Christians?

4. Ministry to the Incarcerated

For years we of the Sandia church prayed that God would help us to begin a prison ministry. Then God sent us Fred Rodriguez, an exciting young Christian who now serves as our associate pastor to the Valley Campus. He developed a vision for a prison ministry. It is currently one of the most fruitful ministries in the church. My favorite story from that ministry is that of Cody Posy, who was incarcerated at age fourteen for the deaths of three family members on a ranch in Hondo, New Mexico, six years ago. Cody was in the youth detention center where Pastor Fred and others ministered. Cody gave his life to Christ, was baptized, and joined the church this year along with several other youth from the center. Cody recently felt a call to ministry and is serving God faithfully as he works to prepare.

Conclusion

There are risks in writing a story like this.

1. **The first is to think**—*This is good for Sandia, but we are doing fine— thank you very much.* We are under no illusion that the types of programs and ministries we are doing are right for every church or every community. One thing that is clear is that we all must be in the redeeming-the-world business. If your church is having only a marginal impact on its community, may the thoughts presented here stimulate you to pray and seek God for future direction.

2. **The second is to think**—*We do not have the resources to make this kind of transition.* Let me remind you that we never had the resources to make this transition. We decided we would rather die trying to have an impact than to die having no impact.

3. **The last is to think**—*We don't have the skills and gifts to take our church to a missional level.* Neither did Moses have the skills and gifts to deliver the people of God. He had to depend on God. I have been operating above my abilities for my entire ministry. I learned with Paul that God's strength is made perfect in my weakness. My answer is simple: pray more and depend on God more. I can't do it without constant dependence upon Him. I have to pray much more than most.

God wants to do great things through your church. God can cause you to look beyond what can be seen, to reach beyond your grasp, to walk beyond your footing, to live beyond your strength, and to give beyond your resources.

Carol Anne Eby is a retired missionary, having served twenty years in Papua New Guinea. She is the former district Missions president of the Tennessee District, General Missions Council member, professor of English at Trevecca Nazarene University, author of four mission books, and contributor to Mission Education curriculum as well as WordAction curriculum. Carol Anne continues to be active in missions, serving as a local president and speaking for Faith Promise and mission gatherings. She and retired missionary husband, Lee, live in Nashville. caeby@comcast.net

McArthur Jackson and wife, Millie, are both ordained elders in the Church of the Nazarene. McArthur is the senior pastor of Memphis Holiness Tabernacle Church of the Nazarene, a multifaceted ministry that has grown from zero to ministering to hundreds of people in Memphis every week. The 181 membership of the church represents only a small fraction of the lives that are touched daily. McArthur and Millie are both graduates of the Memphis Bible Institute, which prepares men and women for ordination in the Church of the Nazarene. The Jacksons live in Memphis. MillieJackson@bellsouth.net

■■ 15 ■■
MULTIPLYING MINISTRIES
WHERE PEOPLE LIVE

CAROL ANNE EBY WITH
MCARTHUR AND MILLIE JACKSON

Nightfall comes to Memphis. The curtain of darkness hides the disheveled youth grasping his crack pipe as he hides in the alley. The shadows disguise the scantily dressed young woman preparing to make her scheduled tryst. The homeless man grabs his bottle of liquor as he lies on the park bench hoping the darkness will assure an undisturbed night's rest. In the darkness, but up on the hill, a light shines that promises hope, transformation, and rescue. As David once sang, "You are my lamp, O LORD; the LORD turns my darkness into light" (2 Samuel 22:29).

Pastors McArthur and Millie Jackson of the Memphis Holiness Tabernacle Church of the Nazarene in Memphis know the depth of that darkness, and having been delivered and transformed, are passionately committed to flood the St. Elmo area of Memphis with God's glorious light.

Millie had come into contact with JoeAnn Ballard and her husband, Monroe, when Millie was only twelve years old, having moved into the neighborhood with her grandparents who raised her. When her parents and brothers and sisters moved back to Memphis from Chicago, they lived at the end of the Ballards' street. Every day Millie's mother, Laura Brewer, and Millie's siblings would pass by the Ballards' house and watch while bread and milk were distributed from the back porch of the Ballards' house, but they would never ask for anything.

One day Monroe asked Millie's mom if she would like some bread. She gratefully accepted the bread and an invitation to attend the Ballards' church, Memphis Friendship Church of the Nazarene. The family began attending regularly. Millie's mom got saved and became a faithful member and steward of the church and still serves the church today at Holiness Tabernacle alongside McArthur and Millie. Millie wasn't raised in the church; she was already an adult by the time her parents had moved back to Memphis. She relocated to Chicago shortly after her parents returned to live with an older sister who still lived there. It was there she became heavily involved in drugs.

157

It was July 1987, and she had returned to Memphis on the day before her birthday. She went to the filling station to buy a bottle of beer. Even though it was her birthday, she was very depressed and wanted to cheer herself up. There she met McArthur, who was filling his car with gas. He was attracted to this lovely young woman. They talked and exchanged numbers, but Millie really wasn't interested in a new relationship. She had had bad luck with men and already had a daughter. However, they started hanging out together, both very heavy into drugs, and finally began living together. After four months they got married, and Millie became pregnant. It was a tubular pregnancy, so she had to have surgery and lost the baby. Very depressed, she found a copy of the Book of John in the hospital and read it through. She began thinking about God, but after leaving the hospital she was still deeply involved in drugs. Finally, Millie got sick of it all, and in God's timing she finally agreed to go with her mom to church. She felt she didn't have decent clothes but remembered she had left a dress at her grandmother's. When she went to get it, she discovered it was dirty, so she found one other skirt and decided to wash it out and wear it. When she went to put it in the washer, she knocked a bottle of bleach into the machine and ruined the skirt. She felt this was Satan really trying to keep her from going to church. She grabbed the dirty dress from her grandmother's house, put it on, and went to church. When they gave the altar call, she wanted to go but felt she had cement boots on.

Her mom grabbed her arm and helped her to the altar. She wept uncontrollably and was determined to make things right with God. A lady came to the altar and said, "Don't worry about tomorrow—just do what you need to do today." That confirmed to Millie that she could accept salvation.

She had a voracious appetite for the Word, but after she was saved, the Jacksons' power was turned off because they didn't have the money to pay the light bill. She was so distressed that McArthur rigged up a light from the car battery so she could read her Bible. God delivered Millie from drugs, but she was still drinking some. Once at a party, she met a friend whom she had been praying for and to whom she wanted to witness. Shamed that her words were slurred, she asked God to deliver her from alcohol. Still smoking but trying to witness to her husband, God again convicted her. One night McArthur said, "You're trying to tell me about God, but every time you get upset, you reach for a cigarette." She never touched another and praised God that He had delivered her from drugs, alcohol, and tobacco almost instantaneously.

Millie finally realized that she could not browbeat McArthur into a religious experience. God's promise to her was *You want me to change your husband. Let me change you, and he will follow.* After about a year, one night McArthur was drinking but sat down on the floor beside Millie and started crying; he felt he was losing her because of the way he was living. He said, "I'm going to finish this quart, but after that I'm not going to drink anymore! Later he told God, "You are not going to put on me more than I can bear," and God delivered him from alcohol. A pastor, Robert Cole, prayed for McArthur over the phone so that he could get home with his check and not spend it on liquor. One night at a revival at First Tabernacle church under Pastor Cole, McArthur came in and sat in the back crying. He made his way to the altar and was gloriously saved. He was twenty-seven years old. Millie would testify, "He's twenty-seven and on his way to heaven."

Growth in Christlikeness and a Call from God

The Jacksons stayed with Pastor Robert Cole, who pastored an independent congregation for six years, and became good workers in the church. McArthur became a deacon, and Millie taught Sunday school. But in 1996 Millie began to feel that God was calling them to deeper ministry. McArthur felt the same way, but they wondered how they were going to tell Pastor Cole that they were going to leave his church. They went to tell him, and before they could get it all out, he said, "God has called you into ministry, hasn't He?"

They had no building, no money, and no congregation. One day they pulled over to the side of the road to pray, and the Holy Spirit impressed them that they should go talk to JoeAnn Ballard. They did, and when she saw them she said, "I know why you're here—you want to start a church."

Holiness Tabernacle Church of the Nazarene Is Born

JoeAnn gave them permission to begin in the foyer of the Neighborhood Center, and they had about fifteen in attendance at the first service. They stayed there about three months and then found a storefront on Chelsea Avenue that was rat-infested and dirty. However, the proprietor said, "If you clean it up, you can have it." Members worked and turned it into a delightful little sanctuary. They were twenty-five members in a home-type mission.

The congregation grew and began to fill up the sanctuary, so soon they realized that they needed to move. The church acquired a new facility in 1998 at 1879 Pinedale with the help of Dennis Johnson, district superintendent of the Tennessee District; JoeAnn Ballard; and the Tennessee District Board. They organized on Easter Sunday with fifty-one members. Their name became Memphis Holiness Tabernacle Church of the Nazarene. They truly wanted to go back to the community they had come out of to minister to the drug addicts, the homeless, and the downtrodden. They felt they could identify with that community and focused their ministries to bring light into that darkness.

The St. Elmo Blessing

God blessed the ministry, and soon again they outgrew their building. They thought of adding on to the building, but they were landlocked. They began praying earnestly that God would direct them to a new location. Dr. Ballard joined with them, and many prayers ascended to the Father. Pastor Allen Canley, a friend and colleague in ministry, went to an auction and discovered the property on St. Elmo was in foreclosure. It was a beautiful sanctuary with fellowship hall and Sunday school rooms and a large two-story, forty-room educational/administration building as well. The asking price was $550,000. JoeAnn said, "We've got to pray that price down!" With the district's blessing and a miraculously lowered price, the Jacksons were able to acquire the property that is now appraised at a million dollars. In July 2005 they moved onto the new property. With the help of many work teams from the district along with the members, and much encouragement and hard labor from Bill Wiesman, the Memphis Holiness Tabernacle Church of the Nazarene truly became a light set upon a hill that cannot be hid.

A Tool Used for God

From the beginning, the Jacksons desired to use their church building to multiply ministries in their community and beyond. Competition was a word that was not in their vocabulary. The Realtor who was trying to sell the Pinedale property put Bryant Walker in touch with the Jacksons. Rev. Walker was beginning a New Start church, and the Jacksons were happy for him to use the Pinedale property. But when a buyer came available and Rev. Walker's group could not buy the property, the Jacksons welcomed Rev. Walker's congregation to their empty upstairs. The Look at God Restoration congregation came under the "Nazarene umbrella," stayed a year, and then moved into their own building.

Restoration Tabernacle

Derrick and Carla Brown were young people who started coming to the church when it was located on Pinedale. Derrick had gang affiliations and the couple were very young, unmarried, but were living together. Derrick took to McArthur as a father figure. Carla would cry every time they came to church. They said they couldn't afford to get married, but the Jacksons helped them, and they had a lovely little wedding. Both were saved, sanctified, and nurtured under the loving tutelage of the Jacksons. After months of serving in the church, Derrick and Carla felt the call of ministry, and Rev. Jackson sent them out to establish the Memphis Restoration Tabernacle. The ministry is thriving, averaging thirty-five to forty, and both Derrick and Carla are working on ordination.

Hope Center and Hope Tabernacle

To help with expenses of an expanding ministry, Millie became a manager at an apartment complex. One day she discovered a stolen car left on the property. Searching the car, she found the owner's information and discovered it belonged to a Donald Washington. She called Mr. Washington. He came to get the car, and she invited him to church. He was struggling with drugs and had been imprisoned as a result of his involvement. Donald did come and was saved and delivered from drugs. Eventually Arlene, now his wife and whom he had met when she installed his telephone, came with him. The Washingtons got married in 1994. Both became Christians and served faithfully with the Jacksons for about twelve years. Donald had left prison with a great burden for the incarcerated. He felt there was no one to help him, but he promised God he would do what he could for those he left behind.

In 2008 Donald's burden for those imprisoned fulfilled a call to go into full-time ministry, and he and Arlene, with the blessing of the Memphis Holiness Tabernacle congregation and pastors, set forth to make their dream a reality by opening Hope Center. They bought a house that had been condemned and with volunteers from the neighboring churches such as Memphis Grace and Memphis Calvary, other volunteers from churches across the district as well as students from Trevecca Nazarene University and even volunteers from Alabama, began repairing the house a little bit at a time. The center opened in April 2010. The center is for females leaving prison and reentering society. Presently there are two occupants, one of whom is attending college. Hope Center becomes their support system, providing lodging, food, clothes, and family. They work to find them employment so they can give their fair share. The project has also birthed another New Start church, and Hope Tabernacle now averages twenty-five to thirty in attendance.

Memphis Christlike

The Jacksons met Stanley Douglas through JoeAnn Ballard. Rev. Douglas needed a place to begin a ministry, and again the Jacksons offered their now-empty space and the Christlike congregation was formed. The space has been enlarged to allow more growth for the new congregation.

The Mother Church Continues to Grow

One might wonder with all the coming and going of congregations how the mother church is surviving. Holiness Tabernacle currently has 183 members and is very active spreading the light of the gospel and the message of holiness to their community. Prison ministries both for male and female inmates continue once a month, led by ministers Marquinn Carson and Deborah Holloway. This ministry led to meeting Michael J. Appleberry. He came faithfully to the prison services and promised to come to church upon his release. When he got out of prison, the next day he was in church and has been attending ever since. He wasn't married when he came to the church but met a lady there and soon fell in love. Both became committed Christians, married, and now have a lovely blended family with her five children, his three, and the beautiful child of their marriage. Terry, his wife, is a registered nurse, and Michael has become a prosperous businessman.

Tamon Jackson came off the streets as a member of a gang and a heavy user of drugs. He was so entangled in drugs and crime that he was looking at a long prison sentence, but God answered prayers and intervened. Tamon came to church and was saved. He met his wife, Mardi, there. They now have a beautiful baby, and both are very committed to God and the church.

Lisa Dunbar has gone every month for the last six years to minister to thirty elderly people. She has a beautiful voice and sings, prays, and preaches to her nursing home congregation faithfully and devotedly. Lisa was living out of wedlock but following a sermon preached by Rev. Jackson on getting your house in order, went home, and came back the next Sunday legally married and ready to fully commit to God and His service.

One of the thriving ministries the Jacksons have is called C.O.R.D. (Couples Overcoming Relationship Difficulties), working with couples who are living together out of wedlock or single. Rev. Jackson has performed some twenty weddings.

Millie runs a large program of children called P.E.A.S. (Pupils Empowered for Academic Success). Each summer she runs a summer camp with sixty or seventy students involved for ten weeks to keep them off the streets. She finances it herself, working extra in the winter to provide funds for the summer. She also runs an after-school program, printing off homework sheets and tutoring the children, giving them educational and spiritual help.

The church is a community center where many volunteers come to do community service as they are receiving government assistance with food stamps and so on. This is a great source of community outreach.

The church always adopts a family at Christmas to provide toys, gifts, clothes, and other items for those in need. This year's recipient is a young girl from Atlanta who is pregnant and has been taken in by the church family as she has no other support.

Another effective ministry that has been started and led by Mr. Appleberry is called the Empowerment Hour. He sets up three chairs symbolic of inviting God the Father, Jesus, and the Holy Ghost to be present in their meeting. Recently a member of the church, Beverly White, who cares for an autistic child, attended the prayer service. At first the child was unmanageable, kicking and screaming. He got away from Beverly and came and sat in the chair of the

Holy Ghost. He quieted and afterward came to Millie saying, "Ghost, Ghost, Ghost." He let Millie pray for him and has been calm ever since.

Another lady came in crying, desolate and distressed. She was prayed with and has since gotten a job and become regular in services and now is so joyful, attesting to the continuance of God's blessing upon this ministry.

Millie also serves as a chaplain and goes to hotels and companies to pray for their businesses and pray for personal needs. A truck driver at one of the businesses came over to her and said, "How do I get the Holy Ghost?" She continues to be overwhelmed at God's opportunities for witnessing. To her own sixteen-year-old-niece and to the many young people whose lives she touches she says, "When you're pressured to do drugs, engage in sex, are overwhelmed with the things of the world, just know you haven't missed a thing! God is so good."

The Jacksons are wonderful models of God's multiplication of ministries by unselfishly allowing the use of their unoccupied space and their promotion of compassionate ministries to meet the needs of the community in which they live.

Trevecca Community Church of the Nazarene

Light is spreading and ministries are being multiplied not only in Memphis but also in Nashville. Trevecca Community Church, "on the hill," is a beacon of light to the darkness surrounding it. Located on the edge of the Trevecca Nazarene University campus, the church is using its building and a vast number of volunteers from the church and the university to bring hope and a future to recovering addicts and to disenfranchised children living in the nearby housing project of J. C. Napier Homes.

The Mitchells Arrive from Ohio

In 2002 because of a job transfer, Billy and Tina Mitchell moved from Ohio to Nashville. Upon their first visit to Trevecca Community Church, they knew this was to be their new church home. They felt it was reaching out to their immediate community to make a difference. Crime was rampant; drug trafficking and prostitution were operating on virtually every street corner; and quality children's programming aimed at breaking this cycle was in short supply. For twenty-two years the church had sponsored a "King Kids" ministry one night a week, reaching out to the children of the J. C. Napier Projects. Every Thursday from November to March, fourteen men spent the night at the church in a Room in the Inn program set up for homeless men who were working but unable to establish themselves in their own lodging.

A Fresh Vision from God

This was effective, but God gave Tina a vision that would encompass so much more. One day as she was returning from a hospital visit at Vanderbilt Hospital in early spring, suddenly as she traveled the road back to the church, she became aware of the homeless, the prostitutes, the drug dealers, all within sight of her church, so near yet so far from God. In tears she went to her pastor and said, "We've got to do more." For a year because of the lack of funds to make her a part of the staff, she worked as a volunteer with no pay. After that, she was put on part-time and then full-time as pastor of evangelism. In these eight years God has miraculously multiplied Trevecca Community Church's ministries in Tina and Pastor Dwight Gunter's commitment to God—"If You'll open the doors, we will walk through them."

CrossBRIDGE

An Access to Recovery grant enabled many programs to be set up. The church sponsored the start of CrossBRIDGE, a nonprofit organization committed to individual and community transformation. BRIDGE is an acronym standing for the following: Build—Building leaders through direct, hands-on involvement with children and youth in our community. Restore—Restoring lives destroyed by the scourge of addiction through dedicated recovery ministries. Invite—Inviting people into the warmth of meaningful, caring relationships with God and others. Develop—Offering life skills classes such as parenting, computing, GED, money management, conflict resolution, and anger management. Give—Creating a culture of community reinvestment, giving back, with a special emphasis on reinvesting human resources. Elevate—Lifting people out of shame, restoring in them the image of God, conveying and imparting intrinsic value to all.

Journey to Wholeness

Trevecca Community Church became a provider for Davidson County General Sessions Treatment Court X, better known as Drug Court. Each Sunday morning more than eighty people gather in a spiritual support group for people in recovery during the Sunday school hour. On Sunday night, relapse prevention classes, averaging about seventy, are held with paid counselors. On Wednesday evening about seventy-five gather in a twelve-step Journey to Wholeness in a meeting called the Bridge, which is bridging recovery and authentic Christ-centered spirituality. This is a one-of-a-kind program with nothing else quite like it anywhere.

A "Welcoming Place"

Trevecca Community Church has partnered with Phases Recovery for Women and four Restoration Houses for men to provide food donated monthly by the congregation of the church as well as weekly deliveries from Second Harvest food warehouse to each of the women's and men's houses. Clothes, rental assistance, bus passes, employment skills classes, and anger management classes are also provided. Trevecca's congregation is a loving, accepting, grace-filled community of believers that welcomes the recovery groups as family. Trevecca Community Church is considered a "welcoming place"—a place that loves in spite of, a place where people can be authentic, not perfect but striving to draw ever closer to God.

Ministries Extending

Many ministries have evolved from extension of the recovery program. "Jammin at the Jail" is an annual event involving over nine hundred people, seven hundred fifty inmates, and two hundred Trevecca Community Church musicians and attendees, worshiping together behind the fences and razor wire of a jail.

An annual egg hunt for inmates and their families is held with the church's teens filling 6,000 plastic eggs. At Christmas 1,700 Christmas candy bags are distributed to inmates. Backpacks are distributed to inmates' children at the beginning of the school year.

KidPower

Future generations have not been forgotten. KidPOWER began in October of 2010. POWER stands for Purity in body and mind; Others—community service; Wellness—physical fitness and nutrition; Excellence in academics and arts; and Reconciliation through peaceful means. This program is beginning with twenty-five second graders from the J. C. Napier community who are brought to the church four days a week after school to have one-on-one tutoring with Trevecca Nazarene University students and to participate in physical fitness, character education, and conflict resolution classes. A class in the arts and opportunity for service projects is also provided.

New Life Café

Trevecca Community Church has also opened its facility to be used five days a week by New Life Café, open to the community with proceeds funding CrossBRIDGE, which is committed to the transformation of the south Nashville community. Their brochure states, "Your patronage at New Life Café provides you a wonderful meal and helps the men, women, boys, and girls living in a community suffering the effects of generational poverty."

God's Blessing and Faithfulness and a Call to Do More

Presently almost twenty ministries have emerged in the eight years from Tina's vision of "We must do more!" From all departments, the congregation of Trevecca Community Church participates in some one hundred sixty ministries. Whether a small or a large church, to multiply ministries takes servants of God fully committed to His will, eyes that look around them to see what Jesus sees, and a passion to use what God has given them, consecrated to His service and possessing a vision "to do more."

Matt Friedeman is the founding pastor of DaySpring Community Church of the Nazarene in Clinton, Mississippi. Matt earned three degrees from the University of Kansas (bachelor's, master's, and doctorate). He also has an MDiv degree from Asbury Theological Seminary. DaySpring has grown from zero attendance in 2001 to 221 in average worship attendance in 2010. Matt and wife, Mary, live in Jackson, Mississippi. mfriedeman@wbs.edu

FOLLOWING THE LEADER

MATT FRIEDEMAN

The Saturday after our new church had its public launch, I found myself outside a Jackson, Mississippi, abortion clinic wondering how I had gotten myself in such a predicament.

For years I had written a biweekly opinion column in the statewide newspaper and hosted a daily radio talk show that urged people to get involved in the problems of their communities. Specifically on the topic of abortion, I had sanctimoniously declared on a regular basis that if local pastors would take the lead on this issue and head out to the abortion clinics to stand up for the unborn, the people of their churches would follow suit and the tragedy of abortion would end in our state.

I was now a pastor.

I now had pressure on my soul to be more than a talker.

I was now, regrettably, a pro-life activist.

Either that, or I would be a bald-faced hypocrite.

And that was only the beginning of my reluctant journey into "Follow me" leadership. Reluctant or not, it would become the mode of operations of our fledgling body's leadership.

Biblical Foundation

This wholistic approach to faith has a strong biblical precedent. The Hebrew word for "know," *yada*, perhaps more accurately means "to experience" or "to encounter." It is first seen in Genesis 4:1. As Scripture puts it, "Adam knew Eve his wife" (KJV). In other words, he experienced or encountered Eve sexually. From there the word appears in many contexts throughout the Old Testament narrative, but at its most profound level it expressed the desire of God that His people would *know* Him—not just intellectually but in a much more intimate sense. They would experience and encounter Him and would act on His behalf, including *knowing* their neighbors in sacrificial acts of love and kindness. Marvin Wilson in his discussion of *yada* notes:

The idea of knowledge thus embraced the whole human personality. A grasp of so much information was not enough; it also implied a response in the practical domain of life, in behavior and morals. . . . In short, for the Hebrew, to "know" was to "do." . . . [It] went far beyond mere intellectual activity; it was to act. It included down-to-earth activity or personal know-how applied to various realms and experience of life.[1]

The life of Jesus exemplifies this paradigm of active, modeled faith. In Matthew 4 Jesus calls His first disciples; directly thereafter He begins His march through Galilee, teaching, preaching, *and healing* (v. 23). From that point forward, His teaching includes words like "let your light shine before men that they may see your good deeds" (5:16) and "everyone who hears these words of mine and puts them into practice is like a wise man" (7:24). The Gospels portray a vital correlation between the words of Christ and His actions—with His disciples in tow. Christ's ministry is punctuated by strong teachings on the importance of faith expressed in acts of obedience. He explicitly warns that not all who expect to reach heaven will, but only those who possess an active faith—giving sustenance to the hungry and thirsty and aid to the stranger, sick, and imprisoned (25:31-46). He describes His "family" as those who do the will of His Father (12:50). He said of himself, "Do not believe me unless I do what my Father does" (John 10:37) and "the world must learn that I love the Father and that I do exactly what my Father has commanded me" (14:31).

Indeed, Jesus' last command to His disciples in the first Gospel is to "Go and make disciples . . . teaching them to obey everything I have commanded you" (Matthew 28:19-20). His life was reflective of this priority, and He commanded His students to go and make faithful followers who would do likewise. Robert Coleman summarizes Christ's leadership style and the implications for ministers in his seminal work *The Master Plan of Evangelism*:

> When it is all boiled down, those of us who are seeking to train men must be prepared to have them follow us, even as we follow Christ. . . . We are the exhibit. . . . They will do those things which they hear and see in us. . . . We must take this truth to our lives. There can be no shirking or evading of our personal responsibility to show the way to those we are training, and this revelation must include the practical outworking in life of the deeper realities of the Spirit . . . mere knowledge is not enough. There comes a time for action.[2]

DaySpring Community Church

And so by reluctant default, as pastor of DaySpring I felt compelled by public declarations and biblical data to lead by doing. While the first Saturday after the public launch of the church put me where I initially didn't want to be, that and subsequent other involvements have deepened not only my life but also the lives of my family and church. This active leadership approach is informed by two statements of DaySpring Community Church: our mission statement and the Habits of a DaySpringer.

First, our mission statement, which we recite corporately in every worship service:

DaySpring exists to excite men and women, boys and girls, about a life-changing relationship with Jesus, and to release these disciples for ministry in this community and around the world for the glory of God.

Through this statement we explicitly express and frequently affirm vital faith and outreach as a foundational value of our congregation. As our numbers have grown, so has the number of outreach ministries, which are listed weekly in the bulletin.

The Habits of a DaySpringer is a statement reflective of fundamental means of grace as John Wesley called such habits. It summarizes the basic disciplines taught in DaySpring's membership and discipleship courses, which are organized around the Saddleback church paradigm of membership, maturity, ministry, and mission. The habits are as follows:

- Regular attendance at church
- Daily devotional life
- Giving of a regular tithe
- Involvement in a small group
- Involvement in at least one internal (building up the local church) and one external (compassionate or evangelistic) ministry
- Involvement in the worldwide mission of the Church

"Follow me" leadership means that the pastor is not merely promoting these values but is experiencing them personally and encouraging his or her church to do the same. It involves sharing specific examples from his or her own life with the congregation. The pastoral staff, small-group leaders, and church board members are committed to leading by example in this manner as well. The many contexts for interaction outside of worship services—through small groups and side-by-side in outreach ministry—allow those who attend DaySpring to see the core values lived out in the lives of their leaders.

Follow Me as a Disciple-making Strategy

The strategy of leading by example was initially expressed in two different arenas: outreach and family life.

Outreach

Early emphasis on compassionate outreach proved to be a draw toward membership and involvement in DaySpring. I encouraged our congregation to join me at the abortion clinic, and many did. From pro-life ministry, outreach soon expanded to include weekly evangelism and discipleship at the county detention center, which houses upwards of seven hundred inmates. Often people seemed more willing to become actively engaged when they saw the preacher not merely exhorting them to involvement but rather inviting them to share the journey with him. Others had previously felt stifled by pastors who preferred to confine ministry—theirs and their congregation's—within the four walls of the church building. In the context of an active congregation, these members blossomed. Said one member, "This is the first church that actually trusted me to do ministry."

DaySpringers are encouraged to listen to God's call to new avenues of outreach. This has resulted in a plethora of outward-bound ministries, many of which are lay-led. The average number of church members involved outside the church building in weekly compassionate ministry is eighty, reaching approximately seven hundred persons through these ministries. Current ministries include—

- Prison ministry (the pastor is a deputized chaplain)
- Penal farm Bible study (we have started baptizing inmates at a church service once a month)
- Abortion clinic counseling (loving approach—no yelling, jeering, exhibiting signage with aborted fetuses; many children and youth are involved)
- Crisis Pregnancy Center outreach
- Ministry to the elderly and infirm at two nursing home facilities (many children involved here)
- Celebrate Recovery
- Angel Food ministry (once a month; many teens and children are involved)
- Biennial free garage sale to benefit the needy (many teens and children are involved)
- Adopt-a-school—book buddy program, tutoring, student enrichment activities
- Work and Witness ministry (regularly in-state/out of country; teens frequently involved)

The pastor obviously cannot be involved hands-on in every outreach ministry. I am a bi-vocational pastor with a full-time job as a seminary professor; I host a daily radio talk show and have other family commitments such as coaching a couple of soccer teams. My congregation knows I am busy, even overextended, but they also know that evangelistic and compassionate outreach is a joint commitment of our church life. They enjoy seeing that fruit in my life, and I expect to see it in theirs.

Having a pastoral team that leads by example has fostered a culture of others-centered ministry at DaySpring. This in turn continues to attract new attendees to our church; in many cases their initial contact is as a recipient of one of the above ministries. When they become members and then engage in ministry themselves, the cycle is complete. For example, a former inmate and his family, now gloriously converted, have become vital, active members of our congregation and are involved in ministries in our church.

Family Life

The second arena in which the "follow me" dynamic has had significant impact involves family life. At the time of the church plant, my wife and I had five children; shortly thereafter, the sixth was born. Early in the life of the church, many members expressed that the reason so many parents with children came to DaySpring was the reputation of the pastoral family ("Wow—they have lots of kids!") or the child-friendliness of the church once they arrived.

While the age span in our church ranges from birth to older members in their 80s, many of those attracted to our fellowship seem to be younger families. Parents today are hungry for leadership and notable examples in the area of family life, especially those who are from broken homes or who were not raised in a Christian environment. They want to establish a godly home but often lack the tools or an example. My wife and I were thirty-nine and forty-one, respectively, when DaySpring launched, and our children ranged from *in utero* to age eleven. So we were older parents but with young children near the ages of many target families' children. Because our children love Jesus and were actively involved in the life of the church from the outset—helping to move equipment into our rented facility and assisting with setup and breakdown each week, running PowerPoint for worship services, and so on—these families took notice and made frequent comment of the children's work ethic, their jovial attitudes, and their passion for the church.

They trusted the teaching on family life they heard from the pulpit and bought into the Habits of a DaySpringer and the mission of the church because they saw it modeled in the life of our family. My wife and I function as a ministry team, and this also proved beneficial to the church. In this day and age of broken families and rampant divorce (even in clergy homes), people are eager for someone committed to lifelong marriage who will say, "Follow us." We give God great praise for His grace at work in our lives. And please understand—it is hard to share these things, because my intent is not to tout the virtue of my family but to underscore the vital importance of modeling in all aspects of leaders' lives. In the case of our church, marriage and family life has simply, in retrospect, turned out to be a powerful impetus to growth.

We have been blessed that our children continue to be actively involved in both internal and external ministries (as all DaySpring members are exhorted to do). They currently serve in several capacities on the multimedia team, lead worship, play in worship bands, and assist with children's ministries in the church. They also regularly participate in the nursing home and abortion clinic ministries and in mission trips.

There is a reason God through Timothy exhorted that an overseer must be "the husband of but one wife" (1 Timothy 3:2) and "must manage his own family well and see that his children obey him with proper respect" (v. 4). Especially in the contemporary climate, it is a powerful witness to both believing and unbelieving families and a validation of the church's ministry.

Conclusion

Before you can make a disciple, you must know what a disciple is. DaySpring tries to articulate these characteristics through its mission statement and Habits of a DaySpringer list. The basic disciple definition clear, the pastor must lead the way by living into that list of qualities so critical to the aspirational church culture. Through teaching and leadership, he or she must challenge the congregation to do the same.

A founding pastor and an ensuing leadership team willing to lead by example have proved essential to the ongoing health and growth of our congregation. Daily Bible study and prayer; full participation in church life through worship, giving, and small groups; and regular involvement in outreach ministry are all key components to the "follow me" leadership style. As leaders both articulate and demonstrate the key qualities of a disciple, our church has increased both in discipleship and in numbers. The outreach component has been an especially effective growth indicator; as our congregation has cultivated an others-orientation, new people are attracted to our fellowship, and those who attend are inspired to a deeper level of discipleship as they put hands and feet to their faith.

If there is no common understanding or clear example about what a disciple is, the congregation is apt, over time, to assume the style of the pastor both spiritually and behaviorally anyway. The pastor must be "saved, sanctified, and sent" and have a congregation that will see and hear the challenge to be the same. A pastor who says, "Follow me as I follow Christ" is a key component to the initial success and continuing vitality of the church body.

Other Information

Church Web site: www.dayspringonline.org

Average worship attendance: 250

Style of worship: contemporary with live band; occasional hymns via band

Other staff: Jim Joyce, associate (full-time); Mary Friedeman (children's/part-time); Tim Burnett (youth/part-time)

Prayer meeting: Every Wednesday night. We open with a song, then read a Scripture passage. We follow the ACT paradigm and spend ten minutes of extemporaneous prayer on each segment (adoration, confession, and thanksgiving), prefacing each prayer period with a relevant song. We then split into separate groups (men, women, boys, and girls, the latter two groups being led by men) for intercessory prayer. This is a very important part of our church life and, we have found, unique. Rarely are prayer meetings exclusively about prayer anymore. We have gained a reputation as a church you definitely want on your side in time of need. Healings are frequent, miracles abundant.

No Sunday school: We use children's church and small-group meetings in the evening to fill the educational and fellowship gap.

Building: We started in a skating rink and after three years purchased and moved to an old furniture warehouse (metal building—12,000 square feet). We have some convictions here, too. Nazarene founder Phineas Bresee:

What must He think of His people today, spending their time and strength and the money which would feed the hungry and clothe the naked and send the gospel to the unsaved, in placing stone upon stone, building massive towers, carving forms of beauty, adding elaborate and expensive adornments, putting thousands of dollars into grand organs, and all tending necessarily to drive the poor from the portals of the so-called house of the Lord? . . . We want places so plain that every board will say welcome to the poorest. We can get along without rich people, but not without preaching the gospel to the poor. . . . Let the Church of the Nazarene be true to its commission; not great and elegant buildings; but to feed the hungry and clothe the naked, and wipe away the tears of sorrowing; and gather jewels for His diadem.[3]

Dress: Very casual. Pastor leads here by wearing no tie, usually no coat, and preaching in running shoes or sandals.

Missions: We typically send twenty or more people per year on short-term mission trips. The walls of our worship area are covered with flags of the nations where we have gone to minister or from which people have come to be part of our fellowship. Currently around thirty flags are displayed.

Biggest current problems: (1) inadequate parking; (2) pastoral time (as a full-time seminary professor, radio talk show host, and father of six, I am way too busy with other things); (3) need of a capable leader to plant a new church.

Walter Argueta is an ordained elder in the Church of the Nazarene and pastor of Owings Mills, Maryland, Latin American First Iglesia del Nazareno. Walter is a graduate of Colegio Internacional de Cristo (BA). In the seven years of Walter's ministry the church has grown from seventy-seven in average worship attendance to four hundred sixty while adding two hundred thirty-eight new Nazarenes for a total membership of two hundred fifty. Walter and his wife, Doris, live in Owings Mills, Maryland. latin.nazarene@gmail.com

Roberto Hodgson serves as the Hispanic Ministries director for the USA/Canada Region Church of the Nazarene and as district superintendent of the Southwest Latin American District. Roberto pastored churches in Costa Rica, Washington, D.C., and Maryland. He is a graduate of the Nazarene Seminary in Costa Rica (Licenciatura in Theology), Wesley Theological Seminary (Master of Theological Studies), and Graduate Theological Foundation (DMin). He and his wife, Carol, live in Shawnee, Kansas. rchodgson@aol.com

▪▪ 17 ▪▪
MAKING CHRISTLIKE HISPANIC DISCIPLES
ROBERTO HODGSON AND WALTER ARGUETA

The Church of the Nazarene is now ministering in one hundred fifty-six world areas. As noted earlier, it is estimated that representatives of 80 percent of those people groups to whom we have sent missionaries are presently residing within the borders of the United States and Canada. God has brought the mission field to us. Will we be true to this opportunity? We must open our arms to them and love them here, as we love them there.

If our churches will open their eyes, they will discover the thrill and excitement that new people can bring to the family. The largest new people group among us is the Hispanic group.

Hispanics by the Numbers

Consider these striking numbers from the United States Census Bureau.

48.4 million: the estimated Hispanic population of the United States as of July 1, 2009, making people of Hispanic origin the nation's largest ethnic or race minority. Hispanics constituted 16 percent of the nation's total population. In addition, there are approximately 4 million residents of Puerto Rico, a Caribbean United States territory.

The Hispanics are one of the most diverse ethnic groups in the U.S. They (or their forebears) came from two dozen countries, and their racial ancestry ranges from pure Spanish to mixtures of Spanish blood with native American, African, German, and Italian, to name a few hybrids. While most are bound by a common language, many Hispanic Americans speak only English.

3.1 percent: increase in the Hispanic population between July 1, 2008, and July 1, 2009, making Hispanics the fastest-growing minority group.

132.8 million: the projected Hispanic population of the United States on July 1, 2050. According to this projection, Hispanics will constitute 30 percent of the nation's population by that date.

22.4 million: The nation's Hispanic population during the 1990 Census—less than half the current total.

2nd: ranking of the size of the United States Hispanic population worldwide as of 2009. Only Mexico (111 million) had a larger Hispanic population than the United States (48.4 million).

66 percent: the percentage of Hispanic-origin people in the United States who were of Mexican background in 2008. Another 9 percent were of Puerto Rican background, with 3.4 percent Cuban, 3.4 percent Salvadoran, and 2.8 percent Dominican. The remainder were of some other Central American, South American, or other Hispanic or Latino origin.[1]

Window of Opportunity

Over one-half of the growth in Hispanic population between now and 2050 will come from net in-migration.[2] Strangers in a foreign land face a myriad of challenges that the Church of the Nazarene must be prepared to meet. Often the basics of life—food, clothing, housing, and employment—are the most immediate needs. The median income of Hispanic households in 2008 was $37,913, down 5.6 percent from the previous year after adjusting for inflation. The poverty rate among Hispanics in 2008 was 23.2 percent, up from 21.5 percent in 2007. Remember that this is a diverse group from many different countries with significant cultural differences even though they speak Spanish. For example, 62 percent of Hispanics twenty-five and older had at least a high school education in 2009 and 13 percent had a bachelor's degree or higher.[3]

Churches must discover and develop tangible methods to demonstrate the love of God for the stranger. New immigrants do not remain new. There is a window of opportunity to reach out with love and compassion.

Nazarene Response

To reach this fertile Hispanic/Latino mission field; the Hispanic Ministries Office as an integral unit of the USA/Canada regional office has been developing resources to support the efforts of districts and local churches to make Christlike disciples. There are several discipleship materials available, such as: *En Sus Pasos* (*In His Steps*), by Rev. Leonel deLeon; *Operacion Cornelio* (Cornelius), by Rev. Javier Paniagua; and *The Master's Plan* (12 Steps), by Rev. Obed Jauregui. Information about these materials can be found on the Hispanic Web site www.nazarenosusacan.org.

The Hispanic Strategic Readiness Team (HSRT) is comprised of a representative from each of the university regional zones plus the three Hispanic district superintendents. The main purpose of the HSRT is to serve as an advisory committee, to strategize, to develop resources and events, and to support the Hispanic/Latino ministries. The HSRT is structured into three committees: evangelism/discipleship; communication; and education.

The Education Committee has been working in collaboration with Clergy Development to translate the twenty-four modular studies courses leading to ordination in the Church of the Nazarene in the USA/Canada. The modules have been translated into Spanish, allowing many of our eighty USA/Canada districts to offer courses in Spanish for pastoral and leadership development. They are available on the Hispanic or Clergy Development Web site.

ENTE (Specialized Nazarene Theological Education) provides ministerial preparation for ordination using the modular curriculum and has graduated three classes.

There are other educational efforts in collaboration with our Nazarene educational institutions such as: Nazarene Bible College is developing a Hispanic Pastoral Ministries major, culminating in the bachelor of arts in ministry degree. Dr. Alberto Guang, Hispanic ministry coordinator, Northwest Indiana District, and Dr. Alan Lyke, chair of the Church Ministries Department at NBC, are serving as the program's facilitators. Olivet Nazarene University offers a master in ministry degree in Spanish and graduated its first class in May 2010. Rev. Wilfredo Canales is the facilitator of the program.

For more information about Hispanic ministerial education visit www.nazarenosusacan.org.

The Hispanic Nazarene family in the USA/Canada has experienced a significant growth. Out of the eighty districts in the USA/Canada, sixty-two have Hispanic ministries outreach. In the last ten years the numbers of congregations have almost doubled to five hundred with thirty thousand members. At the annual Hispanic Strategic Readiness Team meeting in October 2009 a goal was set to double again in the next ten years (by 2020) to one thousand congregations.

In this USA/Canada mission field God has enabled many Hispanic/Latino pastors and churches to reach their communities effectively in partnership with districts and English-speaking churches. One such church is Primera Iglesia Latinoamericana, pastored by Walter Argueta.

A First-person Account of an Effective Hispanic Ministry— Walter Argueta

The Owings Mills, Maryland, Latin American First Iglesia del Nazareno was organized in 1989. The church struggled for fourteen years for stability, varying between twenty-five and sixty in attendance. Between 2003 and 2010 the church grew to four hundred sixty in worship attendance. What made the difference?

A New Pastor

In 2003 I was ordained and appointed pastor. The faithful members had overcome many obstacles to remain open. They sincerely wanted to grow and reach the people around us for Jesus. We met in a basement room that had no heat, no air conditioning, and very low lighting. As we began to grow, people sat in the hallway and up the stairs. We were crowded and too cold or hot. But the Lord blessed. We were located in an area with a large Latin American population. The local Latino stores and community began to learn about our church.

A New Focus

Our first priority became prayer. In addition to our regular services, we gathered on Monday and Friday to pray and seek the Lord. Everything we did began with prayer. The faithful base who was there when I arrived believed in prayer and were ready to follow my leadership. Pray, pray, pray!

After we began to pray, the Lord led us to do street evangelism. After every Sunday worship service we would go out into the streets and do personal evangelism. We met Latinos where they were. We went to the local stores—supermarkets, Home Depot, and everywhere else we saw Latinos. With our small group of trained leaders we really emphasized sharing our faith with others. And the Lord blessed. In answer to our prayers He gave us divine appointments, and many people came to Jesus.

A New Building

We grew rapidly to one hundred twenty-five in attendance during those first three years. Crowded, hot, and cold, we soon realized that we needed a new building. In 2004 we set our goal of raising $100,000. The Lord again answered prayer, and we did it! God enabled us to meet that seemingly impossible goal. In 2006 the Lord enabled us to buy our present building valued at one million dollars. Latino congregations in our area were known to rent from other churches. But now we had our own building. It gave us increased credibility in the Latino community. Since moving to our new building in 2006, we have grown from one hundred twenty-five to four hundred sixty in average attendance.

New Ministries

God has continuously reminded us to keep our eyes on the lost. Once in the new building, we set new goals and began new ministries. Our building stays open almost all the time with many community activities. We have worship services on Sunday and on Saturday night.

Recognizing the importance of prayer and how God had blessed, we expanded our prayer ministry. We continued the Monday and Friday prayer times and added Tuesday, Thursday, and early Saturday at 5:00 AM. First Sundays became a day of fasting, and Last Fridays became prayer vigil days.

We continued with our street evangelism and added family groups and cells. Our goal is to reach to one thousand in attendance by adding strategically placed cells across the Baltimore area wherever Latinos are found.

We recognized the need for discipleship of new believers, so we added our Baseball Diamond discipleship plan. We have been inspired by the Master's Plan from the House of Prayer Church of the Nazarene in Cali, Colombia. We developed departments within the church (men, women, youth, and children) to facilitate our ministries outside the church. Our youth developed a *NazCafé* coffeehouse ministry and have added Tuesday night Bible studies. We have twenty-five different cell groups of approximately ten each meeting throughout the city.

Our usher's ministry is vital. Our well-trained ushers act as greeters, parking lot attendants, and informational guides. Our worship team ministry has expanded to add a second group to help provide an atmosphere conducive to great worship.

We organize big events. We invite visiting preachers, organize concerts, and celebrate our Hispanic heritage. We do everything we can to touch the lives of as many people as we can.

God is calling some into a deeper leadership role. So we have started teaching in Spanish the modular course of study for preparation for ordination in the Church of the Nazarene. We have an average of thirteen enrolled and meeting once a week.

Our vision and mission to make Christlike disciples extends to all nations. Our Nazarene Missions International group is very active. We believe in world missions. We have invited many missionaries to inspire and challenge us. We are very strong in receiving Alabaster Offerings to help construct new buildings on the mission field. We have a mission in El Salvador that we support with workers and finances.

New Goals

God has answered prayer over and over. This gives us the faith to believe that He will do it again and that we can accomplish anything that He wants us to. We have set goals for 2015. We want to:

1. Use our building continuously.
2. Be involved in our community in as many different ways as we can.
3. Average one thousand in attendance.
4. Close the back door by better discipleship.
5. Have one hundred cell groups.
6. Start an inner-city ministry in Baltimore.

7. Increase the number of our students preparing for ordination from thirteen to twenty.
8. Develop a bilingual ministry by hiring an English-speaking youth pastor.
9. Double our youth group size.

Our Future

Owings Mills has a large population of Latinos with significant needs that God wants to meet through our church. We are a diverse group from a number of different Hispanic heritages, but we are one in Jesus. We see ourselves as continually renewing the vision of sharing the good news of new life in Jesus to the lost in our greater Baltimore area.

The journey that God has led us on has been one that has made our faith in Him stronger and stronger. We believe that God answers prayer. He has done it for us over and over and over. We have not grown comfortable as a congregation, even though we have grown in numbers. We are not satisfied. We are totally surrendered to Him and His will. We are a church of Spirit-filled, God-believing ambassadors for Jesus, an army that will continue to reach new and needy people with the love of Jesus.

Today our church is active, busy, and enjoying the presence of God. We will continue to honor His name in all that we do.

Strategy No. 5
MULTIFACETED NEW CHURCH DEVELOPMENT

We need to foster an environment and enthusiasm
for starting new churches through districts
and local churches.

The fifth strategy is absolutely essential for the future of the Church of the Nazarene in the United States and Canada. New works must be continually started, because individual churches don't live forever. Today we are unable to find the New Testament church at Philippi or Thessalonica, but that doesn't mean we should not start new ones. Each church has a life cycle. This was the passion of Paul. He started many new works and prayed for his friends to do the same. He said, "Pray for us, too, that God may open a door for our message, so that we may proclaim the mystery of Christ" (Colossians 4:3). We are praying that God will open up many new doors for our work in this region.

The purpose of strategy number five is to help us discover how to start new works. Somehow we must free up our pastors and people for this essential ministry. And the district superintendent must continually point us in that direction. In our early days, our congregations were not only building their own churches but also always thinking about how to start something in "the next town." May God help us to be captivated by "the next town." With Paul we pray for "open doors" and brave hearts. In the next chapters you will discover exciting reports on how this is already happening in our region.

Chapter 18: Multiplying Organic Church Networks, by Darrell MacLearn

Darrell MacLearn, a fourth-generation Nazarene pastor, challenges us to plant hundreds of organic churches by making disciples who make disciples who make disciples, by leaving our comfortable "barns" and planting "out there" in the harvest fields ripe for harvest. Darrell reminds us that the same Spirit who came at Pentecost is blowing a fresh wind upon the church in the United States and Canada. Can you be Nazarene *and* organic? The answer is a resounding *yes!*

Chapter 19: Starting High-Impact Churches, by Stephen Gray

Stephen Gray compares planting a high-impact church (one that reaches two hundred in attendance in fewer than twenty-four months) with storming the beaches of Normandy in World War II. Stephen challenges us to consider the $200,000 to $300,000 start-up cost as an investment that when well-done will generate enough momentum to decisively establish a foothold in a community and give a new church the ability to transform the very fabric of the culture in which it was launched.

Chapter 20: Developing New Churches on a Shoestring, by Bill Wiesman

Bill Wiesman offers a contrast to Stephen Gray. Because the Lord of the harvest has told us that the harvest is ripe (John 4:34) and the harvest is plentiful (Luke 10:2), we must harvest. And if we must harvest, then we must develop strategies of harvesting that are not dependent upon finances. It is possible to begin new works, ministries, and churches literally on a "shoestring" budget.

Chapter 21: Building a Great Future, by Stan Reeder

Stan Reeder shares the challenge of churches sponsoring new churches. Prior to becoming district superintendent of the Oregon Pacific District, while he was pastor of the church in Westminster, Colorado, his church developed a vision and plan for sponsoring many new churches.

Chapter 22: Planting a Church in Kalkaska, by Marilyn McCool

Marilyn McCool shares how she and her church planter husband, David, launched out in faith in the adventure of starting a new church. As I first read Marilyn and David's story of faith and sacrifice, I was moved to tears by the faithfulness of God to provide for those whom He calls. It's a heartwarming story that has been repeated over and over again throughout the rich history of the Church of the Nazarene. Ordinary men and women called of God have stepped out, trusted God, and have become "giants of the faith."

Darrell MacLearn is a fourth-generation Nazarene pastor serving on the Dallas District and is the director of the Nazarene Organic Church Network, launching a network of organic or simple churches that focus on building relationships, serving the community, and making disciples who make disciples. Darrell has served as a pastor in Oregon, New Mexico, and Texas. He holds an MA degree in theology from George Fox University Seminary. Darrell also works with New Church Specialties as a national coach and consultant for districts and church leaders desiring to plant nontraditional churches and start organic-type ministries. Darrell, his wife, Robin, and two daughters reside in McKinney, Texas. dmaclearn@gmail.com

▪▪ 18 ▪▪
MULTIPLYING ORGANIC CHURCH NETWORKS

DARRELL MACLEARN

"You will receive power when the Holy Spirit comes on you; and you will be my witnesses in Jerusalem, and in all Judea and Samaria, and to the ends of the earth" (Acts 1:8).

"The Lord added to their number daily those who were being saved" (Acts 2:47).

"Those who accepted his message were baptized, and about three thousand were added to their number that day" (Acts 2:41).

"Many who heard the message believed, and the number of men grew to about five thousand" (Acts 4:4).

"More and more men and women believed in the Lord and were added to their number" (Acts 5:14).

"In those days when the number of disciples was increasing . . ." (Acts 6:1).

"The word of God spread. The number of disciples in Jerusalem increased rapidly, and a large number of priests became obedient to the faith" (Acts 6:7).

"Then the church throughout Judea, Galilee and Samaria enjoyed a time of peace. It was strengthened; and encouraged by the Holy Spirit, it grew in numbers, living in the fear of the Lord" (Acts 9:31).

"The churches were strengthened in faith and grew daily in numbers" (Acts 16:5).

Has this "people multiplication movement" ended, or is the same Spirit of Pentecost multiplying His disciples and churches around the world? Terry Barker, a Nazarene missionary to Africa, stated recently, "It is like Pentecost every day on the continent of Africa. Entire villages are getting saved." Each month an estimated twelve hundred new churches are started in Africa.[1] "The work of the Church of the Nazarene in the Horn of Africa can be described most aptly as a movement of the Holy Spirit. Growth has been

New Testament-like. From 2005 until 2008, membership grew from fifteen thousand to ninety thousand. Attendance grew from forty-two thousand to two hundred and fifty thousand. Congregations grew from five hundred thirty-nine to two thousand five hundred thirty-five. In the midst of this phenomenal growth, the Church of the Nazarene so far is working in only three of the seven hundred languages spoken here."[2]

"Churches are being planted at such a rate that Rev. John Yaul Nguth, mission coordinator for the Horn of Africa Area One, spent almost three months walking across this area to document Nazarene churches. As Nguth traveled to count the churches already established, he started new churches as he preached along the way. Consequently, the number continued to rise."[3]

"We are witnessing history and future," said Gustavo Crocker, director of the Eurasia Region. "What we are seeing in Bangladesh is the result of the missiology of the twenty-first century: A group of national leaders, fully supported and equipped by committed and capable nonresident missionaries, and embraced by our entire denominational missionary system, has seized the moving of the Holy Spirit in this nation. As a result, the work that I first visited in 1994 has grown to the point of becoming a model of indigenous church multiplication."[4]

This is one of the greatest periods of disciple-making in history, and yet at the same time that we celebrate what God is doing around the world, we weep for the harvest that is plentiful and ripe all around us because there are not enough workers. At the same time that we celebrate, we witness the closing of church doors and the empty cathedrals that scatter the hillsides, communities, and urban centers in our world.

There is hope, however. The same Spirit of Pentecost, Africa, and Bangladesh is blowing a fresh wind upon the church in the United States and Canada and is calling missionaries to leave the comforts of their Evangelical culture and go out into the cultures that surround them and make disciples who make disciples and plant churches that plant churches.

Led by the Spirit, missionaries are rising up in the same organic nature as found from the Horn of Africa to Bangladesh and following the Spirit out of the barn and into the fields ripe for harvest. Not allowing the weeds of our culture to hold them back, they are rediscovering what it means to be missionaries in the United States and Canada.

Organic Church Planting—A Missionary Way of Thinking

Jesus said, "The harvest is plentiful" (Luke 10:2a) and "The fields . . . are ripe for harvest" (John 4:35). He also said, "The workers are few" (Luke 10:2b). As I ponder these biblical truths, I am struck by the reality of two locations. One location is where the harvest is, and the other is where the workers are. The harvest is in the field, not the barn, and the workers are in the barn, not the field. Could it be that we have gotten very comfortable at the barn dance celebrating the year we were harvested and have neglected the harvest that is ripe and plentiful today? Is the shortage of workers today a result of a salvation that removes the saved from the harvest field into the safety and security of the barn? When we look at the movement of God described above, one of the things noticed by those who have studied these movements is the immediate expectation and Spirit-led compulsion for a new believer to go and personally engage in mission.

If we are going to make new disciples and not just spend our time "discipling the disciple," we are going to have to get out of the barn. Luke 10:2 says, "The harvest is plentiful, but the workers are few. Ask the Lord of the harvest, therefore, to **send out** workers into his harvest field. **Go! I am sending you out**" (emphasis added). The Lord of the harvest is calling His workers out of the barn and into the harvest fields.

Phineas Bresee said it well in 1899:

What the world needs today is cheap, commodious places in every center of population, where the gospel is preached in the power of the Holy Ghost and men are crowded to the cross of Christ. . . . We don't need **forts** and **barricades**; we need a **marching, conquering** army, who sleeps on their arms and in the morning **presses the battle**, filling the world with the redeemed and blood washed people. . . . There is far too much building fortifications for little bands to fortify themselves in the enemy's country.[5]

This is a missionary way of thinking. Ponder this question: *Is it the responsibility of the sinner to leave his or her culture to get Jesus or the responsibility of the missionary to leave his or her culture to give Jesus? Is it the responsibility of a sinner to enter a Christian's life to find Jesus or the responsibility of a Christian to enter a sinner's life to love him or her to Jesus?*

When we train missionaries, we train them to leave the comforts of their culture, go into another culture and learn the language, live among them, learn their history and their customs, and help them find Christ in the midst of their culture. Our Evangelical subculture is surrounded by unique and distinctive cultures. We tell those in the cultures around us to leave their culture, come into our church culture, learn our language, sing our songs, wear our clothes, practice our customs, and in the midst of doing so we hope they will find Jesus. Organic church planting is about our becoming missionaries and leaving our culture and entering one of the cultures that surround us, whether it is ethnic, economic, or a subculture and loving them with the transforming love of Christ as we plant gospel seeds into the fertile soil of their lives.

Jesus Goes to Levi's House, Heather to Main Stage, and Mark to the Mall

A story repeated in Matthew 9:9-13, Mark 2:13-17, and Luke 5:27-32 is of Jesus eating with sinners and tax collectors at Levi's house. As I read this story over and over, I am struck with the question, "Why did Jesus eat with them?" a question asked by the Pharisees and teachers of the Law. "Why didn't He just go to Levi's house and put a professionally done glossy on the door inviting him and his sinner-friends to the new church they were starting down the street?" Jesus' missionary way of thinking led Him to have table fellowship, which meant *relationship* and *acceptance,* in order that the sick might find healing.

Jesus went to Levi's house; Heather went to Main Stage. Main Stage is one of five strip clubs in the Fort Worth area that Heather and a team of "missionaries" have entered. It is a unique culture filled with "sinners and tax collectors" who need a doctor or a missionary to love them to Jesus. Heather and her friends are welcomed by the owners and managers, and when they go, they love the girls. They give them manicures and pedicures and pray with them as they wash their feet. Why do they wash feet at Main Stage? Why don't they just go to the door with some creative, churchy, glossy invitation cards and invite all the girls to the church they are starting down the street? Because washing feet is about acceptance and relationship in the same way that sharing a meal with Jesus was. As they wash the girls' feet, they pray for them and talk with them and encourage them. They are now ministering to approximately sixty girls a month. Some have accepted Christ, and many have left the sex industry altogether. Heather reports, "There is no shortage of girls who want out; there is just a shortage of workers to show them the way." Sound familiar? "The harvest is plentiful, but the workers are few."

Heather is in the process of planting a church. In order to fully understand this, maybe we need to rethink what we mean when we say "church" and "church planting." I am always asking people to define the word "church." Only a couple of times has someone defined it by a meeting place and time. What I hear over and over, and what holds true in Scripture, is that the church is a group of people. In an effort to simplify and communicate, Acts 1:8 helps me in the definition of church.

> "**You** will receive **power** when the Holy Spirit comes on **you**; and **you** will be my **witnesses** in Jerusalem, and in all Judea and Samaria, and to the ends of the earth" (emphasis added).

The church is *the people of God, empowered by the Spirit of God on the mission of God in His world.*

So when we say, "*Church* planting," we are not talking about planting buildings, structures, staffs, and programs. We are talking about planting people; the people of God, clothing the Spirit of God, functioning as His body in the world.

Heather is a missionary who has left the comfort of her church culture and entered a culture where she is reaching a pocket of people who are not banging down the doors of our churches. She is making disciples and discipling them to make disciples. It will be these girls who will return to the ripe and plentiful harvest field as indigenous missionaries loving their fellow sisters the way they were loved.

Jesus ate at Levi's house, Heather washed feet at Main Stage, and Mark is going to the mall.

Mark is a missionary in Michigan who is planting an organic church using the *JESUS* film in a shopping mall filled with great ethnic diversity. Two large-screen TV sets positioned in a kiosk display the life of Jesus in one thousand and ninety languages and dialects for shoppers to view. Counselors are available to pray for seekers in the marketplace. When we plant people instead of buildings, the possibilities are as endless as the creativity of the Creator who indwells us.

Organic Church Planting—A Missional Way of Living

The mission of the Church of the Nazarene is *to make Christlike disciples in the nations.* The mission of the Nazarene Organic Church Network is *to make disciples who make disciples who make disciples.*

Making disciples is our mission. It is what drives us and is our purpose. Organic church planting is about simplification and getting back to basics. It is in this context that the word "organic" begins to make sense to me. Organic farming has to do with the natural growth process without the employment of chemically formulated fertilizers and growth stimulants. Organic crops are naturally grown without additives and preservatives. The natural outcome of seed planted in good soil is a crop thirty, sixty, and even one hundred times what was sown. Organic church planting is about simplifying and getting back to the mission that has often gotten lost in the clutter of additives.

Many churches today spend all their time discipling the discipled and have not made a new disciple in years. Therefore, the Nazarene organic church is lowering the bar on how we do church and raising the bar on what it means to be a disciple.

Jesus said, "Therefore go and make disciples . . . , baptizing them in the name of the Father and of the Son and of the Holy Spirit, and teaching them to obey everything I have commanded you. And surely I am with you always, to the very end of the age" (Matthew 28:19-20, emphasis added).

This is not something we are commanded to do once per week in a church classroom down the street. This is something we are to live. It is a missional way of living as we clothe the Spirit of God and walk Him through our cities and out into the harvest fields around us.

Neil Cole writes, "Where you go, the king goes, and where the king goes, people bow."[6] Take a moment and grasp the power of that statement. If we are truly the temple of God, filled with the Spirit of God, then where we go He goes, and He wants to eat at Levi's house so that Levi might know Him and that the King of Kings might move from his house to his life as the temple. It is when the world around us is in the presence of the King of Kings at work in our lives that new disciples are made.

Have you seen the bumper sticker that reads, "God, I love your Jesus, but I don't like your people because they look nothing like your Jesus"? I have discovered that most people I meet don't have a problem with Jesus—they just have a problem with His representatives. It is when Spirit-filled people, who embody the power and presence of the living God, get out of their barricades and begin to love like Christ loved, go where Christ went, and serve like Christ served that new disciples will be made, and this bumper sticker will be rewritten to read, "God, I love your Jesus, and I love your people—because they look, love, and live like your Jesus."

Jay and Jodi Become Missionaries

Jay and Jodi discovered the truth of this when they became missionaries and began to readjust their "church" time to "mission" time, and God has transformed them as well as their neighbors across the street. For years, Jay and Jodi left their neighbors to go minister to someone else's neighbors. Their time was consumed three plus days per week commuting through three cities to get to their church, where they would spend the majority of their time "being fed" and ministering to believers. When God called them to become missionaries to their neighbors, they made a decision to take the same amount of time that they were spending on the road and in the ministries of the church and reinvest it back into their neighborhood, loving their neighbors to Jesus. They are now not just making new disciples but also discipling them to make new disciples. This has so transformed Jay and Jodi's lives that they are simplifying their lives even further, selling their suburban house and moving into another harvest field that is plentiful and ripe, a place where Jodi can use her college training intentionally for the mission.

Missional living doesn't just make new disciples—it transforms and continues to shape the discipler as well. When Jay and Jodi's focus shifted from *going to church* to *being the church on mission* in their neighborhood, God's Word began to come alive in new and transformational ways for them and their children.

Organic Church Planting—A Multiplication Methodology

The Great Commission gives us a picture into God's heart for multiplication. It is about making new disciples who can make new disciples. I have grown tired of making disciples who can say, "Come meet my pastor. He can help you." I want to make disciples who can say, "Come meet my Jesus. He can transform you." We have made too many disciples who are more interested in helping people find their "church" than they are helping them find Jesus.

The Great Commission is not the job description of the pastor but the job description of a disciple. God calls His Bride to *Love Him with all her heart, soul, strength, and mind.* God calls His Bride to *Love her neighbor as herself,* and God calls His Bride to *get pregnant and give birth to fertile children.* God did not marry a sterile Bride, but throughout Scripture we see the heart of the husband of the Church to be fruitful and multiply. When God's seed is planted in fertile soil, it *will* produce a multiplying crop thirty, sixty, and even one hundred fold (Mark 4).

The Great "Go-mission" says, "Therefore **go** and **make** disciples . . . , **baptizing** them in the name of the Father and of the Son and of the Holy Spirit, and **teaching** them to **obey everything** I have commanded you."

Notice in the chart below the multiplication that takes place in this great "Go-mission" cycle.

THE GREAT GO-MISSION CYCLE

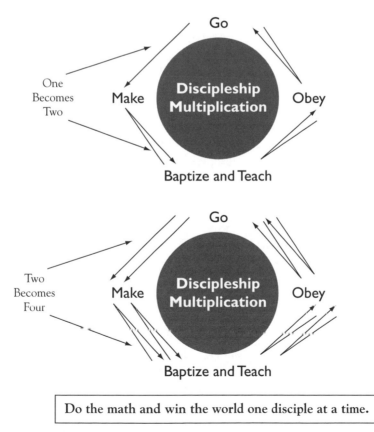

Do the math and win the world one disciple at a time.

I am commanded to go and make a disciple and to baptize him or her and teach him or her to obey. Now the next word is important. He or she is to be taught to obey everything commanded. There are many commands summed up in the all-consuming love for God and others, and in that vertical and horizontal love is a command to go and make disciples. Therefore, if we teach them to obey everything, we are teaching them to go and make a new disciple. Now we both go and we both make and baptize and teach, and the cycle continues, multiplying exponentially.

What would happen if every believer were discipled to make disciples? Are the programs of your church producing disciples who can make disciples, or church attendees who can invite friends to meet their pastor? What needs to be eliminated from your church "programming" for you to give emphasis to making disciples who make disciples? Who is discipling you, and who are you discipling to make disciples?

What would happen if every church sent out missionaries who planted missional churches as we defined "church," who made disciples who made disciples who would intentionally then send out missionaries and plant more churches, thus saturating our cities with simple, reproducible missional churches?

Our mission in the Nazarene Organic Church Movement is to make disciples who make disciples. Our vision is to have a "church" within walking distance of every person in the world. In order to fulfill this vision, churches must multiply. For churches to multiply, these disciples, new and old, must be intentional about planting simple reproducible churches. It is not enough for church and denominational leaders to want to plant churches or have a vision, budget, and even a plan to plant churches. Denominational leaders, church leaders, and even new disciples must work together to intentionally plant churches that have a DNA to intentionally plant churches, multiplying and saturating the cultures around us until there is a church within walking distance of everyone in the world.

John Plants Nomad—Churches Without Homes

John Huddle, an organic church planter in Los Angeles, knows what it means to make disciples who make disciples and out of that plant churches that plant churches. He is beginning the process of saturating his world with churches that have a DNA of planting simple and reproducible churches.

It began in a Suburban at 4:47 P.M. on a Friday as John and Terrence began to pick up a bunch of people for organic church at an apartment off of Adams and Crenshaw in central Los Angeles. Terrence is a college student, and John a college instructor and church planter. John and Terrence had known each other for about four weeks and were in a Life Transformation Group (LTG) together. In the Suburban on a Friday night, John led Terrence to Christ. A week later, Terrence found Mark, a homeless man he met in the parking lot of a grocery store washing windows for money. Terrence had an urgent sense in his stomach that he was supposed to meet this person on this day at this time for a reason.

Terrence led Mark to become a follower of Christ one week later, sitting on a hill overlooking Lake Piru. He would stay clean for a couple weeks and then fall, and he was as homeless and alone as you can get, but every week he was at LTG. He opened up the world of the park. They saw the LTGs grow quickly, and a church was born simultaneously. The church was a mixture of working marrieds, singles with kids, homeless married couples, homeless singles, homeless single with a kid, high schoolers, middle schoolers, and elementary schoolers. They had no target group. Meanwhile, the church that John had already started at Adams and Crenshaw kept going, but after the day they met Mark during LTG, it became clear that the church was being born in this park with Mark.

They started with three people. Then everything happened quickly. John begat Terrence (with Marcus joining them), Terrence begat Mark, Mark begat Dave and Deena, Dave and Deena begat Kara, Kara begat Stan; then Mark begat Kellie and Gracie, and along the way Bob and J. B. joined them, as well as the Skeltons and Tijari and Howard and Nora and Fran and many, many others, including John's next-door neighbors, who swore to him they would never talk "God or religion," and yet, they found out, had been involved in redemptive action with Dave and Deena. When they found out about this church that had been born in the park, Jesus gave them many chances to share His love and His story in their lives with them.

In five weeks the church at the park grew to twenty-five or more, and that was getting too big. Since then, they have seen a simple church happen in the bowling alley bar across the street, a KFC, and two more coffee shops.

This happened in 2009. The previous year, 2008, they were in three locations, and at that time someone made the comment, "Where we meeting next week? Hey—we're kind of like nomads, huh?" From then on it was, "Are you going to Nomad?"

John and the Nomads in Los Angeles are making disciples that are making disciples, and out of that they are intentionally planting churches that are planting churches, multiplying and saturating their world for Christ.

Organic Church Planting—A Movement to Reach Today's World

This may not look like what we are used to: church in a park, a bowling alley bar, a KFC, coffee shops, strip clubs, malls, and houses in the neighborhood. It may be uncomfortable, because we "have never done it that way before." However, "The harvest is plentiful, but the workers are few." The harvest is plentiful, and one way of planting churches will never reach the multitudes waiting for a missionary. It is time for us to begin to think like missionaries and leave our culture and intentionally enter into the pockets of people that surround us and live the mission of making disciples who can make disciples. It is time for us to saturate our world with the church and plant churches that plant churches until we have groups of disciples who are empowered by the Spirit on the mission of God planted within walking distance of everyone in the world.

Values of Planting Organic Churches

- Little to no financial investment
- Increased missional giving
- Increased ministry dollar capacity
- Increased ministry people involvement
- Increased focus on reproductive discipleship
- Self-sustaining feasibility in resource-poor environments
- No geographic, cultural, structural, or logistic barriers
- Simple and reproducible
- Natural and relational leadership development
- Can quickly adjust missional strategy to the ever-changing culture

"Ask the Lord of the harvest, therefore, to send out workers into his harvest field."

Thousands of us across the country have set our alarms for 10:02 every day to pray Luke 10:2. We are praying for fellow harvesters to join us in the field. We are praying for you.

"Go—I am sending you out."

It takes all kinds of churches to reach all kinds of people. What kind of people will you reach?

Over the last twenty years **Stephen Gray** has been involved in transitioning, restarting, and planting new churches. Stephen is the church planting facilitator for the Western Region of the Free Methodist Church of North America. Stephen received his DMin degree from Asbury Theological Seminary and has published several books on church planting. He has consulted with multiple denominations and written numerous church-planting guides and tools for church planting organizations. STGray67@gmail.com

▪▪ 19 ▪▪
STARTING HIGH-IMPACT CHURCHES
STEPHEN GRAY

On June 6, 1944, the Allies landed on the shores of northern France. The world held its breath as the long-awaited emancipation of Europe from Adolf Hitler's oppressive regime began. After a seemingly hopeless fight in the European theater, thousands of Allied troops stormed the shores in order to break the back of the German war machine. Many brave men lost their lives that day in an attempt to overwhelm the enemy and create a strategic surge that would generate enough momentum to decisively establish a foothold that would ultimately give the Allies the ability to win the war.

Although it may sound strange to you, I believe that planting a high-impact church is a lot like storming the shores of Normandy. You need critical mass, momentum, and dozens of individuals willing to put everything on the line. Launching a large, high-impact church promises enormous positive potential, yet it carries a burden of potentially catastrophic failure. However, when done well, a high-impact church will generate enough momentum to decisively establish a foothold in a community and give a new church the ability to transform the culture in which it is launched. Launching a large, high-impact church is one of several ways to plant an effective new church in a community.

Why Launch Large High-Impact Churches?

Planting a high-impact church is not simply about the numbers. It is more about the ability to impact and transform a seeker, a city, a county, and a country. Let me suggest five reasons for planting high-impact churches.

1. Breaking Growth Barriers

Breaking growth barriers in a church is very hard. The best way to break any growth barrier is to do it quickly. One of the most significant growth barriers in the life of any church is two hundred. Breaking this barrier will be a significant momentum-shifter. A new church has many barriers to overcome.

If it is launched with fewer than two hundred people and remains stagnant for any length of time, it will fight just to stay alive. Attention will be diverted away from the primary role of evangelism toward survival and maintenance. According to Peter Wagner, a church plant should "expect to pass through the 200 barrier within about twelve months after going public. If you are not through it in two years, something is going wrong and your chances of ever doing it are greatly diminished."[1] So just how quickly should a church plant expect to reach two hundred? Some have said that it should happen in the first year; others teach that a new church should reach two hundred within the first eighteen months.

In 2007 I conducted a research project to discover what made a fast-growing church plant tick. In order to accomplish this task, I surveyed two sets of church plants, those that were growing rapidly and those that seemed to have stalled out. The process was intended to compare struggling church plants with those that seemed to be exploding. (You can read more about this in my book *Planting Fast-Growing Churches.*[2])

I discovered that seventy-seven percent of the fast-growing church plants reached an average weekly attendance of two hundred by the twenty-fourth month. Only twenty-three percent of these fast-growing churches broke the two hundred barrier after that time. It is statistically significant to understand that if a church plant has not broken this barrier within the first two years, it increases the likelihood that it never will.[3] Momentum is a major issue that will work either for or against a new church.

The size of a new congregation will set the agenda for its future viability and effectiveness. Please understand, I am not questioning the commitment and call of a new church that does not reach the two hundred mark. Nor am I attempting to say that smaller churches are not effective and valid. I am simply stating what twenty-plus years of experience have taught me. Unless a new church hits the two hundred mark quickly, the possibility increases that ministry will be slowed, and it will fall prey to fighting for survival.

2. Larger Churches Are Easier to Control

Larger churches are easier to control. I know this may be counterintuitive, but it is true. The larger a church grows, the easier it is to control, the greater the involvement of discipleship, and the more opportunity exists for worshipers to engage in close relationships. The scientific world calls this phenomenon "power scaling."[4] In essence, the theory states that the larger an organism, the less energy it takes to keep it alive.

For years scientists expected that the energy used to keep a mouse alive and moving was much less than that of a larger animal like an elephant. Contrary to popular belief, the facts reveal just the opposite. Power scaling reveals that the larger an organism, the less energy is needed to keep it alive.

George Johnson, a science writer, reports, "As organisms grow in size they become more efficient. That is why nature has evolved large animals. . . . It's a much better way of utilizing energy. This might also explain the drive for corporations to merge. Small may be beautiful but it is more efficient to be big."[5] While humanistic scientists believe this phenomenon to be an effect of evolution, we understand it as part of God's created order.

What does that have to do with the church? Simple. Smaller churches take more resources and greater effort to keep alive and moving forward than do larger churches. Relationships are more forced; decisions are often more difficult to make in a way that keeps everyone happy, and discipleship becomes stalled.

Church growth is a mandate. In fact, it is a natural happening of a healthy organism or organization. If a church is healthy, it will grow. As the church grows, management is easier, takes less energy to keep alive, and creates greater opportunity for effective outreach in the community. We should celebrate and encourage churches to grow rapidly and larger.

3. Credibility

New churches are sometimes viewed as disgruntled splinter groups with an axe to grind. The years' worth of community interaction does not exist, and that makes it difficult to create a sense of stability. In a small community, credibility is even more important. Rapid growth of a new church can create enough buzz on the street to help give it the credibility it needs.

4. Finances

Established churches have had decades to build loyal and habitual givers. The established church has the advantage of traditional and institutional tithing. A new church does not have that luxury. New believers, as well as those who simply come to rubberneck in a new church, rarely have the spiritual maturity to understand the need to give to God's work. Naturally, it will take a greater base of givers to keep a new church afloat. Without a large constituency from which to draw resources, a new church stands a greater chance of becoming financially anemic. The simple acquisition of tables, chairs, sound systems, computers, and the like can become an insurmountable financial burden and divert funds from the real Great Commission work of the Church.

5. Corporate Esteem

Momentum is a tricky thing in a new church. Positive momentum can ignite passion, excite members, and drive more attendees to join in the rush. Negative momentum, on the other hand, can have just as a profound effect on a new congregation. It can generate a depressing emotional fatalism that can take over the hearts and minds of those who dreamed big dreams.

This is one of the most difficult problems for a new church to overcome. Crowds attract crowds. Why? New church plants are infused with a heightened expectation for success. Those who become part of a new church are driven by and excited by a passionate vision to change the world. The very vision that drives them also makes them more vulnerable to low morale. When a new church does not live up to an expected experience, a palpable discouragement can set in. That discouragement can be a fatal blow for a new church.[6]

What Is a High-Impact Church?

Okay, so now that we have explored why planting high-impact churches helps to overcome certain barriers, allow me to answer a more basic question: What exactly is a high-impact church plant? If it isn't all about the numbers, what is it about?

On January 25, 2009, in West Plains, Missouri, Genesis Church launched its grand opening service with over two hundred twenty people in attendance. Within a few short months, this new church celebrated over forty conversions, baptized thirty-five, and witnessed dozens of individuals reconnect to Christ. On Easter Sunday 2010, a little over one year after its grand opening, Genesis Church launched its third service and welcomed over 530 in attendance. Since the day this new church launched, it has touched thousands of lives and has had a major impact on the community of West Plains. They are now in the process of building their first facility, and they have dreams of launching numerous other churches in the surrounding communities. You can visit their Web site at www.genesiswired.org.

On September 10, 2006, in Zephyrhills, Florida, New Walk Church launched its grand opening service with over three hundred twenty people in attendance. On Easter 2010, New Walk hit a historic number of eighteen hundred in attendance in five services. The church is now averaging over eight hundred fifty in weekly attendance and has witnessed the transformation of hundreds of new believers. Three times in the last year alone, Gary Baldus, lead pastor of New Walk, has held baptismal services at a local beach in Clearwater, Florida, and baptized over ninety people each time. The church has now purchased an eleven-acre plot and will soon build their first facility. We are confident that with God's help and blessing this church will continue to grow and celebrate tremendous impact on the community it serves. You can discover more about this church at www.mynewwalk.com.

Launching a high-impact church is not easy. Yet if done well, it will produce enormous results for the kingdom of God. Please understand—it is not all about big numbers, but every number represents a life, so talking about numbers should never be frowned on. In order to launch a fast-growing church that will make significant impact on its community, I believe it will need to have seven components in place.

1. Passionate Worship

Passionate worship is a necessity. Notice I did not say "contemporary" worship. I think that we need to get beyond the argument that pits traditional against contemporary. Notice that I did not say "music." Worship is more than the format of music. Worship is holistic! Worship involves music, fellowship, preaching, and serving. In fact, Romans 12:1 indicates that worship is not to be relegated to one day a week. Rather, it is to be the sum total of our life: "I urge you, brothers, in view of God's mercy, to offer your bodies as living sacrifices, holy and pleasing to God—this is your spiritual act of worship."

If a church is to become a high-impact church, it must develop a culture of passionate worship. Passionate worship is defined as exciting, engaging, transformational, and vibrant. A passionate worship service is designed to help people experience and connect with God in a way that will help them engage and serve as missionaries in their own personal context. This is not a matter of contemporary vs. traditional; it goes much deeper than that.

2. Critical Mass

As mentioned earlier, if a church is to gain momentum in the community, it must grow rapidly in order to break barriers quickly. Critical mass will change according to the setting in which the church launches. It can be best described as the existence of sufficient momentum to fuel further growth, which leads to a self-sustaining, self-governing, and self-propagating church.

3. Proper Funding

Launching a high-impact church is not cheap, and therefore many are afraid to attempt it. According to the research I completed in 2007, which can be found in my book *Planting Fast-Growing Churches*, a fast-growing church plant will need $200,000 to $300,000 within a two-year period.[7] Can it be done any cheaper? Yes! However, you get what you pay for. Don't forget that the things we find so necessary, in order to do business in an established church (buildings, chairs, office equipment, as well as multiple other items) have to be built into a high-impact church quickly.

Look at it this way: "Churches over fifteen years of age win an average of only three people to Christ per year for every one hundred church members. Churches three years to fifteen years old win an average of five people to Christ per year for every one hundred church members, but churches under three years of age win an average of ten people to Christ per year for every one hundred church members."[8] The average size of an American church is between seventy to eighty in weekly attendance and is more than fifteen years old. That would mean that the average church, according to the above data, is reaching one person per year for Christ. A church of seventy to eighty people will (according to the place of ministry) average around $125,000 a year as an annual budget. Over a two-year period, that church will spend around $250,000 and celebrate the salvation of two people. The average cost of doing ministry is around $3,000 per person over a two-year period.

A high-impact church, on the other hand, that reaches two hundred in its first two years is much more efficient. If this new church uses $250,000 over a two-year period and has two hundred people, the cost of ministry is roughly $1,200 per person. A new church will spend the same amount of money, win more people into the Kingdom, and cost less per person to do ministry.

4. Strong Leadership

If a high-impact church is going to make a difference, it will need to be led by a high-quality leader. As with any organization, a new church will rise and fall on leadership. A plant of this kind will need to be led by a "level 5 leader." (This terminology comes from Jim Collins in his book *Good to Great*.[9])

5. Good Discipleship Systems

If a church is built on numbers alone, it is not a high-impact church plant. A high-impact church plant will have excellent discipleship systems. The purpose of the church is not to get people saved but to create "Christ-like" disciples. This can be done only as intentional systems are developed to move first-time guests to become lifetime servants of Christ.

Most churches in the United States struggle to engage people at a deeper level and foster personal commitment to lifelong discipleship. Churches are full of those who can quote scriptures, know much about ancient biblical history, and can share theological concepts of the death and resurrection of Jesus. We don't have a knowledge problem in today's church—we have an *application* problem. We know more and do less.

Discipleship is not about knowing—it is about doing, sending, and living the life of Christ. Anyone can know a set of facts, but the true disciple puts them into practice. A high-impact church is one that puts intentional systems into place to create an atmosphere of growth, service, and transformation.

6. Constant Outward Focus

Too often once a church launches, it stops doing outreach and focuses on managing growth. A high-impact church will unashamedly keep a continual outward focus. Why do I say "unashamedly"? Because many well-meaning people will try to convince the leaders of a new church that they have grown too fast and now need to slow down and close the back door. In other words, they want the pastor to stop the focus on growing and take care of those already in the church. That is one of the quickest ways I know to kill a new church.

7. Structured for Growth

I have heard Nelson Searcy state that "most churches want guests, but few know what to do with them when they show up." High-impact churches structure for growth in several ways: (A) They develop good systems that allow for quick decisions and change without constantly involving entire committees or congregational voting. (B) They have a good assimilation process in place to quickly involve new guests. (C) They are constantly restructuring staff responsibilities and involving volunteer staff. (D) They are not afraid to hire or fire new staff quickly. (E) The pastor is able to change his or her leadership style to fit the growth of the church.

One of the biggest growth barriers in any church is the pastor. The second usually has to do with basic functional structure of the church. If the pastor is not allowed to lead or the structures are cumbersome, growth will be difficult.

Conclusion

Planting a High-Impact church is more about "Why" than "How." In a speech to educators in 1985, former United States Assistant Secretary of Education Diane Ravitch stated, "The person who knows 'how' will always have a job. The person who knows 'why' will always be his boss." In other words, to know "why" is always a higher calling than knowing "how."

When done well, a high-impact church will generate enough momentum to decisively establish a foothold in a community and give a new church the ability to transform the culture in which it is launched.

Bill Wiesman serves as the director of Evangelism Ministries and New Church Development for the USA and Canada Region of the Church of the Nazarene. Prior to his present position, he served in Tennessee and Alabama with district responsibilities for new churches and church health. Bill is the founding pastor for four churches, the sponsor pastor for four churches, and has served as coach to more than fifty new church pastors. Bill is a graduate of Johns Hopkins University, Nazarene Theological Seminary (MDiv), and Fuller Theological Seminary (DMin). Bill has five children. He and his wife, Sharon, live in Gardner, Kansas. bwiesman@nazarene.org

▪▪ 20 ▪▪
DEVELOPING NEW CHURCHES ON A SHOESTRING
BILL WIESMAN

Developing new churches on a shoestring not only is possible but is happening all across the United States and Canada. After graduating together from Nazarene Theological Seminary, Kim Richardson and I went to Buffalo, New York, First Church. We were both convinced that the starting of new churches was the most effective method God had given to His Church to reach the thousands of unchurched people who surrounded Buffalo First. We developed the "Buffalo 20-20 Vision," to plant twenty new churches in twenty years. We did not make it. But God helped us to grow First Church and to start four new churches that impacted the lives of many new disciples for Jesus! In those early days we had no money to invest in church planting, so we planted on a shoestring. In these later days most of our new church leaders, sponsoring churches, and districts still do not have extra funds to invest in church planting. To begin many new churches, to seriously impact the harvest field, we must develop strategies that will yield reproducible indigenous churches; and that means developing new churches on a shoestring.

I. Our Mission

The mission of the Church of the Nazarene is to make Christlike disciples in the nations. The Holy Spirit desires to make thousands of those Christlike disciples in the United States and Canada—and He is not finished with the Church of the Nazarene! I am absolutely convinced that we are on the edge of the greatest days of harvesting in the history of the USA/Canada Church of the Nazarene! An African proverb says, "In the desert there is one crime worse than murder. That is to know where the water is and not tell others." Priceless truths have been entrusted to us. Life-giving water has been placed in our hands. Jesus put it no less directly when He said, "From everyone to whom much has been given, much will be required" (Luke 12:48, NRSV).

II. Our Heritage

Inherent in the Great Commission is the starting of new churches. Going and making disciples means there must be baptizing and teaching. New churches were started rapidly in the Early Church as believers spread out from Jerusalem. The Church of the Nazarene stands squarely in that apostolic stream of new church planting. Paul Orjala declared,

> In fact, the Church of the Nazarene owes its record of rapid growth more to rapid church planting than to any other factor. In 1907, there were 99 churches and 6,198 members. In 1908, at the end of a consolidation year and launching of the denomination, there were 288 churches and 10,414 members. Then in rapid order we multiplied churches. The 288 churches doubled in four years to 576, and doubled again nine years later when 1,145 were reported. By 1936, the number of churches had again doubled. By 1959, the denomination had 4,696 churches and membership totaled 311,299. But the number of total churches had leveled off at around 5,000.[1]

From 1909 to 1944, the districts of the Church of the Nazarene in the United States and Canada averaged at least three newly begun churches each year. In 1945, the rate dropped to 2.8, and by 1948 it was only 2.2 new churches per district. Beginning in 1960, not only did the new churches per district drop by half (less than one per district most years), but also the number of districts reporting new churches dropped significantly. Up until 1960, at least 70 percent of districts reported new churches each year, and most years the figure was 80 percent or higher. In 1960 the ratio dropped to 67 percent and continued to decline through the mid-1970s. By 1978 only 35 percent of Nazarene districts in the United States and Canada reported any new churches, making an average of less than one new church per every *two* districts.

When church planting slowed, the total number of active Churches of the Nazarene stabilized. At the same time, total attendance stopped climbing, as did the number of new Nazarenes reported each year.

In 1994 the NewStart Initiative was launched with a renewed emphasis on new churches. In the fifteen years 1994 through 2009, we have begun 1,661 new starts in the USA/Canada Region. But in that same fifteen years we have closed 1,696, for a net decrease of thirty-five.[2]

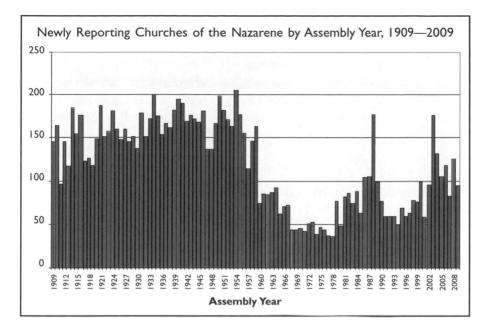

Newly Reporting Churches of the Nazarene by Assembly Year, 1909—2009

USA/Canada Growth, Comparative Statistics, 1999-2009

Growth from New Churches

- 1,065 churches started since 1999; 697 new churches still active in 2009
- Over 28,000 members in new churches
- Nearly 36,000 in worship in new churches
- 780 older churches no longer active: 15 percent of active churches reporting in 1999
- Churches begun by 1999 lost 7,000 members during decade
- Churches begun by 1999 lost 26,000 worshipers during decade

Growing Churches 2008-9

These churches outpaced the denomination in worship growth in 2008-9

- New churches (started in 2000 or later)
- Churches under 50 in worship
- Culturally specific churches (best: Chinese, Hispanic, Native American, Haitian)
- Churches over 1,000 in worship

To Simply Maintain

A district or denomination must add 3 percent new churches every year

- For 50 churches = 1.5 average

- For 75 churches = 1.75 average
- For 100 churches = 3.0 average
- For 5,000 churches = 150 average

We dare not become a "maintenance" church. Our task is clear—we must find strategies to make Christlike disciples in the United States and Canada. We must start many new churches, and many will be developed on a shoestring.

III. Our Nine Key Assumptions

Assumption One: We will use a variety of models. The approach in each situation should vary. These new churches will take on a variety of identities—rural churches, urban churches, suburban churches, multisite churches, multicongregational churches, culturally specific churches, multicultural churches, organic churches, cowboy churches, and so on. These churches will be started by both districts and local churches. Some will begin immediately as new churches, and some will begin as ministries or small groups and perhaps someday become organized churches. Three things are certain. Each one will be unique. Each one will *not* last forever. And each one will win new people to Christ, and their souls *will* last forever with Jesus.

In the organic church model, homes are often used for meetings. New churches have started in chapels and fellowship halls of existing churches; fire halls; funeral chapels; community rooms in banks and apartment complexes; music venues; city recreation centers; elementary, middle, and high schools; cafeterias and restaurants; storefronts; movie theaters; and so on.

Assumption Two: There will be financial constraints. We dare not assume building, land, and a full-time paid pastor. Too much support can actually hinder the health and stewardship of a new church. The resources are in the harvest field. People who do not yet know the life-giving Savior will contribute to the advancement of His kingdom once they have met Him in a life-changing encounter.

A local church leader with a great vision will inspire people to get involved in an adventure with God, and the money follows the people. The proper sequence is always *vision, people, $$$*.

In cases in which financial support is given by a sponsoring church or district, one example of financial restraints is to require that the budget of the new church be balanced within six months.

Illustration—Balance the Budget in Six Months or Less

- Definition of balanced budget: Expenses = Income
- To balance must either cut expenses or increase income
- No fixed subsidy

- Monthly grants for up to six months based upon income and projected expenses

Assumption Three: Leadership is essential. Leadership must be loyal to our movement. This has to do with mood and style and basic commitment. The key to loyalty is new birth—people tend to remain very loyal to the church where they were reborn as children of God and nurtured in the faith. The best place to find leaders for new churches is within the sponsoring churches.

Assumption Four: People must be reached in their own language and culture. The world has come to our doorstep. We are able to proclaim the gospel to the peoples of the world without leaving the shores of our own country. Waves of immigrants are coming from countries where the United States and Canada once sent missionaries. The story of Pentecost is the story of a God who came to people of many different nations in such a way that each heard and understood in his or her own language. We can do no less.

Assumption Five: People respond best to a workforce from among their own people. There are those with the gift of doing cross-cultural work, of being from one culture and being able to so love and identify with others that they are able to win those from other cultures. But the early goal must be to identify leaders from each people group, train them, and trust them to lead.

Assumption Six: Not all efforts will succeed. We must be willing to try some things that may fail. The histories of church planting show that some do not make it. Some die; but others, growing out of an effort, emerge strong. At the outset we need to say, "They will not all fly."

Assumption Seven: A "seed group" is not required. There may be times when we have a seed group or fellowship from our own movement. But this is not essential. Experience insists that there does not need to be a group from our own movement.

Assumption Eight: There should be a sponsor church or cluster of churches. It is helpful if there is a parent church or a cluster of churches that can provide a support structure. Physical and moral support can be terribly important. The number one reason new churches fail is that the planter leaves. The number one reason the planter leaves is discouragement.

Assumption Nine: There should be a coach and/or mentor for every new church pastor. A coach has "been there." A coach for a new church pastor will have started new churches. A mentor is a friend who has ministry experiences, but not necessarily new church experience.

IV. Our Two Biggest Apparent Obstacles

The two biggest apparent obstacles to beginning a new church on a shoestring are money and workers; how are we going to pay for this, and where will we find a leader?

The Wrong Use of Money

The wrong use of money causes dependence. A monthly *fixed subsidy* paid to a new church can cause dependence. Subsidies can dilute the dignity of the new believers, causing them to think that they are not a part of a real church. If a new church is to start on a shoestring, it must learn to depend in faith upon God and not on the mother church or the district or the denomination. God has the resources, and the new church must develop her faith muscles as soon as possible for continued health. Financial *grants* from sponsoring churches or districts can provide for start-up costs and an operating safety net for a set period of time.

The wrong use of money can stifle the freedom of new believers. A new church that receives regular subsidies senses that approval is needed from the source of the money before new initiatives can be started. In fact, some sending agencies insist upon subsidies as a means of control. A new church started on a shoestring will have local ownership and local control of initiatives to continue to reach new people with the love of Jesus.

Charles Brock has stated, "Money is usually a greater hindrance than help in multiplying reproducible churches."[3] Often a disciplined, redemptive love must say no to wants if eternal needs are to be met. We have learned on the mission field in developing nations that the flashing of a dollar forever damages the potential spiritual vision of the unbelievers. The end result will be a group of new churches that cannot or will not attempt any important project unless someone outside helps them. The same is true in the United States and Canada. New churches begun on a shoestring recognize that developing relationships and building bridges must have priority.

Material crutches appear to be a blessing but can actually cause stymied, stunted, irreproducible growth.

Lack of Workers

Jesus says in John 4:35, "Do you not say, 'Four months more and then the harvest'? I tell you, open your eyes and look at the fields! They are ripe for harvest." The leaders of a new church must behaviorally demonstrate that they believe the Lord of the harvest when He proclaims that the harvest is ripe. It is not possible to overemphasize the importance of believing Jesus, Lord of the harvest, when He proclaims that the harvest is ripe. Starting a new church is a faith venture—not faith in programs or in our own abilities but faith in the Lord of the harvest. It is faith in Him and His promises that brings results in the Kingdom. And He has said, "The fields . . . are ripe for harvest." Do you believe Him?

Jesus has said the harvest is ripe. That means that we are in a time of harvesting. There is only one reason given by Jesus for not harvesting. In Luke 10:2 He told them, "The harvest is plentiful, but the workers are few. Ask the

Lord of the harvest, therefore, to send out workers into his harvest field." So in John 4 the Lord of the harvest tells us the harvest is ripe, and in Luke 10 the Lord of the harvest tells us the harvest is plentiful. Do you believe Him? The harvest is ripe and plentiful. So why are we not harvesting more?

The only reason given by Jesus for not harvesting is the lack of workers. *"The harvest is plentiful, but the workers are few."* But He also gives the solution: "Ask the Lord of the harvest, therefore, to send out workers into his harvest field." Shepherds or pastors of existing churches are the gatekeepers to His harvest field. We are to pray and ask the Lord of the harvest to send out workers—not to "raise them up," as I have prayed for years, but to "send them out." We thus become part of the answer to own prayers. It is His harvest field. And shepherds are the gatekeepers. Where will the workers come from? From our existing churches. New church leaders are the associates, the Sunday school teachers, the youth workers, the board members, the lay leaders, the unassigned elder in our churches, the newly called minister, the retired elder, the businessperson who wants to do more for Jesus.

So if shepherds are the gatekeepers, how do we open the gate?

1. **Identify** those who have leadership ability.
2. **Recruit** them in the sense of giving them ample opportunity to respond to God's call on their heart and life. Why is it that so many are called to the mission field when a missionary comes to share and invite people to respond?
3. **Train** them.
4. **Deploy** them. We should be especially in tune with God's call on the life of new disciples with their much-wider circle of unchurched friends.

We must be willing to send out those that God has called into His harvest field as an answer to our own prayer. If we ask the Lord of the harvest to send out workers, we must be prepared to open the gate and release those workers into His harvest field. We must be willing to deploy workers into our Jerusalem, Judea, Samaria, and the ends of the earth.

Consider This Dramatic Change

1. Identify
2. Recruit/Select
3. Deploy
4. Train

The suggestion is to reverse the last two from Train and Deploy to Deploy and Train. This focuses on empowering rather than screening. The only way to learn leadership is to lead. Never select a leader based upon potential, but based upon performance. If a leader can build a small group, start a new class, a ministry, a business, and so on, then he or she can start a new church. But maintaining does not indicate a church planter.

The role of existing leadership becomes more one of qualifying the new leaders that are already emerging. "By their fruit you will recognize them" (Matthew 7:16) allows leadership to evaluate not so much the call of a prospective minister but the fruit of his or her work. None of us are 100 percent. We have all empowered leaders who disappointed us. We always need a reverse gear to change an ineffective leader. In the end, however, the work will progress best if the focus is on empowering rather than screening. Cull the nonfruitful ones as the fruitful ones are trained.

A New Testament Model—Lay Pastors

"A new church experiencing the power of the Holy Spirit and motivated along New Testament lines, can multiply cells of believers without dependence on missionaries or ordained ministers. Local men, gifted by the Holy Spirit, were given on-the-job training by the apostles and other leaders, and thrust out to work."[4]

Think About It

- Why don't we see rapid growth here in the United States as we do in other world areas?
- Do we have the faith to believe that the harvest is ripe and plentiful?
- Do we believe it for our mission field?

I sat next to Sukamal Biswas at the neighbors conference in Amsterdam in April 2010. Sukamal is the district superintendent of the Bangladesh District. At his 2009 district assembly he reported 1,220 churches—a growth from one hundred churches in 2002. Four general superintendents attended the district assembly to ordain one hundred and ninety-three new clergy, thirty of them women. We are the only denomination in Bangladesh to ordain women. A total of six hundred and ninety-five new district licenses were issued. At one point at the conference in Amsterdam, after realizing who he was, I turned to Sukamal and asked, "Your growth has been so rapid, how many of your new churches have buildings?" His answer: "I don't know. Our focus is not on buildings. Some do have buildings. We are more concerned with boldly sharing the gospel with everyone in Bangladesh and training and sending out new pastors."

It is beginning to happen in the United States and Canada. As we learned earlier in this book, Memphis Holiness Tabernacle began in a building lobby in 1996 by McArthur Jackson and his wife, Millie. Today they average about 200 in worship. McArthur Jackson's congregation has been instrumental in beginning three other new churches, and he has a fourth meeting in his educational building now. Three additional planters are in training as a part of

McArthur's unpaid staff. They affectionately call McArthur "Bishop," not as one who is elected to a position but rather a person who demonstrates leadership by sending out one or more disciples to begin a new church.

Each of these churches started on a shoestring. McArthur's church provided a leader, mentoring, prayer support, workers to help get started, use of facilities, and small amounts of money. McArthur does not believe in subsidies. He believes that God will provide if He is in the new ministry. And God has blessed with the making of many new Christlike disciples.

I am excited about what the Lord is doing all across the USA and Canada Church of the Nazarene. And we must do more. He is helping us to catch a glimpse of the vision of what He really wants to do through developing new churches on a shoestring.

V. Our Resources

1. 5,000 Churches
2. 80 Districts
3. Global Ministry Center Support
   - Nazarene New Church Task Force
   - Nazarene Multi-Congregational Task Force
4. Educational Opportunities
   - Nine Liberal Arts Universities; Nazarene Bible College; Nazarene Theological Seminary (NTS)
   - On-line Module Program Leading to Ordination at Northwest Nazarene University
   - On-line Module Program Leading to Ordination at Nazarene Bible College (NBC)
   - Four On-line Courses at NBC Leading to a Certificate in Church Planting
   - Inter-term Intensive at NTS in Church Planting
   - Many District Training Centers Offering Module Programs Leading to Ordination
   - Leadership University for New Church Leaders: http://leadershipu.nazarene.org/
5. New Church Evangelism Web site: www.nazarenenewchurches.org/
6. Nazarene Cowboy Church Network
7. Nazarene Research Department: http://map.nazarene.org/
8. Nazarene Organic Church Network (NOCN): www.OrganicNazarene.net
9. Partnerships
   - Jesus Film Harvest Partners: www.jfhp.org

- New Church Specialties: www.newchurchspecialties.org
- Mapping Center for Evangelism and Growth: http://www.mapping center.org/

10. MisLinks: www.mislinks.org

VI. Our Challenge

Developing new churches on a shoestring not only is possible but is happening all across the United States and Canada. To begin many new churches, to seriously impact the harvest field, we must develop strategies that will yield reproducible indigenous churches; and that means developing more and more new churches on a shoestring. Will you pray for two BHAGs (Big, Hairy, Audacious Goals) as we ask the Lord of the harvest to send out workers into His harvest field? First, will you pray for an increase from an average of eighty to three hundred plus new churches per year in the United States and Canada? And second, will you pray that every leader, every pastor, every church and every district would be actively involved in developing new churches?

Stan Reeder is the superintendent of the Oregon Pacific District Church of the Nazarene. Prior to being elected district superintendent in 2009, he pastored in Canada, Arizona, Michigan, and Colorado. Stan is a graduate of Manitoba University (AB), Canadian Nazarene University (ThB), McMaster University (MDiv), and Fuller Theological Seminary (DMin). Stan and his wife, Janet, live in Salem, Oregon. StanReeder@orpac.org

■■ 21 ■■
BUILDING A GREAT FUTURE
STAN REEDER

My first encounter with starting new churches came through the denominational emphasis "Thrust to the Cities" in the 1980s. Toronto, Ontario—a nearby city to where I was pastoring in Hamilton—was targeted for a ministry blitz. All the pastors in the surrounding areas were asked to consider the possibility of starting a new church as part of the campaign. My problem with starting a new church was that I thought I needed to grow my church before I could possibly create an effective new work. Notice the key words:

My problem . . . I thought . . . I needed to grow . . . my church.

The Lord needed to do some work in me before He could use me. I was the one with the problem, not the Lord. It was my faulty thinking—my bad theology. "My problem" in God's economy is "His opportunity"—"For when I am weak, then I am strong" (2 Corinthians 12:10). I'm not the one who grows the church. I plant or water, and God grows the church. It is not "my" church; it is *Jesus'* church. I was not responsible to create an effective new church. The Lord is the one in charge of the "creating" department. Jesus is the one who promises, "I will build my church; and the gates of hell shall not prevail against it" (Matthew 16:18, KJV). I needed to listen to what the Lord has to say:

Indeed I have spoken it; I will also bring it to pass.
I have purposed it; I will also do it. (Isaiah 46:11, NKJV)

The Lord started to melt my heart and give me faith for church planting through Bill Sullivan, who talked about the heritage of planting churches that we have as a denomination. Since the start of the church in the early 1900s up until the 1950s, we were continually starting new congregations, and we were closing very few. He noted that all churches have a lifespan roughly similar to that of a human. They typically live anywhere from fifty to one hundred years with an average life of sixty years. The problem we were facing in the 1990s was that all the churches we planted between 1900 and 1950 were starting to age and die. He predicted that many of those churches would start closing in the next fifteen years. He was right.

George Barna believes that about 20 percent of Americans attend church every Sunday. We must have a renewed sense of urgency among Christians and among our churches! The Lord invites us: "Call on Me, and I will answer you, and show you great and mighty things, which you do not know" (Jeremiah 33:3, NKJV). We can have confidence that He will see us through. "In all these things we are more than conquerors through Him who loved us" (Romans 8:37, NKJV). Henry Blackaby writes,

> When a church realizes it all depends on God . . . and will together yield their lives fully to Him, God begins to work. It doesn't depend on numbers, status, skills, or even resources. The future depends on God and on His people who will hear Him, believe Him, and obey Him.[1]

What We Give the Lord

Before becoming a district superintendent, I was a pastor for many years. I know what makes a pastor's ministry easier. It's as easy as ABC:

- ATTENDANCE. Being a pastor is much easier while the attendance is going up.
- BUILDINGS. Being a pastor is much easier while the buildings and technologies are up-to-date and in good repair and everything looks great.
- CASH. Being a pastor is much easier when the offerings are strong and there is money in the bank.

We tend to measure success using the ABC method listed above, but we must understand the urgency of the gospel, and we need to lay all on the altar. Whatever is laid on the altar is never lost; it is invested into the Lord's hands so He can use it in supernatural ways. Let's not think "loss" in these areas—let's think investment that will bring tremendous Kingdom return.

Members

The last I checked, the number one question people still ask when they want to know how a church is doing is "What are they running now?" When you become a church that plants churches, you are going to invest people. It may mean some loss.

Help people understand that *everyone* is called to plant. Some are called to *go* and be part of the new core group. Others are called to *stay* and stabilize the parent. Regardless of the role—everybody is called.

Money

One of the members the Lord called into starting another work was the church's largest donor. It was a transition that the Lord helped us to make— and the doors of the church remained open. The year we fully parented our first plant, our income was lagging several thousand dollars behind the budget. A board member expressed his concern about giving away fifty tithers when we were already running in the red. We did not "lose" anything that year—we "invested" it, and the Lord brought the single greatest increase in the giving history of the church that next year.

Mud

A parent church invests turf and territory. In five years we assisted in the planting of five churches. Four of them are within driving distance from the mother church. Now when people move into the area, they have a choice of which church to attend!

Ministry Resources

During a board meeting one of the members was concerned about "giving away" ministry workers to a new work when we did not have enough workers to meet the demands of ministry in our own church. We had a faith talk during the board meeting that night. We reminded ourselves that it is Jesus' church, and Jesus will provide for His church! Interestingly, that same board member is now a member of one of the church plants. He is likely their number one worker!

Momentum

Being a pastor is a lot more fun when you have the big "MO" working for you. Let me be clear: The parent church must sacrifice momentum for a daughter church. After the new church has started, the mother will often have a "postpartum depression." It takes time to get through this.

There is a gap between the resources you have invested and the rewards the Lord is about to increase, but this gap is the place where you will experience the touch of Jesus' miraculous power as you never have before. Are you ready to step into the gap?

What the Lord Gives Us

Ripple

The Lord will give a ripple effect every time you throw a pebble into the pond of His kingdom. The ripple is always so much bigger and more expansive than the pebble.

The Lord put a vision in the heart of Westminster Church of the Nazarene: To be a holy, positive, impact church that over the next fifty years plants five hundred churches and reaches five hundred thousand people with the good news of Jesus Christ.

How is that possible? The 5-7-5 strategy: If we plant one reproducing church every five years, and that church after its first seven years starts planting a reproducing church every five years, in fifty years we will have five hundred churches and will have reached five hundred thousand people with the good news of the gospel! The Lord had us take part in the planting of five churches in a variety of ways, not just the one we planned. Parenting a church is planting a seed. Only God knows what tremendous fruit will result.

"Anyone can count the number of seeds in an apple, but only God can count the number of apples in a seed."[2]

Replenishment

"Without faith it is impossible to please God, because anyone who comes to him must believe that he exists and that he *rewards* those who earnestly seek him" (Hebrews 11:6, emphasis added).

As we have earnestly sought the Lord in this matter, He has rewarded us. We have His word on it; He will reward those who earnestly seek Him.

The Replenishment of Attendance. Throughout the five years of our endeavor to plant churches, the Lord doubled the size of the mother church. The year after we gave fifty people away to start our first fully parented church, we saw the largest jump in attendance in the history of the church. Simple math would indicate that we should have shrunk by fifty people. Instead, the Lord worked the "miracle of replenishment," and the worship attendance grew by over one hundred the next year. All of God and none of us!

The Replenishment of Buildings. Our present facility is pretty cramped. We have a Saturday night service and three Sunday morning services. We wondered if we would be giving up the future of a larger facility if we engaged in church planting. Since we started on the planting venture, the Lord has provided us access to an eighty-acre site located at the interchange of the two busiest highways in north Denver. All of God and none of us!

The Replenishment of Cash. The year we started our first fully parented plant we were running in the red. That did not seem like the time to give away a bunch of strong tithers! The next year we saw the largest jump in income in our church's history. The Lord doubled the income of the church during the five-year period of church planting. All of God and none of us! He is a good and gracious God who is faithful to His promise. He rewards those who earnestly seek Him!

Relevance

With a love for our churches I say, *most of our churches are irrelevant to large segments of society.* I have been very slow to recognize this. I have been very stubborn in my dream to maintain a multigenerational church that ministers to everybody in the same way all at the same time. I have had to adjust my dream. We are still multigenerational but ministering in a variety of ways. There are some profound cultural shifts that have taken place in the last generation— some in the last few years! I see three factors that have changed everything.

Cable TV. I would venture to say that very few people could name the anchors for the major networks: ABC, NBC, CBS. Thirty years ago, people knew who these people were. What has changed? Cable TV. The networks are dying! Society wants what they want. When I was a kid, we got one channel. It was the local channel in Hamilton, Ontario, and I never got to watch it, because I was the youngest of four boys. I was the one standing behind the TV set holding the bunny ears in just the right position. Today some TVs have hundreds of channels and have access to hundreds of movies, and we still complain, "Nothing is on!" Why? Because we don't like to bother with something we don't like.

The iPod. In the past, if you wanted to hear your favorite song, you would have to listen to twenty-five other songs that you did not particularly enjoy before you heard the genre and style you really liked. This forced people to have a fairly wide taste of music. Today you do not have to listen to any music that you do not like. You don't even have to have the group's whole CD—just the particular songs you enjoy.

It will not work any longer to have a blended style of music in the church that tries to have a song that the eighty-year-olds will enjoy, one for the sixty-year-olds, one for the forty-year-olds, and one for the twenty-year-olds. Because of our cultural shifts, there is a growing intolerance to the music and styles of other generations.

Mass Customization. Twenty years ago Burger King started saying, "Have it your way." Everybody has had to adjust. Even McDonald's had to cave to the pressure, so now I can order my Big Mac without onions. It didn't use to be that way. Culture has changed.

There used to be "ego" cars like Porsche or Mercedes. People would buy them even though the interior color choice for a Porsche was black or black. Mercedes went way out on a limb and gave you tan or black. That is not the case anymore. You can go online today and design your own car with thousands of different combinations so it's exactly the way you like it.

The days of offering one product for everybody are gone—everywhere, that is, except in the church. We still say to twenty-year-olds and to eighty-year-olds, "Have it our way" or too bad. As a result, there are very few twenty-year-olds going to our churches, and the eighty-year-olds feel disenfranchised. Church planting allows existing churches to do ministry in new ways without upsetting its traditional base. As a result, we are relevant to a whole new group of people.

Reach

Because of the freedom in a new plant, it can reach different people that the mother church cannot. Our newest plant started because God put the desire in a couple of laypeople to reach their neighborhood that was beyond driving distance to mother church. They invited their friends to a small group in their home. Their first meeting had eight couples, which quickly grew to sixteen. Then, there were over one hundred people, and they did not even have a pastor. The Lord is blessing us with a reach that we never would have had on our own. One week when about one hundred fifty people showed up for "small group," the lay leader contacted me in a panic and asked, "Should I tell our people to stop inviting people?"

Forty percent of new Nazarenes come from churches less than fifteen years old. It takes over fifteen people at churches started before 1940 to see one person saved per year; it takes only three persons at new churches to see one person saved per year.[3]

The Lord honors church planting churches with a reach they would never have otherwise.

Reward

"His master replied, 'Well done, good and faithful servant! You have been faithful with a few things; I will put you in charge of many things. Come and share your master's happiness!'" (Matthew 25:21).

A Closing Challenge

As you finish reading this chapter, you may think, *Well, that would be great, but I'm part of a smaller church, and we don't have the resources to do any of this.* Henry Blackaby may have an additional challenge for you.

Starting new works was in Henry Blackaby's blood. As a boy, his dad was a Christian businessman who was often relocated. In one location, a small town in British Columbia, his layman dad rented the dance hall and started a church. His dad preached, his mom played the piano, and he and his brother served as ushers—because it was eight months before they had their first adult visitor. With slow growth and much prayer, they were able to get their first pastor after *eight years*.

When Henry grew up, he became a pastor. As a young man, he was called from a prospering ministry in Los Angeles to a fledgling church in the western Canadian prairies. When he arrived at his church in Saskatoon, Saskatchewan, there were ten members that were holding it together, but they had already put a "for sale" sign on the front lawn. They had decided that if Blackaby did not accept the call to be their pastor, they were going to close the church. They were on "life support."

The good news is that the attendance on Blackaby's first Sunday was not just ten people—it was fifteen; the bad news is that five of those fifteen had arrived together and were visiting from Prince Albert (a small town ninety miles from Saskatoon). They were in the church in Saskatoon because they sensed the Holy Spirit's direction to attend. Those five individuals had been meeting in a home in Prince Albert and had been praying that God would help them start a new work in their town. After Blackaby's first service in Saskatoon, they asked him if he would be willing to start driving the ninety miles to Prince Albert on Sunday afternoons to preach in their home. Blackaby talked with his church board, and they all agreed if the Lord was opening a door, they should walk through it.

For two years, Blackaby made the one-hundred-eighty-mile round trip to preach at that new work. One Sunday he braved a winter storm to make the trip only to have no one show up at church. There were many times when they could have given up, but after two years that new work had enough people and enough resources to call its own pastor.

Over the next twelve years of ministry, their small Saskatoon church made the simple commitment to the Lord that if He opened doors, they would walk through them. The Lord honored their commitment and over the next twelve years opened doors for the starting of thirty-eight new churches.

It is an amazing mathematical formula. If one church starts one new reproducing work every five years, and that new work, after its first seven years, starts planting new reproducing works every five years—in fifty years there will be five hundred new works reaching over fifty thousand people with the good news of Jesus Christ. All you have to do to reach fifty thousand people is start one new work every five years!

After I embarked on the journey of starting new works, I started the daily practice of offering the Lord a very simple prayer. It's based on the Lord's instruction for Peter in Luke 5:1-11. After catching nothing all night, Peter was instructed to let down his nets into the deep water. Peter obeyed, even though he could have made all kinds of objections. The Lord provided such a catch of fish that the boat began to sink, so they had to call for the assistance of James and John to fill their boat. Both boats were so full that they were sinking. Will you make it your prayer? *Lord, fill our boat and another too.* Ask the Lord to bless your obedience to His call to start another work in such a great way that both churches will be filled.

The end result could be five hundred thousand souls in heaven some day!

Marilyn McCool was elected in 2002 as the first woman general treasurer of the Church of the Nazarene. She is a former Northern Michigan banker of twenty-seven years, community services leader, pastor's wife, and church planter. Marilyn has a master's degree from Central Michigan University and a doctorate from Olivet Nazarene University. She and her husband, David, have three daughters and nine grandchildren and live in Overland Park, Kansas. mmccool@nazarene.org

PLANTING A CHURCH IN KALKASKA

MARILYN MCCOOL

It was a knock at the door that changed our lives forever.

The evening began as an ordinary ending to an ordinary work and school day for a father, mother, and three daughters (ages eleven, fourteen, and fifteen). When we opened the door of our little six-year-old house we had built on land we cleared on a remote unimproved Kalkaska County road, we didn't know it was God calling.

I always thought that one heard and answered God's call during an altar call at a church service, revival service, missionary rally, or youth camp bonfire; so I didn't recognize at that time that God can also call you in your own home in the middle of the woods.

"Hello. We are from the Church of the Nazarene, and we would like to talk to you. The International Church of the Nazarene in Kansas City is beginning a focused campaign to plant new Nazarene churches in the United States. We are establishing a pioneer district in Northern Michigan and would like to know if your family would be interested in attending a church in Kalkaska should we plant one there."

The newly appointed district superintendent of the pioneer Northern Michigan District and the pastor of the Traverse City Church of the Nazarene shared their vision for Northern Michigan, specifically starting with Kalkaska, a new community for a Nazarene church plant.

Because we had been Nazarenes for sixteen years, we assured them that our family would welcome a chance to once again worship in a Nazarene church, especially in our childhood hometown where we chose to raise our family.

As the conversation drew to a close, we mechanically but politely asked the simple questions of when, where, how, and who. It was then we learned that neither the general church nor the district had resources with which to begin this project. There was no core congregation, no building, no financial resources—no pastor.

We were encouraging them with words such as "Please keep working on your plan" and "Let us know when things work out," when I heard my husband, David, speak. "Should you need someone to fill the pulpit for a few weeks until you find a pastor, I have a local minister's license and would be willing to manage my work schedule to donate my time to provide Sunday messages if you wish."

What? His words stunned me. Time stood still as racing thoughts crashed in my head. Help? Help whom? Do what? We can't do this! We don't know how! We've never done anything like this before! We don't have time! We have no place to meet! People of the community won't understand. People will make fun of us. We can't take our children out of their active youth group. We can't have church with only one family—ours! I like the big churches we have attended, with lots of people, music, nurseries, youth programs, and family networking relationships!

I have no memory of subsequent conversation until the parting words of the district superintendent: "We would like you to hold the first service in Kalkaska on the first Sunday of November [1983], four weeks from now, if you can find a place. We will be in touch."

Our front door closed with its classic squeak. All was quiet. We looked at each other. No one spoke. Each of us was alone with our own thoughts. Was God calling? If He was, He must have a plan but forgot to leave us a copy.

A commitment had just been made that would lead us into years of uncharted territory and change our lives forever.

God Provides

We didn't make it. That is, not the originally requested date for the first service of the Church of the Nazarene in Kalkaska. Be we did start.

From the date of God's housecall we spent four months meeting with church officials, identifying community people who may be interested in a Church of the Nazarene, finding a suitable meeting place, and developing an advertising strategy.

As a wife and mother, I became increasingly concerned about the obvious time commitments of church plant responsibilities not being compatible with my ten-year career responsibilities and college studies in Traverse City. It seemed impossible to add this to the list, especially with driving time.

With most issues and concerns still pending, we chose Sunday, March 4, 1984, by faith, for our first afternoon service in Kalkaska.

On Friday, March 2, 1984, the personnel director at the bank where I worked asked to see me. He said, "Our Kalkaska Branch Manager just resigned. Today is his last day. How do you feel about leaving the Traverse City Office and working in Kalkaska? It would really help the bank if you would take this promotion and report as the manager of the Kalkaska office on

Monday, March 5." *God had provided a time and place for us in the Kalkaska community. Thank You, Lord.*

Sunday, March 4, 2:00 P.M. came. Would anyone come to our first service? My eyes were riveted to the parking entrance of my brother's Seventh-Day Adventist Church we had rented for $50. A blue van signaled an approach. A small group of people with smiling faces and joyful hearts from the Traverse City Church of the Nazarene joined David, our youngest daughter, Amy, and me for our first worship service in Kalkaska. *God provides people of one heart and mind. Thank You, Lord.*

Unaccustomed to associating cost with having a church service, we worried about being able to cover the $50 expense of the day. We were humbled when the offering totaled $52.73. God sent a clear message to us that day that is even clearer today because of its proven truth: *This is My work. The financial matters are Mine, not yours. I will always provide. Do not limit My future provisions by human thinking or worry ever again. Trust Me with the work* and the finances.

God provides the financial resources. Thank You, Lord.

Before they said good-bye, the Traverse City pastor and people reached into their van and presented us with two worn wooden offering plates and a few outdated Nazarene hymnals. "We wish we had more to help you with, but this is a start."

We placed the first tangible evidence of the Kalkaska Church of the Nazarene into our car trunk, where the items would reside between weekly Sunday afternoon services. *God provides offering plates and hymnals. Thank You, Lord.*

"See you next Sunday," we said as the blue van disappeared on West M-72 toward Traverse City. David, Amy, and I stood alone in the parking lot. God was there. The work was launched. It was a very humble start; one small service. *God, remember—we don't know what to do next. We need Your help. Please provide for us next Sunday also.*

At that moment we did not know that in just a short time we would be without a place in which to worship.

God Gives a Vision

The low-cost classified ad was short. "Wanted: People who are interested in a Church of the Nazarene in Kalkaska. Please call 258-5128."

The ring of the one and only call sounded above the din of our busy household. I answered the telephone.

"Hello, I have been praying for a Church of the Nazarene in Kalkaska since 1952. I want to attend services, but I may need transportation. My name is Mary Sherwood, and I am a retired Nazarene minister."

With cautious optimism I shared her message with David. Was the caller serious? If so, she had been praying thirty-two years for this day! God gave her a vision and faith to believe. We did not know then that Sister Sherwood would become an awesome prayer warrior, mentor, and encourager to this faint-hearted couple. She came to the next Sunday afternoon service, and the next, and the next.

Feeling led to hold June revival services in the community, David called his good friend and evangelist William Varian, our former pastor at Kankakee (Illinois) First Church of the Nazarene. "I'll come," Bill said. "No charge. I want to help you and the Northern Michigan Pioneer District get a start." We were so excited about advertising the Nazarene meetings and inviting the Kalkaska community.

Less than one week before the revival services were to begin, we were kindly told that we would be unable to hold it in the church we rented for Sunday afternoon services. We scrambled to find alternate meeting places, but every lead ended in a definite "no" until someone mentioned the old Masonic Temple on Walnut Street.

We quickly contacted the editor of the Kalkaska newspaper, who also handled matters relating to the facility. "Sure," he said. "We can arrange a rental fee for the use of the building. What do you need?" So it was that the old Masonic Temple, originally the first church to be built in the village of Kalkaska and formally opened in 1880 as a congregational church, became a church house once again when we advertised it as the first official address of the Kalkaska Church of the Nazarene.

The revival services happened. We held six meetings with an average of twenty-three in attendance. Brother Varian preached to the small group of people just as if it were a big congregation. He sang his favorite song, "Because He Lives," over and over with fervor, as if he had a special vision of heaven.

Brother Varian had fun with my inexperienced husband and taught him never to forget an offering! Most notably, however, God used this revival to reintroduce a call to ministry to a man who was only "helping out" until a pastor could be found. Over a cup of coffee Brother Varian shared his vision for the Kalkaska work and directed a challenge toward David. "Why don't you enter the Ministerial Studies Program and minister in this work? You have a degree from Olivet. I know you could do it."

It seemed that Brother Varian had vision beyond our scope of understanding at that time. To us he was a God-sent Moses, to help us on our Christian service journey. We didn't know then that he was only seventeen months away, at age fifty-seven, from the last verse of "Because He Lives." His gain in crossing that river was our great loss.

Traverse City Church of the Nazarene continued to support our services on Sunday afternoons with their attendance, but soon we had a vision of moving to a full schedule of Sunday morning and evening services, which was possible for a one-day Masonic Temple rental fee. We were now on our own for Sunday services. In addition, we could not afford a second day's rent for Wednesday service, so we began cottage prayer meetings in our home, eventually moving from home to home of those in our small group.

So it was that I began Sunday mornings by delivering our two teenage daughters to our former church so they could be with their friends. We had promised them that it was their choice to stay or join us. They had chosen not to come with us, and we couldn't blame them. We had nothing to offer. The ache in my heart was unbelievable. How could something so good feel so bad? This was the first time we had been a divided family on Sundays. I would then go to the Masonic Temple with Amy to listen to my husband preach his first messages. God was faithful in His ministry to me. He gave me a vision that all would be well. It wasn't long before my girls quietly said one Sunday morning, "We have decided to go to the Nazarene church."

The first winter in the Masonic Temple was very cold. We paid one heating bill of $300 for two meetings. People sat in services clad in coats and mittens under lap robes. Wisps of breath suspended in the air when greetings were exchanged and songs sung. In search of comfort and less expense, we moved from the main meeting room to the small pool table room in the back. The pool table was immovable, so we placed our chairs around it, and David positioned his little low lectern up against the coat racks. What a sight!

The plumbing was decommissioned for the winter, so running water and restroom facilities were not available on the premises. Crawling over the snow banks in my Sunday dress, without coat or boots, I once prevailed on the good graces of our neighbor for a pail of water to clean up after a child who lost his breakfast in front of the pulpit, in the middle of a service. When I returned with the water, David was still preaching, and people had just pushed their chairs a little farther to the side!

The first winter did pass, and we did survive. On a spring day in 1985 David was driving his old pickup truck down West Kalkaska Road when he came to a stop in the middle of the road. The sign read, "For Sale—60 Acres." At dinner he matter-of-factly stated with confidence, "Today I named and claimed acreage for the Church of the Nazarene in Kalkaska, on West Kalkaska Road. I prayed that God would provide the way. God has given me a vision. I can see it all."

Ten Acres of Jack Pines

"Mornin', li'l lady!"

I looked up from my desk to see Big John standing in the middle of the bank lobby, his grin as big as his Texas drawl.

"Hear your husband is interested in my property for a church. You can have as much or as little of it as you want. Make me an offer. Nothin' down and whatever y'all can pay a month is fine with me. It's on West Kalkaska Road, ya know."

I knew. It was God at work again! I was too embarrassed to tell John that we did not have resources from which to make a deal, not even a modest, good one. But knowing that God did, I replied, "I'll tell David. Thanks."

Our prayer warrior, Mrs. Sherwood, challenged us to pray and fast for four days to seek the Lord's will regarding property for the church. We did. The outcome was one of peace and a reminder to trust God.

Just a few months later, on June 6, 1985, David and I sat across from Big John in the Realtor's office while signatures were placed on a document transferring ten acres on West Kalkaska Road to the Church of the Nazarene. David handed the cash proceeds over in exchange: $3,000 from our little congregation, $5,000 from Alabaster Offering funds, and $5,000 from the Michigan District, via Dr. Strait. God's provisions paid the property in full!

Jack pines were everywhere on the ten acres of Kalkaska sand. They were so thick that only my pioneer husband would venture past the cleared utility right-of-way along the road to see the possibilities for a church site. Mr. Peelman worked hard mowing the brush and weeds along the road to make it look nice for its Sunday afternoon dedication service on September 8, 1985.

We rented a big tent with a yellow-and-white striped top for the all-day meetings and dinner on the grounds. The tent looked great. The trailer was ready to move the piano, chairs, and tables to the tent. Everything for Sunday was in place before the special Saturday night youth revival at the Masonic Temple, which filled to capacity.

A few minutes into the service I was paged to respond to an alarm at the bank. A terrible storm was in process. Black and yellow clouds billowed and raced across the eerie green sky. Sheets of wind-driven rain pelted the car and made it almost impossible to drive. Lightning cracked, and thunder jolted the ground. My fear for the safety of the people in the old Masonic Temple was validated when I returned to find reentry into the building impossible. A lake of water blocked the doorway where three feet of rain had entered the basement. People were still singing, oblivious to the fact a tornado had just passed through the area.

It was then I remembered the ten acres of jack pines. The tent! To our dismay we found all our hard work lying on the ground. Poles were bent, and the yellow-and-white canvas was sagging under the weight of the water. We were dismayed! How could we ever fix this mess before Sunday morning, only a few hours away?

Sunday dawned bright, sunny, and warm. It was a beautiful day on which to dedicate ten acres of jack pines to the Lord for His work in Kalkaska. A wonderful group of people enjoyed services under the tent and dinner on the grounds—the grounds on which a Nazarene church would stand someday. Only David and I knew of the late-hour, frantic adventure in the wet darkness to reprepare for this great day of thanksgiving for the gift that God had given.

In the months to follow, God continued to work quietly but very quickly.

"Could you tell me where I can find the Church of the Nazarene?" I looked up from my bank desk to see who was speaking. "Hi. I'm Gil Dingman. We are Nazarenes and are moving to Kalkaska. I am the new postmaster. My wife and three children will be relocating in January, and we are looking for a Nazarene church home." Unbelievable! The first family with a Nazarene background had been sent to Kalkaska one month after the property dedication.

God showed He was leading by calling people to help: the gift of a piano from Sylvia Hubbell, which replaced our cassette player; the gift of seed money for the building fund; the arrival of Mrs. Guy as pianist and youth leader, at the age of eighty-something; the pledge of prayer support by Barb Cotton, even though she couldn't attend services at that time.

Greater than all the material blessings, however, were the spiritual blessings God showered on the people to meet their needs. The 1986 revival services with evangelist Russell Coffey will always be remembered as a spiritual landmark. The Lord met the needs of many people, including David's mother and father who, at age seventy-five-plus, were saved.

David soon felt led to officially organize the church. On Sunday, May 4, 1986, C. Neil Strait officiated at the organizational service, when we became an official Church of the Nazarene, with twelve charter members comprised of six teens and six adults: the Dingman family, the McCool family, Mary Sherwood, and Leone Guy. It was an unlikely beginning with only three of the adults employed, but God doesn't always require human logic. It was a modern-day "loaves and fishes" miracle.

A few months later, David challenged the little congregation with a construction program for a much-needed church building that would give community recognition to the Church of the Nazarene and provide a more versatile place in which to worship. David prayed that the people would catch the vision. It seemed that there was so much to do and so few to help.

Two years of working a full-time job, taking care of our home, fathering, planning the church, preaching, and now performing the new unfamiliar duties of pastoring and counseling people were all-consuming for David. It was physically and emotionally overwhelming at times. There was not a how-to book, and even the best efforts offered to the Lord were, unfortunately, often subject to criticism. But God was always faithful to bring people alongside to encourage when discouragement from unexpected places appeared to be winning. During these times God sharpened David's vision for the ministry of the church even more clearly, and he continued on.

David could hear the ring of the axe. God had great plans and would soon send workers into the fields—into the ten acres of jack pines.

Little Is Much When God Is in It

"I'll make macaroni salad and molasses cookies. Be at my house Thursday morning at 7:30 sharp!"

When eighty-something Mrs. Guy spoke, everyone listened. She had been serving the Lord for so long that I was convinced He spoke to her often. "If we are ever going to get out of this Masonic Temple into our church, we need to start now. We will start with a garage sale!" When I asked who "we" were, she said, "Who do you think? You and me!"

Spurred by Mrs. Guy's determination and sincerity, I climbed the wall ladder to the loft in our carriage shed, opened the window, and selectively hurled treasures out into the light of day to the ground below. David quickly scooped the stuff into his pickup for delivery to Mrs. Guy's house before I could change my mind. He was delighted!

It was not without skepticism that I participated, because I had financed enough loans in my career to know that it was impossible to hold a garage sale big enough to make even a small dent in a project as big as building a church. But when I had eaten Mrs. Guy's macaroni salad and molasses cookies for three days, between waiting on customers, I learned that the $300 we grossed in sales was an object lesson in vision and faith. Mrs. Guy taught this banker that little is much when God is in it!

A determined woman of faith, some cast-off possessions, macaroni salad, and molasses cookies. Little is much when God is in it!

We earmarked our proceeds for the first window in the church. "There," she said. "Now all they have to do is build the building around it!" I chose not to ask who "they" were.

One day I came home to find David at the kitchen table drawing lines on a big piece of white paper. "It's a multipurpose building," he said. Ever gifted for being able to see into the future, he continued: "It's actually phase one of a three-phase church building project." It was difficult for me to grasp David's big-picture vision, because I was still concerned about having enough money to install a second window in the church house. My absence of faith silenced a response.

One man's vision, a piece of white paper, a pencil, and a kitchen table— little is much when God is in it!

"We're going to start clearing the land—I've asked some of the men to come with chain saws," David proclaimed. Sure enough, in the spring of 1987 the saws whined shrilly, motors revved, axes rang, and the trees leaned to the ground with a swish and a thud until two of the ten acres were leveled, revealing sunlight across the beautiful foliage on the forest floor. On nice evenings we moved the Wednesday cottage prayer meetings to lawn chairs among the ferns, using a stump for a pulpit. Some willing men, some chain saws, and an axe. Little is much when God is in it!

In his report to the district assembly on June 4, 1987, David said, "We have faith that God will honor our stewardship and provide the means for us to construct a multipurpose building before the coming winter. Our faith is such that we have cleared two of our ten acres, and we are prepared to burn brush and pull stumps as soon as the weather permits. God is so good, and we await His will in eager anticipation to see how He will work next in our new church planting." I was in the audience, trying to stretch my faith, hoping that he wouldn't be disappointed.

Two months later, on August 10, Sieting Construction removed the stumps and prepared the site for a building. The little congregation had gathered a modest down payment for the building project and had secured a $45,000, fifteen-year mortgage of $490 a month from Nazarene Headquarters. Now the hard work began.

When we didn't know where to look for help, the Lord miraculously assembled a team of people for us faster than we could handle the details: a Christian architect to convert our kitchen table plans into construction code format; a Christian electrician who would save us money by allowing us to do part of the work; a Christian business owner who would supply ceiling, doors, and, yes, windows—at a discount; a carpet layer who just happened to have a business cancel an order of expensive carpet we could not have afforded otherwise; a pastor friend who said he would give us pews out of his church balcony in Sturgis, Michigan, if we would come after them with a U-haul for storage in our garage; a mother on Social Security who said she wanted us to have a pulpit and gave her tithe to buy oak to construct one; a minister's widow who said she wanted us to have an altar and gave an offering to build it.

A piece of oak, a mother's Social Security tithes, a canceled carpeting order, cast-off pews two hundred and fifty miles away. Little is much when God is in it!

On September 23, 1987, the foundational footings were dug for the multipurpose building. Phase one began with snow less than eight weeks away. Inexperienced in a project of this size, David served as general contractor and carpenter, with a few men from the congregation of primarily women and children. The call went out on the district; more help came, including the district superintendent and the missionary (NMI) president, for whom Grandma McCool served wonderful hot lunches in her garage on cold November days.

We especially remember those who have since passed on to their reward, who helped so willingly to build the church. Their contributions and memories linger on with our thankfulness: Grandpa Dingman, Uncle Glen, Mr.

Penfold, and our prayer warrior, Mary Sherwood, who died during the writing of this series. They are greatly missed.

A pastor, a few willing men and women, strong backs, tools, and good food. Little is much when God is in it!

> *In the harvest field now ripened*
> *There is work for all to do;*
> *Hark! The voice of God is calling*
> *To the harvest calling you.*
>
> *Does the place you're called to labor*
> *Seem so small and little known?*
> *It is great if God is in it,*
> *And He'll not forget His own.*
>
> *Little is much when God is in it!*
> *Labor not for wealth or fame.*
> *There's a crown, and you can win it,*
> *If you go in Jesus' name.*
> —Kittie L. Suffield

May the Lord bless my teacher of this great truth, Mrs. Guy, who at ninety-something is still serving the Lord. Oh, by the way—if you did not have a chance to sample one of her many dozens of big molasses cookies she rolled out on the old porcelain-topped farm table that now resides in my home, you missed a real treat. Just ask Scott Dingman!

"I Surrender All"

I didn't marry a preacher!

"All to Jesus I surrender, all to Him I freely give." I responded to this altar call hymn at a Lake Ann Baptist Camp chapel service. Pastor Brower pled with us to dedicate our lives for service. Since I thought I had no hope of ever going to college, my twelve-year-old mind reasoned that I would need to marry a missionary or preacher in order to be in Christian service. Although from that night to my wedding day I desired to serve the Lord, He did not send me a missionary or a preacher to marry.

Later I returned to Lake Ann Camp with my daughter and grandchildren. It was Saturday. All the campers had gone home. I walked the quiet grounds, and I was twelve again. The aroma of the traditional cinnamon rolls wafted from the whitewashed kitchen. Its same green wooden screen door banged shut with a familiar creak. The fifty concrete steps leading down to the swimming lake were oddly shaped by many years of footsteps and were still covered with grains of sand from glorious sun-filled days.

The old upright piano and brass horns could almost be heard lilting the notes of "Love Lifted Me" through the screens propped open on the chapel. I could feel the anticipation of the dress-up chapel service and the Friday night Glory Bowl, when the flickering firelight would dance across faces of campers publicly testifying about their salvation and dedication commitments. I thought about the many young people who made decisions here that shaped their lives forever. I was one of them.

I was pulled back to the present by my daughter Kirsten, who had also been a Lake Ann camper. Knowingly, she grinned at me and asked, "Where are you?" Then I listened to her share her camp memories with her children, creating great anticipation for the third generation. Since my camp days I have learned that "I Surrender All" even means our children and their children—and our marriages.

Our first real marriage test during the church planting occurred when it became evident that it was impossible for David to work a full-time job, be a pastor, and coordinate and work a church building project all at the same time. After much consideration, in August 1987 we mutually agreed that he commit full-time to the church even though it had always been, and continued to be, a nonpaying position (an arrangement we desired so the resources could be invested in establishing the church).

Cutting a five-member family income and benefits by more than 50 percent, with the same commitments, was a stretch for me. God was faithful and silently worked on my anxiety and fear of insufficient resources. I still have the yellowed, dog-eared envelopes God used to help me allocate my income to run our household. When I finally realized that God's resources were much greater than our frail ones and that He does not withhold what is needed, amazing things happened. He provided for us beyond what we could have even imagined. I learned that "I Surrender All" even means fear, dependence on self, and yes, money.

David plunged headfirst into the church interior finishing project. On Christmas Eve 1987 David and I worked in the unfinished church building warmed only by a roaring, fuming salamander. As David shaped pieces of window trim I would stain them. Light bulbs hung from orange cords, casting weird shadows. Our little portable radio played programs from Moody Bible Institute. I can remember thinking that we would never make it to the end. When David drilled through the palm of his hand while constructing the pulpit and ended up in the emergency room, I was *convinced* we would never make it! A neighbor named Marge Findley stopped by the worksite occasionally to radiate sunbeams of encouraging words and to offer prayer support for the endeavor.

Finally, all the interior work was done. David finished the construction of the pulpit, altar, and Communion table. We hired one of our friends to help us clean the entire building to ready it for carpeting. The pews were rescued from our garage and put into place.

The first building of the Kalkaska Church of the Nazarene was dedicated to the Lord on a Sunday afternoon in February 1988. It was a wonderful service, attended by over one hundred people from the community, including our district superintendent and business people who helped us with the project. It was an exciting day. We had officially moved out of the Masonic Temple!

Well, there you have it. In just less than four years the church was planted, organized, ten acres purchased, and a forty-by-sixty-foot multipurpose building constructed and readied for community worship.

It had been a long road, but it had been accomplished. I thought that the task given to us in 1984 had been completed in 1988. I was sure that David saw it that way also. I was tired. In addition to my job, I completed my bachelor's degree in 1985 and my master's degree in 1986, which were commitments in process prior to the church planting. Our children were beginning to graduate from high school and were entering college. I thought now we could get on with our lives and return to a normalcy, whatever that was! I was about to *find out* what it was. I learned that "I Surrender All" even means our plans and wishes.

"The Lord has not released me from the work. I have a vision of the Kalkaska Church of the Nazarene being a Holiness community church of two hundred or more. I can see it. Further, I feel led to finish the ministerial studies for ordination and also enter the Pastoral Counseling Master's program at Olivet." As David spoke these words, I remember thinking that he was very serious about the ministry for his life, but that I didn't know how to be a minister's wife. Remember—I didn't marry a preacher! Moreover, I was not familiar with the unwritten expectations for pastors' wives I had tripped over during the past four years. Life from the other side of the parsonage door had held many learning experiences for me. I needed help!

Two years later, in May 1990, David received his master's degree in pastoral counseling from the School of Theology during the graduation ceremony at Olivet Nazarene College. Then one year later, in June 1991, David and I knelt at the altar in the Cheboygan Church of the Nazarene while General Superintendent Eugene L. Stowe prayed for us during the ordination service in which David became an ordained minister in the Church of the Nazarene. That day I remembered the altar commitment of a twelve-year-old girl at camp. Although not in time for my wedding, God *did* send me a preacher!

In the meantime, the church phased in a pastoral remuneration program, the first in five years. More Sunday school classes were organized, a long-term care ministry was launched, revival services were held, and Vacation Bible Schools were conducted. Professions of faith were made, baptisms were held in Torch Lake, and people joined the church. A spiritual highlight memory is of David's aunt who started attending services and asked David to lead her to the Lord one Sunday morning after everyone had gone home. They prayed together at the new altar. She was the first one to accept the Lord in the new church building.

Remember when we carried everything the church owned in the trunk of our car? Over the years, God continued to lead faithful people to donate to the church: an organ, a sound system, new hymnals, a Communion set, a pulpit Bible, kitchen appliances, a piano, folding partitions, to name only a few. We did, however, need better advertising and signage. One day I was cleaning the bedroom after our houseguest from Arizona had gone home and found an envelope containing a sizable check and a note that read, "Use this for material to build a church sign." David did—in my house! We had learned long ago to surrender all our needs to God and watch Him work!

One of our biggest needs in the church was for musicians. David and I prayed for eight years that the Lord would send people to minister in music, because we felt it was such an important part of worship. When Mrs. Guy moved to Flint with her daughter, we no longer even had a pianist. One Sunday the Singing Men from Grand Rapids offered us a free concert during our Sunday school hour. It was so wonderful to hear great music in our little church. I remember pleading with the Lord during the concert not to let us go any longer without the blessing of wonderful music in our church. I was very specific in my prayer. I asked for the best.

What I didn't know was that God had sent Mark and Milly Fiedler as visitors to our service that day also. But God didn't stop there. He called them to our church! I had to apologize to the Lord for my impatient petition. He was just waiting for the right time to bring us the very best! He continued to send vocalists and instrumentalists who ministered in so many ways in our worship services.

Then God sent Mary Ferris, who shared the burden and the enthusiasm to start junior church services. We were thankful for her vision and for the wonderful Christian education materials she developed.

During a fall revival Evangelist Elaine Pettit challenged us to get serious about the power of prayer by touching the heart of God. Prayer commitments were made, and things began to happen. People in the church experienced miracles of healing. People began praying specifically for five families with children. Donna Koontz was burdened to pray that God would send committed men to the church who would take an active role in the spiritual leadership of their families and the church. Again God was faithful.

It is not surprising to report that the fifteen-year mortgage was paid off in eight years, at which time the mortgage was burned. The old pews were donated to a local Christian ministry, and one hundred-plus new chairs were purchased for the worship area. The building fund for the new addition doubled its original goal, and a new addition began with many people with willing hearts and hands giving of their time, talents, and energy to make it all come together. God continued to send many wonderful people who were willing to minister in so many ways. On March 30, 1999, at 7:00 A.M., the equipment broke ground for the second phase of the church building plan, including a forty-by-sixty-foot worship area, a foyer, and two offices! An additional one hundred chairs were ordered.

Thank You, Lord, for a group of people at the Kalkaska Church of the Nazarene who were saying "yes" to being used by You to build Your church, even in Kalkaska.

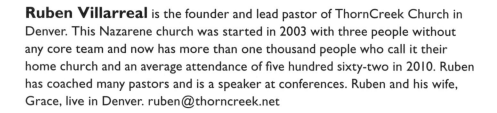

Ruben Villarreal is the founder and lead pastor of ThornCreek Church in Denver. This Nazarene church was started in 2003 with three people without any core team and now has more than one thousand people who call it their home church and an average attendance of five hundred sixty-two in 2010. Ruben has coached many pastors and is a speaker at conferences. Ruben and his wife, Grace, live in Denver. ruben@thorncreek.net

EPILOGUE
RISKING IT!
RUBEN VILLARREAL

Just a few weeks after a trip to a church conference, God gave me a quote that changed my ministry life. I was sitting in my office in Colorado Springs when God showed me a quote from A. W. Tozer—"God is looking for people through whom He can do the impossible. What a pity we only attempt the things we can do on our own."[1]

This one quote forced me to do a serious inventory of myself. I did a careful evaluation of my ministry and came to grips with the fact that 90 percent of the things I endeavored did not require the assistance of God's Holy Spirit. In other words, I was not attempting things in my life that would fail if God did not show up. I was not attempting those seemingly foolish things that were all riding on God's intervention. I just was not there. I was more concerned with comfort, convenience, and—dare I say?—pleasure. I put my head on my desk and asked God for forgiveness. At that moment I vowed to attempt things that could be accomplished only if God showed up. It was an incredible moment for me. I was a pastor serving God, a faith figure, yet my faith was contingent on my own resources, my own intellect, and my own parameters of logic.

I was watching a documentary of Bill Gates. I saw his seemingly unwavering drive and his undying passion. It was all for a product and service that had no eternal value. It made me consider the kind of passion I have for the kingdom of God. Am I willing to risk it? Am I willing to attempt the impossible?

There are two types of pastors I have encountered. One pastor attempts things hinged on his or her intellect, faith experiences, or resources. The results can be wonderful, but it is rooted in that pastor's framework of faith. The other type of pastor is a risky one. He or she is willing to attempt the things that are inspired by God. He or she is willing to be a minority and stand up for a cause for the Kingdom. I have learned that God still blesses both scenarios, but the possibility for exponential growth rests on the latter.

Risking it for the kingdom of God is not an irrational faith step, though it can seem that way. It starts with one's private worship time with God. It stems from the intimate time of reading and drilling down into God's Word. It is not being willing to close the Bible until you understand what that one word, that one phrase, means. Looking closer because you want to know God's will for your life and your hunger for His Word drives you. This is the breeding ground for the seemingly foolish faith. This is the place where your heart is grabbed by the Spirit of God, and you are willing to risk it.

Warning: this is not the easiest path to walk. It requires a commitment to be accountable to God's Word. It requires a heart that is continually open to transformation, regardless of age, occupation, or intellect. It is not for the person who is looking to be noticed by people or enjoys the accolades of praise. There is nothing sweeter than surrendering to His perfect plan for your life where every other circumstance and life experience points to His purpose.

What are you risking that could be accomplished only if God were in it? If you are like me, you might be slow to answer that question. The greatest men and women who have attempted the greatest things in this world started with an honest assessment.

God wants to do more in you and through you than you can imagine or even ask. Ephesians 3:20 is a hallmark verse in my life and the life of the church I pastor—"Now to him who is able to do immeasurably more than all we ask or imagine, according to his power that is at work within us."

God is able to do "immeasurably more" beyond our imagination and beyond our greatest vision. God can do more. What a tragedy to consider that at the end of life there is a possibility that we could have accomplished more for the kingdom of God, but we did not risk it!

Know Who You Are

I love to golf. One of the most important things I learned in golf is that it is imperative that you stay within your swing. You do not try to do more than you should, and you do not do less than you should. You want that perfect swing.

Likewise, ministry is all about staying within your swing. God has gifted every person with unique gifts and strengths. Knowing who you are is the first step to knowing what you can do well through Christ.

I know pastors who are rural pastors ministering in urban settings. I know pastors who are compassionate-driven pastors ministering in suburban areas. I know pastors who love small towns and are ministering in big cities. I know pastors who love the South but are ministering in the North. Now, I'll be the first to say that God can do anything. God can certainly overcome demographic and geographic barriers. He is a big God, but I have learned that our natural preferences, our background, and our passion are all factored into God's mission for our lives.

Learn to be who God made you to be. It sounds so simple and elementary, but there will always be a pull to be someone else or to meet the expectations of others.

I know when I try too hard in golf and I get out of my swing, the ball rarely if ever goes where I want it to go. It usually means I will be spending the next few minutes in rough, in trees, or in some kind of brush. Not fun at all! It is the same in our ministry. When we attempt to do things that are not within our God-given swing, it is just work, and it consumes our time and energy.

Some of the best golfers are the older ones. They are the guys who have been out on the course for years. They know their limitations. They do not hit the ball nearly as far as the "young buck," but they are more consistent than anyone. They hit the ball right down the middle of the fairway. They have learned the reality of what they can do, and they have learned to stay within their swing.

I have learned God always calls us to do things that are in line with our strengths. I could never do what my colleagues do. I am not gifted as they are. The day I realized God wants me to stay within my swing was the day I started focusing on my strengths rather than mastering my weaknesses.

Even with my best attempts, my weaknesses will never catch up to my strengths. They will always be below par. If I focus on my strengths and understand my limitations, then I am strategically positioned to be used by God and get exponential results.

There is only one Rick Warren, one Andy Stanley, and one Bill Hybels. That's okay. There is only one of you as well. I look at myself in the mirror, and I know God has chosen the foolish things of this world to put to shame the wise. I had to come to grips with who I am.

Likewise, the church you lead has to stay within their swing. When your church attempts to be something that is outside of God's purpose, it generates havoc. Do not ignore the gifting of your church. God has given you everyone and everything you need to be successful and advance His kingdom.

At the core of who you are is whether or not you are living that righteous life God wants you to live. Is your life consistent? Are you the same guy on the platform as you are at home? When you focus on who you are, you cannot help but to take serious evaluations of your own motives, gifts, and abilities.

Perhaps one of the greatest verses that helped me realize who I am and who my church is was Romans 11:16—"If the root is holy, so are the branches."

If you are right with God and you have a healthy growing relationship with Him, you can expect to have a healthy church. When your motives are right, your ambitions are in line with God's will, your strengths are in tune with God's direction, you can expect to have a healthy church. Likewise, if you are living a holy life, you can expect your people to have a clear picture of what a holy life looks like. When you are living that holy life, you can expect God to move before you, including with any divisive people.

Something I learned early on is that our insecurities, our fears, our preferences will always bleed into the branches of our church. If you spend enough time at any church, and you are looking with the right eye, you can tell a lot about the spiritual leader. God wants every spiritual leader to experience complete healing, freedom, and holiness. This impacts your ministry.

Ask yourself, "Am I staying within my swing?" God has gifted you beautifully to advance His kingdom. He has strategically aligned you to accomplish His will for your life. When you come to grips with who you are, then you become more successful for His kingdom. Stay within your swing.

How the Message and Culture Live Together

One of the Bible classes I took in college was how to exegete scripture. If you went to Bible college or seminary, that is one of those memorable courses. I remember the first time I heard the word "exegete." I had no idea what the professor was talking about. When you exegete scripture, you basically drill down to the original meaning, context, and history of that passage. Depending on how you are wired, it can be a lot of fun.

God also wants ministry leaders to exegete their culture. This is the gap most ministry leaders wrestle with. Ministry leaders should know more about the culture they minister in than any other person in that community.

Many times the ministry leader determines what kind of ministry best fits an area before he or she ever exegetes that culture. The ministry leader will walk into a location with prearranged strategies and solutions, but he or she has not taken the time to know about who the community is.

When I started ThornCreek, I knocked on doors for about three months. It wasn't fun at all. I felt like a vacuum cleaner sales guy. It was a daunting thing to walk up a sidewalk and knock on someone's door. Of course, they took one look at me and thought I was up to something. In spite of the anxiety, it was an incredible learning time for me.

I learned that the church is organic. As the target area changes, the church must evolve as well. It does not mean we compromise the message. The message is transcendent. It means I am more committed to the culture than an idea. I have learned that the gospel is timeless. It is really the same message no matter how we would like to wrap it. No matter the terminology we would like to use, it still comes down to a loving God who is holy and is reaching out to humanity for the purpose of salvation and destiny. It is a timeless message.

When Jesus ministered in Galilee, it was within the context of Jewish culture. That is why His parables, the customs He adhered to, even His clothes were all in respect to His target area. He was "in" the culture. Jesus did not go in with a Greek mind. He went in with a Jewish mind. The gospel spread from this central context.

The beauty of the gospel is that it is transcendent. Contrary to popular beliefs, a ministry strategy is not driven by a conference or some popular pastor from a growing church, or the latest book. The crux of success comes from understanding your culture and sharing the gospel with that culture in an understandable way.

The best ideas and strategies for your ministry will come from your intimate relationship with Jesus Christ and your awareness of your culture. God will reveal to you the best strategies.

A scripture that has impacted my cultural view of preaching and teaching is a story Jesus told when talking to His disciples. He asked them who they thought He was.

Matthew 16:16-17 says, "Simon Peter answered, 'You are the Christ, the Son of the living God.' Jesus replied, 'Blessed are you, Simon son of Jonah, for this was not revealed to you by man, but by my Father in heaven.'"

Simon Peter was "blessed" because God revealed this to him. If you want to experience a "blessed" ministry, it starts with a commitment to let God be your chief strategist, your chief source for preaching and teaching, and your chief source for encouragement.

With all the available sources in books, the Internet, and conference material, it could become really easy to depend first on other sources rather than on God. The danger is that we become more dependent on that Web site, or that sermon resource—and less dependent on God. God wants us to depend on Him. If we do that, we will be blessed.

Who knows your culture better than God? Isn't God big enough to give you relevant, cutting-edge strategies that will connect your culture with the gospel of Jesus Christ? God wants to do this.

When you have a transformational relationship with Jesus Christ and you understand your culture, the message and the culture live together, and God gives you a clearer vision of what will work.

Do you exegete your culture? It should be a daily task. Your ministry strategies should intentionally and strategically be driven by who you are ministering to and the challenges they face in everyday life. If your goal is to develop strong, spiritually mature followers of Christ, then knowing who you are reaching is essential.

This also means you do not get emotionally attached to any idea or strategy. It means you are more passionate about doing whatever is necessary to reach the lost for the cause of Christ than you are embracing your own idea.

For many churches the tragedy is not the location, the age of the church, or demographics. It is a refusal to grow with the cultural dynamics of their target area and a reluctance to rely completely on God's Holy Spirit. They have simply lost touch. That's why people visit churches all across America and feel as if they stepped into something that is remotely separate from the world they live in, and they don't experience God in a personal way.

Exegete your culture. When you combine this strategy with other intentional strategies and the good news of Christ, God transforms lives.

Deploy Leadership That Takes You to the Next Level

ThornCreek Church started with me, my wife, and my two-year-old son. We had no core team, no parent church, no prior relationships, and we were complete strangers to north Denver. It was one of the scariest times in my life in ministry, but I knew God wanted me to do this.

I quickly learned the value of identifying the workhorses. Horses are incredibly strong animals, and two can exponentially pull more. Growing up, I always wanted a horse named Starbuck. This was before the popular Starbucks Coffee shop was around. I should have gotten royalties from that. The right horses can do a lot for you.

When King David's early leadership team was coming together, they were no slouches. The scriptures say in 1 Chronicles 12:1-2, "These were the men who came to David at Ziklag, while he was banished from the presence of Saul son of Kish (they were among the warriors who helped him in battle; they were armed with bows and were able to shoot arrows or to sling stones right-handed or left-handed."

These guys could have held up on their own, no doubt. If you continue reading this chapter, verse 38 tells us they "came to Hebron fully determined to make David king over all Israel." Wow! Who wouldn't want a leadership team like this? God has the ability to send you the right leaders.

What's important to understand is having the right leadership team is critical, but having the right heart is even more critical. Shortly after this, David came to realize that God made him king because of His mercy for all of Israel. This was a turning point for David. He never faced any battle or any project the same after he came to this awareness. God sent the leaders, and He built up David's character as well. When you have the right horses and the right heart—giddy up!

You have to be secure enough within yourself to surround yourself with strong leaders. You have to be secure with the fact that they may do things better than you. That is tough to do for a lot of people. If you do not know your own strengths and weaknesses, then this is particularly difficult. But it is worth it.

Eighty percent of your time should be focused on spending time with the leaders in your church. They are the ones who can influence those new ministry strategies. If you really want to impact the Kingdom, focus on your key leaders.

This does not mean you ignore the other members. It is important that we minister to everyone and love others with that same love of Christ. God is pleased with this, but you cannot build a ministry on them. It's too much for them to support. From a leadership perspective, it means you recognize who are the key leaders in your church and who can take you to that next level.

Underused gifted leaders will go elsewhere. When good leaders in your church are not challenged and used in a meaningful way that complements their gifts, they will walk. They will not tolerate insecure leaders or leaders who lack vision and strategy. They will quietly walk away.

ThornCreek started with one hundred fifty people on Easter Sunday in 2003. We dropped to about eighty people that summer. Of those eighty people, we had approximately three leaders. It was not much. I learned the importance of coming alongside those new leaders—otherwise I would lose them.

I learned to pray for more leaders. My prayer in the early days was *God, would You send me new leaders? Send me people I can trust, people with humble hearts, who have teachable spirits—and would You send them fast?* God heard that prayer.

It is imperative that you are a growing leader to come alongside other leaders. This means you are willing to do whatever is necessary to become the leader God intends you to be. The river of leadership needs to continue to increase and flow within you. That may mean you read more, spend more time with other strong leaders, and it may mean a review of how you manage your time. Whatever it is, it is worth it to increase the Kingdom.

Faithful with the Small Stuff

I was walking around a local video store sometime ago. As you know, there are some aisles in the video store that do not honor God. I remember looking at one video cover. I stopped and could not believe it was right there in this family video store. Then something told me, "Turn it over —there are more pictures on the back of it." I looked around. There was nobody from my church. I was all alone, but I did not do it. I was so excited that I walked away. It was right then that God spoke to me and said, "Now I know you're ready for the next level."

Jesus taught this incredible leadership principle about the small stuff in Luke 16:10: "Whoever can be trusted with very little can also be trusted with much, and whoever is dishonest with very little will also be dishonest with much." God taught me that being faithful with the small things is where real ministry success starts. It is in the seemingly obscure moments when nobody is looking. It is when you are at home watching television and it is 2:00 A.M. It's when you are on-line and that pop-up window appears. It is those small moments when God looks closely and watches to see how we are going to handle the small stuff. The success of any ministry leader is not hinged on what you have done, an institution, a résumé, or whatever. It's hinged on your faithfulness with the small stuff.

I have learned that it is more important to be faithful than to be original. In the beginning stages of ThornCreek, I was very concerned about being different from anyone else. I remember talking to a pastor about the kind of church ThornCreek would be. I caught myself saying things like "It's going to be unlike any other church—it's going to be unique, and it's going to be relevant." Caution: I was full of myself in those days. I quickly learned that God moves in many ways and in many churches. God's ways are too big for me to comprehend, and everything is to be done for His glory.

I love creativity. I love thinking out of the box. That stuff comes relatively easy for me, but the need to be original can become your own sacred cow and can become a stumbling block for God's blessings in your life. Too many pastors love the new terminologies, love the new mediums, and love the new and latest visuals.

More important than being creative is being faithful to the little stuff that God throws your way. In fact, I have learned that a strong correlation exists between your obedience in the small stuff and the original ideas that flow through your mind. Are you faithful with the small stuff? The success of our church does not depend on what happens on Sunday morning or Saturday night. It is linked to how I spend my time during the day and the late hours of the night when no one is watching.

Faithfulness is like the foundation for a building. The building will never be bigger than a foundation can support. The strength and size of the foundation will determine the size of the building. Likewise, God will never place something on you that you cannot handle. God will always work on the foundation of your faithfulness first. The more faithful you are, the more you can handle God's purpose. God does not want to break your back. God wants you to be faithful, so He can reveal more of His will to you, and He can entrust you with more as well.

When you are faithful with the small stuff, you can articulate a compelling vision to anyone. When you are faithful with the small stuff, you can lead with confidence. When you are faithful with the small stuff, you can be secure of God's anointing in your life.

One of the prayers we say around ThornCreek is God, we pray to be faithful in the small stuff, and we pray to be good stewards of everything You entrust to us. I have learned that God is pleased with this prayer. We are not praying for something physical—we are praying that our faithfulness be increased.

When you are faithful in the small stuff, God moves in the big stuff. So risk it!

NOTES

Chapter 1

1. Martin Luther King, *I Have a Dream: Writings and Speeches That Changed the World* (San Francisco: Harper, 1986), 197.

2. Ibid., 201.

3. Ibid.

Chapter 3

1. John W. Gardner, *On Leadership* (New York: Free Press, 1993), xix.

2. WIE: Business Transformation Through Chaos Theory <http://www.wie.org/j22/hock.asp>.

3. John Maxwell, *Developing the Leaders Around You: How to Help Others Reach Their Full Potential* (Nashville: Thomas Nelson Publishers, 1995), 2-3.

4. Robert E. Logan and Steven L. Ogne, *The Church Planter's Toolkit: A Self-Study Resource Kit for Church Planters and Those Who Supervise Them* (Carol Stream, Ill.: ChurchSmart Resources, 1995).

5. Gary R. Collins, *Christian Coaching: Helping Others Turn Potential into Reality* (Colorado Springs: NavPress, 2001).

Chapter 4

1. 1898 Constitution of Los Angeles First Church of the Nazarene.

2. Data provided by Richard Houseal, Nazarene Research.

3. Nina G. Gunter and Moody Gunter, "Serving the Lord as a General Superintendent," *New Horizons* (September 2006).

4. Used by permission of Nina Gunter, from her personal notes.

5. NWCC meeting minutes (November 2007).

6. E-mail from Judith Schwanz (September 7, 2010).

7. E-mail from Kelly Yates, minister of Church Development, Oklahoma City First Church (July 16, 2010).

8. Lisa Miller, "A Woman's Place Is in the Church," *Newsweek* (April 12, 2010).

9. W. Edwards Deming, *Out of the Crisis* (Cambridge, Mass.: MIT Press, 1982).

10. Walter Brueggemann, *The Prophetic Imagination* (Philadelphia: Fortress Press, 1978).

11. Larry Bossidy and Ram Charan, *Execution: The Discipline of Getting Things Done* (New York: Crown Business, 2002).

Chapter 8

1. John T. Townsend, *A Liturgical Interpretation of the Passion of Jesus Christ*, 2nd ed. (New York: National Council of Christians and Jews, 1985), 13.

Chapter 9

1. Michael Frost and Alan Hirsch, *The Shaping of Things to Come: Innovation and Mission for the 21st Century Church* (Peabody, Mass.: Hendrickson Publishers, 2003), 12.

2. Brennan Manning's language in his subtitle and throughout the book *The Ragamuffin Gospel* (Sisters, Ore.: Multnomah, 1990).

Chapter 10

1. John Wesley, "Principles of a Methodist Farther Explained," in *The Bicentennial Edition of the Works of John Wesley* (Nashville: Abingdon, 1983—), 9:227, hereafter cited as *Bicentennial Works*.

2. H. Ray Dunning, *Grace, Faith and Holiness* (Kansas City: Beacon Hill Press of Kansas City, 1988), 48.

3. John Wesley, *Bicentennial Works*, 18:250.

4. George Croft Cell, *The Re-Discovery of John Wesley* (New York: Henry Holt, 1935), 297.

5. Unless otherwise indicated, all Scripture quotations in this chapter are from the *New Revised Standard Version* (NRSV).

6. John Wesley, Sermon 43, "The Scripture Way of Salvation" (1765), in *Bicentennial Works*, 2:160.

7. See Sermon 19, "The Great Privilege of Those That Are Born of God" (1748), in John Wesley, *Bicentennial Works*, 1:431-43.

8. See Sermon 40, "Christian Perfection" (1741), in Wesley, *Bicentennial Works*, 2:105-6.

9. John Wesley, *A Plain Account of Christian Perfection* (Kansas City: Beacon Hill Press of Kansas City, 1966), 81.

10. See the exposition of these five points in Paul M. Bassett et al., "A White Paper on Article X," in *Didache: Faithful Teaching*, 10:1 (Summer 2010) (http://didache.nts.edu).

11. John Wesley, Sermon 85, "On Working Out Our Own Salvation," in *Bicentennial Works*, 3:204.

12. Wesley, *Plain Account*, 115.

13. See Donald W. Dayton, "Asa Mahan and the Development of the American Holiness Theology," in *Wesleyan Theological Journal* 9 (Spring 1974), 60-67.

14. See A. R. G. Deasley, "Entire Sanctification and the Baptism with the Holy Spirit: Perspectives on the Biblical View of the Relationship," in *Wesleyan Theological Journal* 14:1 (Spring 1979), 27-44.

15. Sermon 129, "Heavenly Treasure in Earthen Vessels" (1790), in John Wesley, *Bicentennial Works*, 4:165.

Chapter 12

1. Michael Fix, Wendy Zimmerman, and Jeffrey Passel, *The Integration of Immigrant Families in the United States* (Washington, D.C.: Urban Institute, July 2001).

2. U.S. Census Bureau, *Profile of the Foreign-Born Population in the United States: 2000* (Washington, D.C.: U.S. Department of Commerce, December 2001).

3. Excerpted from "CQ for Cross-cultural Ministry Leadership" Assessment, adapted by David Livermore, developed by Linn Van Dyne, Michigan State University, and Soon Ang, Nanyang Technological University, Singapore (http://grts.cornerstone.edu/resources/glc/cqprofile).

4. Ibid.

5. C. Kluckhohn and A. L. Kroeber, eds., *Culture* (New York: Random House, 1952), 181.

6. Howard S. Becker, *Art World* (Berkley: University of California Press, 1982), 133.

7. Geert Hofstede, *Cultures and Organizations: Software of the Mind* (New York: McGraw Hill, 1997), 5.

8. Edgar Schien, *Organizational Culture and Leadership* (San Francisco: Jossey-Bass, 2004), 17.

9. Rick Lawrence, "The 18 Month Myth," *Group* 20, no. 2 (January/February 2000): 24.

10. David Livermore, *Leading with Cultural Intelligence: The New Secret to Success* (New York: American Management Association, 2010).

11. David Thomas and Kerr Inkson, *Cultural Intelligence: People Skills for Global Business* (San Francisco: Berrett-Koehler, 2004).

12. David Livermore, *Cultural Intelligence: Improving Your CQ to Engage Our Multicultural World* (Grand Rapids: Baker Academic, 2009).

Chapter 13

1. http://www.nazarene.org/ministries/superintendents/mission/clarify/display.aspx.

2. H. Orton Wiley, *Christian Theology* (Kansas City: Beacon Hill Press, 1940), 3:103.

3. Ibid.

4. See 1 Corinthians 12, 1 Peter 2, and Galatians 5.

5. Westlake T. Purkiser, Richard S. Taylor, and Willard Taylor, *God, Man, and Salvation* (Kansas City: Beacon Hill Press of Kansas City, 1977), 231.

6. J. Andrew Kirk, "The Kingdom of God in Contemporary Protestantism and Catholicism," in *Let the Earth Hear His Voice*, ed. J. D. Douglas (Minneapolis: World Wide Publications, 1975), 1073; quoted in C. Peter Wagner, *Church Growth and the Whole Gospel* (San Francisco: Harper and Row, 1981), 9.

7. Purkiser, *God, Man, and Salvation*, 232.

8. Wagner, *Church Growth and the Whole Gospel*, 10.

9. William F. Arndt and F. Wilbur Gingrich, *A Greek-English Lexicon of the New Testament and Other Early Christian Literature* (Chicago: University of Chicago Press, 1957), 353.

10. Donald McGavran, *Understanding Church Growth*, rev. ed. (Grand Rapids: Eerdmans, 1980), 223.

11. John Miley, *Systematic Theology* (New York: Eaton and Mains, 1894), 2:390-91.

12. Michael Green, *Evangelism in the Early Church* (Grand Rapids: Eerdmans, 1970), 236-55.

13. Professor Charles Shaver of Nazarene Theological Seminary, Kansas City, personal class notes of author, February 1977.

14. Elmer Towns, *Getting a Church Started* (Lynchburg, Va.: Elmer L. Towns, 1982), 11-12.

15. Ibid., 12.

16. Virgil Gerber, *God's Way to Keep a Church Going and Growing* (South Pasadena, Calif.: William Carey Library, 1973), 18.

17. McGavran, *Understanding Church Growth*, 26.

18. J. Kenneth Grider, *Entire Sanctification: The Distinctive Doctrine of Wesleyanism* (Kansas City: Beacon Hill Press of Kansas City, 1980), 9.

19. Ibid., 11.

20. *Manual, 2009-2013*, Church of the Nazarene (Kansas City: Nazarene Publishing House, 2009), 33. Note: A footnote on the same page as this definition explains that the "words in italics" are revisions "by the 2009 General Assembly" awaiting "ratification by the district assemblies at the time" the *Manual* was printed.

21. Wiley, *Christian Theology*, 2:491.

22. Ibid., 2:502.

23. Ibid., 2:511.

24. *Nazarene Messenger* 12, no. 11 (September 12, 1907), 3.

25. Ibid., 1.

26. See William S. Deal, *The March of Holiness Through the Centuries* (Kansas City: Beacon Hill Press of Kansas City, 1978).

27. Grider, *Entire Sanctification*, 21.

28. John Wesley, *A Plain Account of Christian Perfection* (Chicago: Christian Witness, n.d.), 84; quoted in ibid., 22.

29. *Nazarene Messenger*, 7.

Chapter 14

1. Carl Bangs, "P. F. Bresee: Man of Christian Compassion," compiled from the sermons of P. F. Bresee, n.d.

Chapter 16

1. Marvin Wilson, *Our Father Abraham: Jewish Roots of the Christian Faith* (Grand Rapids: Eerdmans, 1989), 288.

2. Robert Coleman, *The Master Plan of Evangelism* (Old Tappan, N.J.: Fleming H. Revell, 1963), 81.

3. Donald P. Brickley, *Man of the Morning: The Life and Work of Phineas F. Bresee* (Kansas City: Nazarene Publishing House, 1960), 157-58.

Chapter 17

1. Hispanic Americans: Census Facts—Infoplease.com, http://www.infoplease.com/spot/hhmcensus1.html#ixzz15G3D7aYz.

2. Ethnicity and Ancestry Branch Population Division, U.S. Census Bureau. For more information on content, please contact Anna M. Owens (e-mail: anna.m.owens@census.gov).

3. Hispanic Americans: Census Facts—Infoplease.com, http://www.infoplease.com/spot/hhmcensus1.html#ixzz15G3D7aYz.

Chapter 18

1. David Garrison, *Church Planting Movements* (Bangalore, India: WIGTake Resources, 2004), 85.

2. http://www.nazarene.org/ministries/superintendents/news/02172009/display.aspx. Porter celebrates multiplication in Africa.

3. http://www.nazarene.org/ministries/superintendents/news/06152010/display.aspx. Graves experiences Africa on the move.

4. http://www.ncnnews.com/nphweb/html/ncn/article.jsp?id=10009104 Bangladesh District organizes 1,000 churches, votes to become three districts.

5. Phineas Bresee, *Nazarene* (July 3, 1899), 3:4.

6. Neil Cole, *Organic Church* (San Francisco: Jossey-Bass, 2005), 177.

Chapter 19

1. C. Peter Wagner, *Church Planting for a Greater Harvest* (Ventura, Calif.: Regal, 1990), 128.

2. Stephen Gray, *Planting Fast-Growing Churches* (St. Charles, Ill.: ChurchSmart, 2007).

3. Ibid., 61.

4. http://hep.ucsb.edu/courses/ph6b_99/0111299sci-scaling.html.

5. Ibid.

6. Gray, *Planting Fast-Growing Churches*, 65.

7. Ibid., 95.

8. Brian McNichol, quoted in "Churches Die with Dignity," *Christianity Today* (January 14, 1991), 69.

9. Jim Collins, *Good to Great* (New York: HarperCollins, 2001).

Chapter 20

1. Paul R. Orjala, *Get Ready to Grow* (Kansas City: Beacon Hill Press of Kansas City, 1978), 102.

2. Nazarene Research Center.

3. Charles Brock, *The Principles and Practices of Indigenous Church Planting* (Nashville: Broadman Press, 1981), 53.

4. Edward Murphy, "Guidelines for Urban Church-Planting," in *Crucial Issues in Missions Tomorrow*, ed. Donald McGavran (Chicago: Moody Press, 1972), 257.

Chapter 21

1. Henry Blackaby, *What the Spirit Is Saying to the Churches* (Sisters, Oreg.: Multnomah, 2003), 30.

2. Robert Schuller, "Robert H. Schuller quotes," Think Exist.com Quotations, http://thinkexist.com/quotation/anyone_can_count_the_seeds_in_an_apple-but_only/14598.html.

3. Nazarene Research Center. These statistics quoted are for the Global Church of the Nazarene and not specifically for USA/Canada.

Epilogue

1. Quoted in John Maxwell, *The 21 Most Powerful Minutes in a Leader's Day*, (Nashville: Thomas Nelson Publishers, 2000), 27.